Municipal Finance in India

Role of Twelfth Finance Commission

MUNICIPAL FINANCE IN INDIA

Role of Twelfth Finance Commission

Edited by

P S N Rao
G C Srivastava

Indian Institute of Public Administration, New Delhi
in association with
KANISHKA PUBLISHERS, DISTRIBUTORS
NEW DELHI-110 002

KANISHKA PUBLISHERS, DISTRIBUTORS
4697/5-21A, Ansari Road, Daryaganj
New Delhi-110 002
Phones : 2327 0497, 2328 8285
Fax : 011-2328 8285
e-mail: kanishka@mantraonline.com

First Published 2005

ISBN 81-7391-726-4

PRINTED IN INDIA

Published by Madan Sachdeva for Kanishka Publishers, Distributors, 4697/5-21A, Ansari Road, Daryaganj, New Delhi-110 002; Typeset by Sunshine Graphics, Delhi, and Printed at Nice Printing Press, Delhi.

Foreword

The last decade has witnessed many landmark developments in the urban sector with the focus shifting towards local bodies and their finances. The seventy fourth Constitutional Amendment in 1992 has been perhaps the most important milestone in the evolution of the urban sector in India. With this, a large number of issues related to central, state and local finances have come to the fore. It is projected that in a few decades from now, when nearly half of the Indian population will be living in urban areas, the quality of urban service delivery and sustenance will assume tremendous importance.

Newly emerging issues such as role of the Central and State Governments, the National and State Finance Commissions, powers and functional responsibilities of urban local bodies, potential for tax and non-tax revenues commensurate with expected level of services and functions transferred to local bodies need to be discussed in detail, so that we are prepared for the days ahead.

It was with this background that the Twelfth Finance Commission thought it fit that a public debate be arranged on the subject of municipal finances for getting greater clarity regarding the approach that the Commission should take to strengthen the local bodies. With this objective in view, a 'National Seminar on Municipal Finance' was sponsored by the Twelfth Finance Commission. It was organized by the Indian Institute of Public Administration (IIPA) at New Delhi on 29-30 December, 2003. The participants were from the academic as well as professional fields representing different States. Dr. C. Rangarajan, Chairman of the Twelfth Finance Commission presented an overview of the issues involved. Four key papers by experts in the field were commissioned on important thematic areas. Experts drawn from all over the country provided their comments on the papers. The present volume is a compilation of all that crystallized during the seminar.

This volume contains the papers presented and summarises the comments and intellectual inputs provided by the experts. Just as the paper writers have contributed in enriching the literature through the articles/studies, the experts have made valuable contributions by their timely intervention and comments. Ample care has been taken to include the views, suggestions and comments of all the contributors. The proceedings of the seminar prepared as an executive summary by Dr. P.S.N. Rao has been included alongwith elaborate data and information presented by Dr. O.P. Mathur in the form of tables, charts and diagrams. Bringing out in print whatever was presented and discussed during those two days would not have been possible but for the assistance rendered by IIPA in organizing the Seminar and documenting all that transpired.

G.C. Srivastava, IAS (Retd.)
Member–Secretary
Twelfth Finance Commission
Government of India
New Delhi.

Preface

Urban areas in India have been growing by leaps bounds. While in the 1991 Census there were around four thousand urban areas in our country, the number had risen to over five thousand by the year 2001. Further the number of metropolitan cities in India has also increased while we had only 23 one million plus cities in India in the year 1991, their number has risen to 35 by the year 2001. According to estimates in the next few decades, nearly half of India's population is going to live in urban areas. Today two-thirds of the GDP actually comes from the urban areas. Therefore, urban areas and their development assumes a high degree of importance.

It is by and large the urban scene which is witness to major effects of globalisation, privatisation and emerging technologies which are likely to shape the contours of our economy. Our towns and cities are therefore going to be the physical platforms in which the new era of development.

The last decade has witnessed many major changes in the governance paradigm of our urban areas. The enactment of the Seventy-Fourth Constitution Amendment Act in the year 1992 has been perhaps the most important development in the management of the urban sector in India. With this, a large number of issues related to central, state and local finances have come to the fore. On the one hand, urban local bodies have to now cater to a more larger and discerning customers and on the other, they are severely hard pressed for funds. The key question today in the municipal sector is that of finances, their mobilization, management and sustainability.

The Twelfth Finance Commission of the Government of India very rightly thought it fit that a serious deliberation be arranged on the subject of municipal finance so that the same could help the Commission in formulating its policies and recommendations.

Key issues such as the role of the national finance commission, powers and functional responsibilities of urban local bodies, potential for tax and non-tax revenues commensurate with expected level of services, functions transferred to local bodies in the wake of the Constitution Amendment and so on need to be addressed and resolved.

In was with this intention that a National Seminar on Municipal Finance was conducted. We are indeed very thankful to Dr. C. Rangarajan, Chairman, Twelfth-Finance Commission, Government of India to have sponsored the Seminar which was conducted by us on 29-30 December, 2003 at our institute. We also take this opportunity to express our thanks to all the Members of the Twelfth Finance Commission, various paper writers, presenters, discussants and participants from all over India for having taken keen interest in this Seminar and for contributing their ideas and suggestions. A good attempt has been made to document them.

I wish to congratulate Prof. P.S.N. Rao, Professor of Urban Management of IIPA for conducting the Seminar and for efficiently editing this useful volume.

Dr. P.L. Sanjeev Reddy, IAS (Retd.)
Director
Indian Institute of Public Administration,
New Delhi

Contents

List of Contributors

Junaid Ahmed, Team Leader, South Asia Water & Sanitation Programme, The World Bank.

A. Bagchi, Professor Emeritus, National Institute of Public Finance and Policy, New Delhi.

P.K. Chaubey, Professor of Economics, Indian Institute of Public Administration, New Delhi.

Abhijit Datta, Professor (Retd.), Indian Institute of Public Administration, New Delhi.

T.N. Dhar, Chairman, Second State Finance Commission, Uttar Pradesh.

Dalip Kumar Gupta, Additional Secretary (Housing and Urban Development), Uttaranchal.

M.C. Gupta, Advisor, UNIDO, Former Director, Indian Institute of Public Administration and Former Member Secretary, Tenth Finance Commission

Gangadhar Jha, Consultant, IPE Pvt. Ltd., New Delhi.

Ravi Kant Joshi, Consultant, CRISIL, Ahmedabad.

Om Prakash Mathur, IDFC Chair Professor in Urban Economics, National Institute of Public Finance and Policy, New Delhi.

K.K. Pandey, Senior Fellow, Human Settlement Management Institute, HUDCO.

C. Rangarajan, Chairman, Twelfth Finance Commission, Government of India.

M . Nageswara Rao, Director, Tamil Nadu Centre for Urban Studies, Coimbatore.

P.S.N. Rao, Professor of Urban Management, Indian Institute of Public Administration, New Delhi. (Coordinator of the National Seminar on Municipal Finance, New Delhi, December 29-30, 2003) and Joint Editor, *Nagarlok*.

P.L. Sanjeev Reddy, Director, Indian Institute of Public Administration, New Delhi, Former Secretary to the Government of India.

V. Satyanarayana, Infrastructure Specialist, FIRE (D) Project, New Delhi.

K.C. Sivaramakrishnan, Former Secretary (Urban Development), Government of India.

P.K. Srihari, Additional Commissioner, Municipal Corporation of Bangalore.

D.K. Srivastava, Member, Twelfth Finance Commission, Government of India.

G.C. Srivastava, Member-Secretary, Twelfth Finance Commission, Government of India.

1

Introduction

–P.L. Sanjeev Reddy

Since the Seventy-Fourth Constitutional Amendment, the Twelfth Finance Commission is sequentially the third Finance Commission, which will make recommendations and measures for augmenting the Consolidated Fund of the States, with the objective of supplementing the resources of municipalities and panchayats.

The Tenth Finance Commission, although not mandated, as article 283 was amended subsequent to it constitution, made an *ad hoc* provision of Rs. 1,000 crores for urban local bodies. The Eleventh Finance Commission was mandated, according to the amended article 280, and simultaneously the terms of reference also provided that in the event of non-availability of the recommendations of the State Finance Commissions, the National Finance Commission should make its own assessment of the resource requirement of municipalities for making its recommendations. The Commission considered the mandate in its entirety and took the position that the recommendations of the Finance Commissions of the States could not form an adequate basis for determining either the extent of the augmentation, or even a general approach to finances and functioning of the municipalities.

In this connection, the terms of reference of the Twelfth Finance Commission are a little different. While it has mandated the Commission to consider augmenting the State finances for local bodies, in the light of the recommendations of the State Finance Commission, it is silent about any alternative course of action, in the event of non-availability or non-acceptability of the reports of the

Finance Commissions of States. Since most reports of the State Finance Commissions for the relevant period are not available the Commission may have to make up its mind and assess on its own the requirements of the local bodies, including the municipalities.

A major issue concerns the size of the financial support required to strengthen the municipalities, since the financial requirements would differ from state to state. Another major question related to horizontal allocation among the states. The constituency of the urban bodies themselves is undergoing a rapid sea change. The constituency itself consists of very very educated people, discerning and demanding people, always wanting better services at less cost.

It goes without saying that cities are the centers of modern services and incubators of new ideas, as well as entrepreneurship. According to one estimate, urban centers contribute 60 per cent of the gross domestic product of our country and 90 per cent of the government's resources. Since high-skilled workers demand high quality public services, it is important to provide quality civic services to urban dewellers, in order to induce the overall competitiveness of the cities to become centers of knowledge, and attract capital investment on a sustainable basis.

However, a lot needs to be done, as the present position presents a disappointing and dismal picture. There is no sanitation available to 52 per cent of the urban population and individual toilet facilities are available to hardly 24 per cent of the people. About 34 per cent of the urban population does not have any arrangement for drainage of rainwater around their habitat. 60 per cent of the municipal bodies collect less than 40 per cent of the solid waste generated within. If the municipalities have to serve as institutions of self-government, they have to generate their own sources of income, so as to reduce their dependency on the higher tiers of the government. Dependence on grants in aid from the higher levels of government reduces efforts of the municipal bodies to mobilize their own resources.

Since the fiscal decentralization is in the early process of evolution, urban local bodies will still face many problems, such as poor financial status, absence of adequate technical manpower, absence of regular maintenance and high operating cost. Lack of capacity and unwillingness of local government to mobilize resources would result in low level of investment for development of infrastructure.

There has been a general tendency of low cost recovery of services rendered by the municipalities. There is a big resource gap for the municipalities in order to perform even the core functions like public health, sanitation, waste management and water supply.

In order to bridge this gap, all the three levels of government, namely, Union Government, Sate Governments and Local Governments have to cooperate. While the Union Government enacts the policy statement and Acts, the States have to provide the necessary legal and financial base to the municipalities. The actual work has to be undertaken by the municipalities themselves.

The Union Government has announced three programmes in the last Union budget, namely, the Urban Reform Incentive Fund of Rs. 500 crores, the City Challenge Fund and the Pooled Fund for infrastructure development. Preparation for implementing the programmes and pool finances are in an advanced stage.

Various State Governments have attempted differently in this context. A few states have devolved the main functions enumerated in the Twelfth Schedule, along with the power to generate resources and fulfill many of the constitutional obligations, including the timely constitution of the State Finance Commission and acceptance of its major recommendations, like the formation of the district planning committee and conduct of regular elections for municipalities. However, a number of states have yet to take sufficient measures to ensure the smooth process of devolution for decentralization.

Given the absence of transparency in operation, firm data on municipal revenue and expenditure are not available. However, it is assumed that the per capita expenditure on municipal services is relatively low. If municipalities can take good measures, the estimate of per capita expenditure that the states would need to incur for providing and maintaining the minimum of core services like water supply, waste management, roads, street lighting, primary health and primary education, can be easily assessed.

To what extent these services are financed from the municipalities' own resources? This would include a host of taxes and user charges. What is the potential revenue raising capacity of the municipalities in the state? What would be the gap between estimated expenditure that the municipalities have to incur for the minium core services and the potential to collect their own revenues or their own revenue base? To what extent the State Finance Commissions can attempt to address these issues? What strategic prevention measures would the Twelfth Finance Commission think of to bridge the gap?

This is the focus of the Seminar. Coming as the Seminar does at the threshold of the New Year, it will bring us a new dawn of hope, inspiring vision and purposeful action. The deliberations of this Seminar, which has been sponsored by the Twelfth Finance Commission, will certainly lead to outcomes and discussions that will help in giving inputs, so that we can make appropriate recommendations and suggest measures, to augment the Consolidated Fund of the State, to meet the incremental demand of resources for urban local bodies.

2

An Overview

–C. Rangarajan

Like in many other federations, local bodies in India are expected to perform may important functions on the strength of their own tax and non-tax revenues as well as the support they receive from their respective State Governments from time to time. These include such essential services as water supply, drainage, sanitation, street lighting and roads. That there is a considerable gap between the requirement and availability of resources for most local bodies for performing these functions is, perhaps, unfortunate fact.

Evolution of Local Bodies

The roots of local bodies in India particularly rural local bodies go back to the ancient times. The history of the Urban Local Bodies also could be traced to as early as the Mauryan period and later to the Cholas and Kings of Vijayanagar under whom mature local self governing institutions are believed to have functioned effectively. However, the representative character of the local self-government comprising a democratically elected body enjoying wide powers of administration and taxation to discharge their functions may only be a creation of the British. The need for decentralization and popular involvement in civic functions was, perhaps, first conceived by Lord Mayo, the then Governor General of India in 1870, when he issued a Resolution aimed at strengthening municipal institutions and to ensure supervision and care in the management of funds devoted to education, sanitation, medical relief and public works. In the wake of this resolution, the elective principle was included in all the municipal laws. However, in their working, the municipalities remained fully dependent on the provincial governments and their officers controlled the working of the committees. A review of this arrangement in 1882 led to the famous Resolution by Lord Ripon, with whose name urban local self government is now associated, that sought to increase the scope of local governments by (*a*) devolution of more functions and (*b*) making local government an instrument of political and popular education. The Resolution conceded non-official majorities in all municipalities. The Chairman was to be a non-official too, replacing the district collector. It placed the management of local functions and services with the municipal committees. It was also laid down that the local bodies would be entrusted with adequate financial resources and frame their own budget. Following this, many provincial governments passed enabling Acts with provision for election, financial resources, etc. The functions handed over to local bodies included: (*i*) maintenance of roads, street lighting, upkeep of municipal property and buildings; (*ii*) Public health, vaccination, sanitation, drainage, water supply and measures against epidemics; and (*iii*) Education. The principal sources of local revenue identified were: (*i*) Octoroi, (*ii*) Property tax on houses and lands; (*iii*) Tax on professions and trades; (*iv*) Road tolls; (*v*) Taxes on carts and other vehicles; and (*vi*) Rates and fees for services rendered like conservancy, water supply, markets, etc. However, the results of the Reforms fell short of the high hopes especially after the exit of Lord Ripon. The efforts were resumed in 1919 by the then Viceroy Lord Chelmsford. The Government of India Act 1919 enlarged the sphere of municipal taxation to include (*i*) oll; (*ii*) Land tax and tax on land values; (*iii*) Tax on buildings; (*iv*) Tax on vehicles and boats; (*v*) Tax on menial and domestic servants; (*vi*) Tax on animals; (*vii*) Octroi; (*viii*) Terminal tax; (*ix*) Tax on trade, professions and callings; (*x*) Tax on private market; and (*xi*) Tax on municipal services-water supply, lighting, drainage, public conveniences. It also gave certain other powers to the local bodies intended to make them independent of government control. It is noteworthy that subsequent developments in local finance have not introduced any better scheme of local taxation than this. Following this, every province passed new legislation to reform local administration. However, while the system of elections improved, in their day-to-day functions and services the municipal bodies were faced with several handicaps including raising their own funds.

The Government of India Act, 1935 envisaged a federal constitution. The subject of local self-government was assigned to provinces. In this arrangement, the legal position of municipalities suffered. The civic functions declined because of a resource crunch. Lapses and failure of municipal functions were met with dissolution of municipal committees. Thus, the institution of local self-government failed to grow in the right direction despite the best intentions of the various legislations.

Post independence, the Indian Constitution adopted the model of the Government of India Act, 1935 and assigned the subject of local self-government to the States. The Municipal Acts that followed were, therefore, creations of state legislatures and the lack of uniformity was inevitable. Despite several committees that were appointed from time to time, municipal self-government remained in an undefined state.

The Constitution Seventy-Fourth Amendment Act, 1992 was the culmination of a prolonged debate on the measures required to strengthen the third tier of the government so that it acquires the institutional capability to deal with the problems created by urbanization and urban growth. It was a recognition of the fact that the Local Bodies in many States had become weak and ineffective on account of a variety of reasons including failure to hold regular elections, prolonged supercessions and inadequate devolution of powers and functions. The Act envisages the urban local bodies to function effectively as vibrant democratic units of self-government. It has attempted to put on a firmer footing the relationship between the State Government and Urban Local Bodies with respect to the functions, taxation powers and arrangements for revenue sharing. It also mandates regular conduct of elections and provides for adequate representation for the weaker sections of the society including women in the elected bodies.

The Constitution Seventy-Fourth Amendment Act also envisages devolving to the local bodies, functions relating to preparation of plans for economic development and social justice as well as for implementation of various development schemes. A new Twelfth Schedule has been appended to the Constitution of India which lists out 18 functions including urban planning, regulation of land use, construction of buildings, roads and bridges, water supply and slum improvement tnat could be performed by the Municipalities. However, the discretion allowed to the State Governments to transfer these functions to the Municipalities is still very large with the result that there is considerable variation in the responsibilities assigned to them in different states.

Status of Urban Problems

The urban population of India has grown at a fast rate in the last few decades. While it was 7 crore persons in 1961, it has now increased to about 29 crore. Urban population projections indicate a more rapid growth and a doubling of the population in the next twenty five years. Its repercussions for the municipal infrastructure an easily be imagined. The rampant growth of slums cannot but have deleterious effects on the environment. It is estimated that at present there is no sanitation available to 52% of urban population while individual toilet facilities are available to only 24% of the population. The sewerage system covers but a very small population. The solid waste management leaves much to be desired. A significant portion of urban waste is allowed to decompose and putrefy on the roadsides and around the houses and factories. Much of it goes into the drains, chocking them and creating health hazards for the people. The performance of urban local bodies in the provision of drinking water, street lighting and other essential services has been no better.

Improvement of the civic services in most Municipalities would require substantial capital investments and maintenance costs. The need to empower the Local Bodies to raise their own resources cannot be over emphasized. The Octroi which was the principal sources of tax revenues for the urban local bodies does not exist in many States. It has been replaced by an entry tax or a surcharge on sales tax collected at the State level. While the advantages of centralized collection in terms of efficiency and removal of barriers in the movement of goods are accepted, it is generally agreed that the Local Bodies should be adequately compensated for the loss of this revenue. However, many states complain of lack of buoyancy of the entry tax. The other principal tax of the Local Bodies viz. the property tax needs major reforms. We understand that the Government of India has circulated the guidelines for property tax reforms to States to facilitate action towards area based valuation of property. These would need to be pursued vigorously. Little progress has been reported regarding the levy/enhancement of land taxes. Profession tax levels continue to remain low and have not been assigned to local bodies in many States.

State Finance Commissions

The provisions regarding the constitution of the State Finance Commissions (SFC) for recommending transfer of resources from the State to the local bodies as well as the requirement that the Finance Commission at the national level should also recommend measures for augmenting the Consolidated Fund of the States to supplement the resources of the Municipalities would need to be seen in this context. Under the new fiscal arrangement, every state government is required to constitute, once in five years, a Finance Commission and entrust it with the task of reviewing the financial position of LSGs and making recommendations as to the principles that should govern:

- the distribution between the state and the Panchayats and Municipalities of the net proceeds of the taxes, duties, tolls and fees leviable by the state;
- the determination of the taxes, duties, tolls and fees that may be assigned to, or appropriated by, the Panchayats and Municipalities; and
- the grants-in-aid to Panchayats and Municipalities from the Consolidated Fund of the State.

Besides, the Finance Commission of the State is also expected to recommend measures needed to improve the financial position of the Panchayats and the Municipalities.

Barring one or two exceptions, all States have now set up the State Finance Commission (SFC) as required under the Constitution. Many of the SFCs have submitted their reports and in many States their recommendations are already under implementation. The importance of the SFCs in the scheme of fiscal decentralization is that besides arbitrating on the claims to resources by the State Government and the local bodies, their recommendations would impart greater stability and predictability to the transfer mechanism. However, the convention established at the national level of accepting the principal recommendations of the Finance Commission without modification is not being followed in the States. Even the accepted recommendations are not always fully implemented citing accepted recommendations are not always fully implemented citing resource constraints and this defeats the very purpose of constituting the SFCs. On the other hand, the funds transferred for the implementation of development schemes remain unspent either due to institutional/procedural constraints or diversion to meet other committed expenditure.

Central Finance Commission

The Constitution requires the Finance Commission to recommend measures to augment the Consolidated Fund of the States to supplement the resources of the Local Body on the basis of the recommendations of the SFCs. For both historical and economic reasons, the extent of devolution of functions to the local bodies, their fiscal capacity and expenditure needs vary widely not only across states but even within the states. The lack of uniformity in the approach of the SFCs in terms of the principles laid down for devolution of resources from the state government to the local bodies, the lack of synchronization in the award period of the SFCs and the absence of a rational determination of the gap between normative costs of service delivery and the normative capacity to raise resources from all sources including appropriate user charges in different states makes the task of recommending measures on the basis of the recommendations of the SFC hugely complex. The Eleventh Finance Commission had, in fact, gone to the extent of recommending the deletion of the reference to the SFCs in the relevant clause of the Constitution so that future Commissions did not face similar handicaps. However, our terms of reference clearly require us to consider the issue exactly in accordance with the present constitutional provision.

Before attempting to suggest measures to supplement the resources of the Local Bodies, it is necessary to understand the precise role of the Finance Commission in this regard. The Tenth Finance Commission had expressed the view that such measures to augment the Consolidated Fund of the State need not necessarily involve transfer of resources from the Centre to the States. It had observed that once the SFCs completed their task, the Finance Commission was duty bound to assess and build into the expenditure stream of the States, the funding requirements for supplementing the resources of the Panchayats and Municipalities. The transfer of duties and functions listed in the Eleventh and Twelfth Schedule of the Constitution would also involve concomitant transfers of staff and resources and, therefore, not entail any extra financial burden. The

Eleventh Finance Commission more or less agreed with these views and stated that while assessing the revenue and expenditure of the States, the additional burden falling on the financial resources of the States had already been taken into account and, therefore, no additional provisions were required to be made on this account. The EFC did, however, recommend some grants with a view to re-emphasizing the need for maintenance of essential civic services including primary education, primary health, safe drinking water, street lighting, sanitation, public conveniences etc. The EFC had evolved a formula for *inter se* distribution of the grants among the States which included a weightage for the steps taken by the States towards decentralization. This was considered necessary, as many states were slow to follow up on the legislative and the executive measures required to be taken in the wake of the Constitutional Amendment. The EFC also recommended certain measures which if taken by State Government/Local Bodies would enable them to supplement the resources of the local Bodies.

Conclusion

It is well recognized that local bodies have an important role to play in the democratic process and in meeting the basic requirements of people. The old adage "for every citizen, most government is local government" still holds good. It is also recognized that the financial resources available to the urban local bodies fall short of what is needed by these institutions to fulfill their responsibilities. The role of the Central Finance Commission in this context is one step removed. The primary responsibility rests with the local bodies and the State Governments. The local bodies need to do their best to raise as much resources as possible through the various avenues available to them. At present there is no strong evidence that all municipal authorities have exercised in full the powers given to them to raise revenues. That benefit taxes where there is a direct quid-pro-quo between the taxpayer and the tax authority can be levied more easily has not happened. The States have come to the help of the local bodies in a number of ways. A part from tax assignments, there has also been revenue sharing as well as untied grants. However, the mode of support from the State Government to the local bodies has varied from one state to another.

The Terms of Reference to the Twelfth Finance Commission as already mentioned required the Commission to suggest measures needed to augment the consolidated Fund of the state to supplement the resources of the panchayats and municipalities. "Measures" could be interpreted to include not only financial but also legislative and administrative.

In relation to allocation of financial resources by Central Finance Commission to urban local bodies, several approaches are possible. One is to follow the route of the Tenth and Eleventh finance Commission and provide for an *ad hoc* grant which will go in some way to augment the resources of the local bodies. Another approach can be to settlement the *ad hoc* grants with additional resources to fulfill some basic services such as, say, solid waste management in urban areas. This would be an application of the equalization principle that a citizen should be entitled to certain minimum standard of civic services irrespective of where he or she resides. Each local government must be able to provide a comparable level of services at comparable charges and if there are gaps due to the factors beyond the control of the local bodies, the higher levels of government should come to its aid. Even here one must recognize that the role of the Central Finance Commission must be treated as supplementary rather than primary. Nevertheless, an application of the equalization principle to one or two select services based on normative projections of revenue and expenditure is worth considering. However, the financial implications will have to be carefully studied, given the constraints at the State and the Central levels.

A reference must also be made here to the principles which would underline the distribution among states of resources earmarked by the Central Finance Commission. The Eleventh Finance Commission, as indicated earlier, used a formula which included variables such as population with a weight of 40 per cent, index of de-centralisation with a weight of 20 per cent, distance from the highest per capita income with a weight of 20 per cent and revenue effort and geographical area, each with a weight of 10 per cent. The variable, Index of Decentralisation has come in for some criticism. While recognizing that the states which have actively taken forward the process of decentralization must be rewarded, a critical question is: How to measure it? Mere assignment of functions or taxation powers may not necessarily reflect the extent of decentralization at the ground level. A search for an appropriate measure becomes necessary, is the incentive through additional funds allocation is to achieve its purpose.

3

The National Finance Commission and Fiscal Devolution to Local Bodies

–*Abhijit Datta*

[**Abstract:** The paper discusses of the approaches of the last two national Finance Commissions that dealt with central grants to local bodies in the country, examines relevant international experiences and attempts to clarify the choices before the current (12th) Finance Commission. Thereafter, it examines the current arrangements for central grants to improve civic services, including a suggestion for two new tasks. This is followed by a review of working of the State Finance Commissions, local government access to the national divisible pool of central revenues, methods of central grants to the states for the local bodies, and the need for ensuring municipal fiscal responsibility. The last section summarises the main thrusts of the paper.]

Introduction

The paper is supposed to examine the role of the national Finance Commission (FC) for fiscal devolution to the municipalities in India. While writing the paper, it was realised that most of the issues of local government finance are common to both panchayats and municipalities; therefore, instead of focusing only on the municipalities, the paper had to look into the common problems of the 'local bodies' or 'local governments' in the country. However, while discussing the muncipal corporations in the national cities and the need for municipal fiscal responsibility, the term 'municipalities' had to be specifically mentioned. Similarly, unlike the panchayats, municipalities do not have a staffing problem that threatens their autonomous functioning; therefore, this aspect has not been covered in the context of fiscal devolution to the municipalities.

I. APPROACHES OF THE FINANCE COMMISSIONS

Earlier Approaches

Since the passage of the 73th/74th constitutional amendments, two FCs have attempted to devolve grants for the local bodies (panchayats and municipalities) for basic civic services. The 10th FC rightly pointed out the significance of these amendments before recommending *ad hoc* 'plan assistance' for the local bodies:

> "The panchayats/municipalities are late entrants in our federal democratic structure but their action or inaction is likely to affect the welfare of the people under their jurisdiction more directly than either the actions of the State or the Union.[1]

The 11th FC recommended united non-salary grants (a) for 'maintenance of accounts, audit of accounts and for the development of the database' and (b) to the 'local bodies which have the primary responsibility for maintenance of civic services'.[2] The first group of grant was essentially meant for the states, while the second group sought to assist the local bodies for provision of essential civic services. Apart from allocating these grants, the 11th FC also made a number of suggestions to the central and state governments on a wide spectrum of subjects covering the entire gamut of local government finances.

The states would like to have the entire quantum of grants for the local bodies allocated to the to them to augment their Consolidated Fund to supplement the finances of the panchayats/municipalities in their areas, as provided under Article 280(c) of the Constitution. We consider this issue after first reviewing international practices of the two finance commissions in a pure and a cooperative federation respectively, and secondly firming our views on the desired role of the FCs in India's scheduled federation.

International Practices

We present below the experience of federal fiscal transfers in the three federal countries, other than India, having a constitutionally mandated finance commission; these are Australia, South Africa and Nigeria.

Australia:[3] In Australia the Commonwealth Grants Commission (CGC) was asked in 1973 to advise on the application of a commonwealth general purpose revenue sharing for local government by the Commonwealth government. Since 1974/75, on the basis of the recommendation of the CGC, the Commonwealth paid grants for local authorities through the states in Australia based on the principles of fiscal equalization. In 1976 a system of tax-sharing grants replaced the equalization grants for local authorities. The state governments were required to legislate to establish the State Grants Commission (SGC) for distributing the tax-sharing grants to the local authorities. Initially the amount available to the states for distribution was 1.75% of net personal income tax collection, and since 1980 this stood at 2%. This represents about 25% of total external assistance to the municipalities (see Box-1).

South Africa:[4] Unlike other federal countries, local governments in South Africa have both exclusive and concurrent functional jurisdictions under its Constitution, as indicated below:

Box-1
Australian CGC Tax-sharing Grants to the Local Authorities

The main features of the tax-sharing grants to the local authorities are:

- It will be expressed as a percentage of personal income tax collection in the previous year,
- The states' existing level of grants to the local authorities cannot be reduced
- Not less than 30% of the grant would be calculated on a per capita basis, adjusted by area (Element A), and
- The balance (70% or less) is to be assessed be the SGCs using general equalization principles based on (i) revenue differential, and (ii) expenditure differential of selected eight local services (Element B).

Source: Datta, Abhijit, *State-Municipal Fiscal Relations: A comparative study of Australia and India,* Canberra : ANU Press, 1982.

Box-2
South African FFC Revenue-sharing Grants to the 'Municipalities'

There are four types of national grants to local government as stated below:

(i) Municipal basic services (S) transfer. This is a formula-based, unconditional revenue transfer. For calculating the amount required it is necessary to get the full picture of total national transfers to local government, both revenue and capital. These would be made available to the primary municipalities over a period of five (urban) to seven (rural) years.

(ii) *Municipal institutions (I) transfer.* It is a formula-based, unconditional capital transfer. This would fund only a small number of institutional facilities that are necessary for the operation of local government, e.g. community centres, council buildings etc. Municipal entitlement would be limited to those with an income below a 'threshold level'. This will not be available to municipalities with less than 2,000 people for reasons of institutional availability; they would be encouraged to combine with adjoining municipalities or their functions would be encouraged to combine with adjoining municipalities or their functions would be transferred to the district council to operate as the agent of the concerned municipality. The local authority will receive an amount equal to the difference between the 'threshold level' and its actual revenue. Due to differences in municipal population size, the transfer is made at different size levels.

(iii) Tax equalization (T) transfer. This is a formula-based, unconditional revenue transfer. This transfer aims to equalise the tax base of the lower tier cities/towns within a metropolitan area. The funds will flow to the substructures of a two-tier municipal system.

(iv) Metropolitan or district council infrastructure (M) transfer. This helps communities within a metropolitan or district council to provide infrastructure services that would benefit residents of other communities in their areas. These projects are to be undertaken on a cost recovery basis; i.e. the metropolitan/district council should charge individual municipalities for the project cost.

(Contd.)

Note: The formulae of 'S', 'I' and 'T' transfers are given in the source below.

Source: South Africa (Department of Finance), A Short Guide to the Equitable Share of Nationally Raised Revenue for Local Government, Pretoria, June 1998

"In terms of section 156 of the Constitution a municipality has executive authority in respect of, and has the right to administer, the matters listed in parts B of schedules 4 and 5. Examples of the former are building regulations, electricity and gas reticulation, fire-fighting services, municipal planning, municipal health services, municipal public transport, and water and sanitation services. Examples of the latter are beaches and amusement facilities, cemeteries, cleansing, local amenities, markets and abattoirs, municipal parks and roads, refuse removal, street lighting, traffic and parking."[5]

In 1997 the South African Financial and Fiscal Commission (FFC) explained in a document how local government is entitled to an "equitable share' of national revenue in terms of section 214 of the country's constitution. These transfers should ensure that poor people have access to basic municipal services, and that transfers should only be made to the communities that cannot afford these basic services (see Box-2).

Box-3

Nigerian Revenue Sharing Formula among the federal, state and local governments

- Nigeria's expenditure assignments to various levels of government consist of (a) federal, (b) federal-state, (c) state-local, and (d) local. There is no exclusive expenditure jurisdiction of the states. This has prompted the states to capture the state-local functions and, thus, limiting the role of the local governments despite their constitutional states since 1976 as the third tier of government in the country.
- In Nigeria, under its 1999 Constitution resources are allocated among the three tiers of government - federal, state and local - in the following proportions:

(Contd.)

	Percent
(a) Federal government	49
(b) State governments	24
(c) Local governments	20
(d) Other funds and the federal capital territory	7
	100

This leads to 'common pool problem' – as in Argentina, Brazil and India – where each sub-national government tries to maximize its share of national resources without any regard for its effect on other jurisdictions. This has resulted in soft budget problems at the sub-national level and the federal government becomes vulnerable to sub-national fiscal manipulation.

Source: Khemani, Stuti. "Fiscal Federalism and Service Delivery in Nigeria: The Role of States and Local Governments", *Op. cit.*, July 2001.

Nigeria:[6] The Nigerian experience resembles the Indian situation in its essentials, such as creation of non-viable states and local governments to reduce the bargaining power of the sub-national entities, the states increasing their functional domain by defining the powers of the local governments, and inefficient utilization of the common revenue pool leading to soft budget problem at the sub-national level. Box-3 gives the details of the Nigerian inter-governmental fiscal situation.

Desired Role of the Indian FCs

From the angle of the Indian FCs, the Australian approach has relevance, except that it would be more practical in future to let the State Finance Commission (SFCs) work out the budget equalization methods appropriate for each state, within a broad guideline to be suggested by the FC. The 11th FC's civic services grant is comparable to the South African 'S' transfers and is appropriate for its: (*a*) passthrough requirement, (*b*) clarification of the primary tasks of the local governments, and (*c*) making a substantial, but not an excessive, topping-up of local revenues. In future this grant should be funded from sharing of a central tax, like excise, at a predetermined rate per cent (say 5%). The grant should be first distributed to the states on population basis, for eventual passing on the same to the local bodies on the recommendations of the SFCs to achieve both vertical (state-local) and horizontal (at different tiers/levels of local government) fiscal equalization.

At the state-level, the other three South African grants, viz. the 'I', 'T' and 'M' transfers, are worth looking at by the SFCs in India. The 'I' transfers, in particular, have relevance to deal with small-size local bodies without worthwhile revenue bases (village and town panchayats).

Choices Before the 12th Finance Commission

Under Article 280(c) of the Constitution, the Finance Commission is to recommend "the measures needed to *augment the Consolidated Fund of a State to supplement the resources of the Municipalities* in the State on the basis of the recommendations made by the Finance Commission of the State" (emphasis added). This might be interpreted to mean that: (*a*) no pass-through of central grants to the local governments should be permitted, and (*b*) the FCs' grants for local governments must be linked to the SFC recommendations. As for the 'no pass-through' argument, its future use can not be precluded as any intergovernmental grant may be qualified with conditions for their use.

The 11th FC decided to make its own recommendations on grants for the local bodies in the light of various shortcomings in the SFCs' reports. These were:

(a) non-synchronisation of the periods covered by the SFCs and the FC,
(b) inadequate review of the financial position of the local bodies and by the SFCs and non-adherence to their constitutionally prescribed terms of reference, and
(c) delay in finalizing action by the states on the recommendations of the SFCs.

In view of these problems, the 11th FC recommended "that the words 'on the basis of the recommendations made by the Finance Commission of the State' in ... the Constitution be deleted".[7] It is possible that the 12th FC might face the same difficulities and, in the absence of a constitutional amendment, adopt the same position that the 11th FC took earlier. Alternatively, the 12th FC might suggest a separate share for the local bodies out of a central tax (say 5% of net excise revenue). The state governments would then be entitled only to meet the state-level expenditures for improving the monitoring and supervision tasks on the local bodies-which the states are supposed to do on their own. The local bodies might also demand a part of the earmarked allocation for creating the base data for improved reporting. If, on the other hand, the required information is to be tailor-made for the FCs, then this should be a charge on the central exchequer.

There is also a thinking that the FCs' role should be only advisory in suggesting measures to be taken by the states to supplement the finances of local governments within their jurisdiction, particularly in the context of the heavy pressures on central finances[8]. This is a complete negation of the 73rd/74th constitutional amendments whereby the FC was given a responsibility to recommend grants to improve local government finances. Moreover, tendering advice without recommending grants for the local bodies would be a futile exercise.

II. NATIONAL TASKS OF THE FINANCE COMMISSIONS

Review of Local Government Finance

It would be extremely useful if the 12th starts its report on 'Grants for Local Bodies' with a review of local government finances and activities since the passage of the 73rd/74th constitutional amendment, the approaches and recommendations of the SFCs, an assessment of the utilization of the grants by the previous commission, and identification of the immediate tasks for which national assistance is called for. Such a review is an annual feature in South Africa by its Fiscal and Finance Commission – which is a permanent body. In India a quinquennial review of local government finances and activities would be quite useful for all the three levels of government and other stakeholders of local government.

Maintenance of Basic Civic Services

The 11th Finance Commission was right in allocating the share of grants to the local bodies (panchayats and municipalities) for maintenance of basic civic services in the rural and urban areas. The identified civic services were: (*i*) primary education, (*ii*) primary health care, (*iii*) safe drinking water, (*iv*) street lighting, (*v*) sanitation, including drainage and scavenging, (vi) maintenance of cremation and burial grounds, (*vii*) public conveniences, and (*viii*) other common property resources. Such a clarification of the primary responsibilities of the local governments in India was necessary to bypass the confused list of subjects included under the 11th/12th Schedules. However, there is still a need to relate this grant to those panchayats/municipalities where the provision of these basic civic services is below a minimum national norm, especially the first five items covered under the Planning Commission's basic services programme. For the rest, it would be necessary to work out appropriate norms in consultation with the central ministries of rural/urban development.

Institutional Strengthening of the 'National Cities'

In view of the unique position of the four premier metro-municipal corporations of Delhi, Mumbai, Kolkata and Chennai in the national economy there is a need to accord these a special constitutional status halfway between the states and the municipalities. Earlier, the National Commission on Urbanisation also mooted the idea of a special development strategy for these cities[9]. Here our special plea is to allow these metro-municipal corporations the necessary functional and fiscal autonomy through suitable changes in fiscal management. With a change in the status of these metro-municipal corporations (for instance, if the Delhi municipal corporation is broken-up into smaller municipal corporations), the experiment should be terminated. Depending on the success of this experiment, other second-order metro-municipal corporations could be included in this experiment later.

The Chinese practice of according 'provincial' status to its four metro-municipalities – Beijing, Tianjin, Shanghai and Chonqing "with significant independent powers directly under the central government"[10] might not be quite relevant in the Indian context. The objective here is to promote fiscal viability with responsibility, both in their revenue and capital accounts, of India's four premier metro-municipal corporations for replication in other municipalities in the country. This could be initiated by the 12th FC as an institutional capacity improvement exercise by financing professional technical assistance. A similar scheme could also be initiated by the 12th FC for the second-order metro-municipal corporations (and district panchayats) for implementation by the states.

III. ASSISTING STATES TO SUPPLEMENT MUNICIPAL FINANCES

A Framework for the SFCs' Tasks

The 11th FC did not find the first generation SFC reports to be useful for its purposes and, accordingly, suggested that the future SFCs could cover at least the following areas:

- The SFC's approach,
- An analysis of state finances,
- An analysis of the finances of each tier (panchayats) and each level (municipalities) of local government,
- The principles of distribution of the net leviable revenues by the state to the rural and urban local governments.
- The principles of *inter se* distribution of the net leviable revenues by the state among the different tiers and levels of local government, and
- The grants to be given by the state to the rural and urban local governments.

The 12th FC would have received the second generation SFC reports by now, but it is unlikely that the content of these reports would have improved since the first generation of SFC reports. The 11th FC pointed out some of deficiencies in the working of the SFCs, some of these resulted from the states' reluctance to undertake the mandated tasks of decentralization to the local bodies, but many of these arise from the way the SFCs have worked so far (see Box-4).

There is no easy solution to these problems and one hopes that over time these impediments in state-local fiscal devolution would be sorted out, provided there is an accepted policy at the national level of targeting of local government expenditure as a percent of total government expenditure.

'Divisible Revenue Pool' and the Local Bodies

It may be recalled that the 10th FC recommended grants to the panchayats and the municipalities on different bases – at Rs. 100 per capita (Rs. 4,381 crores) for the panchayats and Rs. 1,000 crores for the municipalities – over a four-year period. The 11th FC, recommended a total grant of Rs. 1,600 crores for the panchayats and Rs. 400 crores for the municipalities, within the "overall limits set for the flow of resources from the Centre to the States"[11] The amounts include state-level expenditure for maintenance and audit of local bodies, and for development of database.

Box-4

Experience of the State Finance Commissions in India

Some of the experiences of the working of the first two generation of the SFCs might be summarised below:

- There has not been genuine efforts by the states to make clear expenditure assignments to the local bodies and corresponding restructuring of states set-up.
- The state government staff transfers to the local bodies have not been accompanied by revenue source transfers;
- The SFCs waste much of their time to collect routine financial data from the local bodies that the states should have collected in a routine manner; collection of qualitative data for policy purposes, e.g., fiscal autonomy/revenue dependency, expenditure/revenue decentralization, is not attempted;
- There is inadequate realisation that the SFCs are supposed to recommend fiscal transfers in aid of local revenues and not finance for creating local infrastructure;
- The SFCs have not paid much attention to improve fiscal administration of the local bodies, which might be more important that fiscal transfers *per se*,
- The SFCs are not required to cover issues of local taxation or borrowings, in case some of these are required to be examined 'in the interest of sound finance' these should be specifically included in their terms of reference;
- The SFCs do not start their work after first reviewing state finances, nor did they suggest significant transfer of, or surcharging on, the state taxes;
- Inadequate attention is given by the SFCs to the adverse consequences of grants on local revenue efforts and local fiscal autonomy;
- The state governments treat the SFCs with scant respect, partly due to their membership composition that includes serving civil servants; and
- The state governments generally take a long time to accept and act on the SFCs recommendation.

Sources: Data compiled by the NIRD (SFC cell), Hyderabad, and NIUA, New Delhi.

Two questions are relevant here: (*a*) how does one decide what is the appropriate level of central grant allocation to the local bodies without increasing the size of local government expenditure as a proportion or percentage of total government expenditure? and (*b*) how can the 'overall limits' of central fiscal transfers to the states be decided without providing for similar transfers to the local bodies at the same time? The future FCs have to determine the quantum of central grant to the local bodies along with that of the states and not as a residual exercise. The Nigerian practice of such a divisible revenue pool is a pointer in this direction, although such a national revenue pool has to be administered at the local government level so as to project local fiscal autonomy as well as promote their fiscal responsibility.

Distribution of Local Grants to the States

The 11th FC distributed the local grants to the states on a formula basis, similar to the formula for revenue-sharing grants to the states.

Box-5

11th FC Criteria and Weights for Maintenance of Basic Civic Services for Panchayats and Municipalities

	Criteria (Indicators)	*Weights (%)*
i.	Population	40
ii.	Index of decentralisation	20
iii.	Distance from highest per capita income	20
iva.	Own revenue efforts of the local bodies, using state's own revenue as an indicator	5
ivb.	Own revenue efforts of the local bodies, using state's gross domestic product as an indicator	5
v.	Geographical area	10
		100

Note: The formulae for these criteria are given in Mathur (2001), cited below.

Source: *Report of the Eleventh Finance Commission*, Para 8.27; Mathur, Om Prakash, *Approach to State-Municipal Fiscal Relations*, New Delhi: NIPFP, 2001, pp. 93-97.

This is a variation of the central plan assistance formula, also known as the 'Gadgil formula'. This formula is inappropriate if the central revenue sharing with the local bodies takes the pass-through route with conditions for its distribution through the SFCs, as suggested already. The 11th FC formula was based on the following criteria and weights, to be applied separately for the panchayats and the municipalities (see Box-5).

It was pointed out that the individual indices (like, decentralization or local revenue efforts) were again weighted by population.[12] One might also argue that from the angle of fiscal transfer it is the normative *target of expenditure decentralization,* and not institutional decentralisation, that is of primary concern to the FC.

Conditions of Central Grant for the Local Bodies

The central grants for local government should be adequate, but not excessive at the same time–e.g. not exceeding 25% of local revenue, leaving room for additional state grants to local bodies with fiscal disabilities. The adequacy aspect of the grant should be considered within a triangular sharing of central revenues under the principles of cooperative federalism, as practiced, for instance, in South Africa.[13] The so-called states' share in the central divisible revenue pool needs to be redefined for meeting the expenditure needs of autonomous local governments.

A necessary condition of the central grant would be that the states should not reduce their own level of grants to the local bodies. Secondly, the states should reallocate the grant on the recommendation of the SFCs, which would attempt to promote horizontal fiscal equity among the different tiers of panchayats and levels of municipalities. One way to achieve this is to compensate the local bodies in the backward districts higher grants for their poorer revenue capacity.

Fiscal Equalization of Local Bodies

The real concern of the FC should be on achieving fiscal equity[14] between the panchayats and municipalities on the one hand, and within the panchayat tiers and the municipal classes on the other, Two types of fiscal equalization of local bodies – vertical and horizontal – would have to be addressed by the FC and the SFCs together. It is up to the SFCs to introduce innovations and sophistication in the fiscal equalization formula to the extent the quality of state-specific data permit. A simplified model to introduce fiscal equalization of the local bodies is suggested below:

- *Vertical fiscal equalization*

  Medium term - To bring revenue expenditure of the local bodies to be at least 10% of total government expenditure within the five-year period covered by the 12th FC, and

  Long term - To raise the revenue expenditure of the local bodies to be doubled to reach 20% of total government expenditure within the next twenty-five-years starting from the 13th FC period.

  In the absence of a constitutionally mandated national revenue pool, as in Nigeria, reallocating the existing central schemes for rural/urban development for this purpose could make a start in this direction.

- *Horizontal fiscal equalization:*

  Medium term - A minimum per capita FC grant allocation for local bodies through the states would favour rural as against urban local bodies, and

  Long term - The SFCs should ensure horizontal fiscal equalization within all the panchayat tiers and all the municipal levels.

Minimum Income of Local Bodies

Specifying a threshold income to have minimum staff-size and office facilities, as in South Africa, has relevance in India as well. A minimum level of income is insisted upon for creating a municipal council in the southern states following the earlier Madras Presidency practice, viz. Tamil Nadu, Andhra Pradesh and Kerala. The 74th Amendment includes this is as an optional criteria for municipalisation, but the 73rd Amendment does not mention this at all with the result that most village and town panchayats in the country are not viable units for tax administration. For a village panchayat the threshold annual revenue could be Rs. 100,000, and for a town panchayat this might be Rs. 200,000. Also, if the FC grants to the local bodies have matching conditions, then two other associated problems would also be checked, viz., (*a*) grant substitution of own taxes of the local bodies, and (*b*) ensuring local fiscal autonomy.

Municipal Fiscal Responsibility

The terms of reference of the SFCs, under the 74th Amendment, do not include an assessment of municipal borrowing and debt burden. Nevertheless, it would be useful for the 12th FC to collect data on the size and structure of municipal debt and the extent of municipal debt servicing. Such information is necessary to assess the municipal borrowing practices vis-à-vis the borrowing capacity.

So far the state governments have adopted a soft budget policy through periodic municipal debt waivers. The municipalities contend that the loan component of the state plan projects is not related to the nature of the assets created. In future, it would be difficult for the municipalities to secure such soft loan from the state governments and without a strong revenue base, the municipalities would find it difficult to secure market borrowing necessary to creat civic infrastructure. In other words, a hard budget regime is being imposed on the municipalities due to the present fiscal crises of the states. Karnataka has passed a Local Bodies Fiscal Responsibility Act, 2003, with the requirement for the municipalities in the state to prepare medium term expenditure framework (MTEF). The 12th FC might suggest a guideline for similar legislations by all the states. This should cover:

- a prescribed debt limit as a percent of municipal revenue expenditure (say, 20%),
- specification of appropriate precautions and sanctions, e.g. debt funding, escrow account, deduction from general grant etc. and
- special provisions for financial emergency, e.g. a court-appointed executive to oversee and give directions to the municipal council in financial matters during the period of financial emergency.

IV. CONSTITUTIONAL AMENDMENTS ON LOCAL FUNCTIONS AND FINANCES

A 'Local List' in the 7th Schedule

The need for reservation of local taxes has been recognized by all the official committees and commissions since Independence. Recently, the Venkatachaliah Commission recommended that:

> "The Eleventh and Twelfth Schedules to the Constitution should be restructured in a manner that creates a separate fiscal domain for Panchayats and Municipalities".[15]

On the other hand, the two consultation papers of the Commission on the panchayats and the municipalities suggested creation of a separate local list. A municipal share in the divisible pool of taxes, on the lines of Articles 268 to 274, was also mooted in the consultation paper on 'Decentralisation and Municipalities'.[16] Any attempt to restructure the 11th and 12th Schedules to make these subjects mandatory would mean restructuring the 7th Schedule by redesigning the present central and state jurisdictions.[17] The genesis of these two clumsy Schedules was to meet the states' opposition to reduce the 7th Schedule domain of the states (State List) by creating a separate 'Local List' for the local bodies.[18] The earlier opposition to a change in the 7th Schedule 'State List' was based on the inviolability of the 'basic structure' of the Constitution. But the main feature of the 'basic structure' is a democratic polity and other features, such as 'federalism', are its secondary features.[19] The problem here is not technical, as the South African Constitution illustrates, but essentially political which the national government and the civil society will have to deal with.

A suggestion recently mooted by the central government is to transfer the 'Local Government' entry from the 'State List' to the 'Concurrent List'; this will enable the centre to legislate on local bodies and thereby clean-up the optional provisions under the 73rd/74th Amendments. However, this would still leave the functional and tax domain of the local bodies under the states' jurisdiction. Therefore, restructuring the 7th Schedule to create a separate 'Local List' cannot be avoided.

Modification of Parts IX and IXA

There is also a need to unify Parts IX and IXA on the Panchayats

> **Box-6**
>
> **Constitutional Changes on Fiscal Decentralisation to the Local Bodies Suggested by the Venkatachaliah Commission (2002)**
>
> - The Panchayats and the Municipalities "should be categorically declared to be 'institutions of self government' and exclusive functions assigned to them" (Paras 9.7.1 and 9.7.2)

(Contd....)

- The Eleventh and Twelfth Schedules to the Constitution, with powers of local taxation, are to be made compulsory. Its operationalisation would involve restructuring the 7th Schedule as well. This suggestion of the Venkatachaliah Commission is discussed already.
- The words "on the basis of recommendation" of the SFCs should be substituted by the words "after taking into consideration the recommendations" to allow flexibility to the future FCs in making recommendations on grants to the local bodies. This is the suggestion of the Venkatachaliah Commission (Para 9.8.3).
- The periodic setting up of the State Finance Commission (SFC) could be every fifth year or earlier. The state government shall place its Action Taken Report (ATR) before the state legislature within six months of the submission of the SFC report. This is the suggestion of the Venkatachaliah Commission (Para 9.8.4).
- Parliament should be empowered to change the upper limit of the 'professions tax', instead of through a constitutional amendment. This is the suggestion of the Venkatachaliah Commission (Para 9.8.5).
- All local authorities may be allowed to borrow from the state government and financial institutions. This is the suggestion of the Venkatachaliah Commission (Para 9.8.6).
- The concept of a distinct and separate domain for municipalities should be recognized. This is the suggestion of the Venkatachaliah Commission (Para 9.21). This is discussed above with the suggestion to include a 'Local List' in the 7th Schedule of the Constitution.

Source: Report of the National Commission to Review the Working of the Constitution, Vol. I, New Delhi, 2002.

and the Municipalities respectively. The two chapters with identical provisions, made for historical reasons, have outlived their political purpose (the panchayats have political clout on which the municipalities have piggybacked). This was unified in the V.P. Singh bill (74th Amendment Bill) introduced by the short-lived Janata Dal government; but later the original Rajiv Gandhi bills (64th/65th Amendment Bills) model of separating the panchayats and municipalities was revived by Narasimha Rao bills (72nd/73rd Amendment Bills). The recent recommendations of a high-power national commission on the working of the Constitution covered the various constitutional constraints and infirmities and made wide-ranging recommendations (see, Box-6).

V. CONCLUSIONS

The paper suggests changes in the approach and design of FC grants to the local bodies. The initial fixation of the total kitty for distribution to the local bodies should be made on the basis of a decentralization target setting of local expenditure as a per cent of total government expenditure, instead of the arbitrary per capita allocation and its variation for the local bodies. A related suggestion is to meet this from central tax sharing; in case a global revenue sharing for devolution to the states, the share of the local bodies also should be decided simultaneously. There is also a case to redesign the 'Gadgil type' formula, originally meant to distribute central plan assistance to the states, and replace this by a revenue block grant with (*a*) a per capita component, and (*b*) an equalization component.

The paper takes the position that the central assistance to local government need not be 'on the basis of the recommendations made by the Finance Commission of the State' and its deletion from the Constitution is necessary. Secondly, the paper also argues in favour of inclusion of a 'Local List' in the Constitution covering both local functions and taxes; this is not only technically feasible, but also desirable under 'cooperative federalism'.

Notes and References

1. India (Ministry of Finance, Department of Economic Affairs), *Report of the Tenth Finance Commission,* New Delhi, December 1994, Para 10.10.
2. India (Ministry of Finance, Department of Economic Affairs), *Report of the Eleventh Finance Commission,* New Delhi, July 2000, Paras 8.18-8.22.
3. Datta, Abhijit. *State-Municipal Fiscal Relations: A comparative study of Australia and India,* Canberra: ANU Press, 1982.
4. South Africa (Department of Finance). (A Short Guide to the Equitable Share of Nationally Raised Revenue for Local Government), Pretoria, June 1998.
5. South Africa (Financial and Fiscal Commission), (Local Government

in a System of Intergovernmental Fiscal Relations in South Africa: A Discussion Document), Pretoria, July 1997, p. 3.

6. Khemani, Stuti. (Fiscal Federalism and Service Delivery in Nigeria: The Role of States and Local Governments), prepared for the Nigerian PER Steering Committee, July 2001.
7. *Report of the Eleventh Finance Commission, op. cit.*, Para 8.11.
8. National Workshop on Implementation of SFC Recommendations and EFC Grants for Panchayati Raj; 'Background Material and Issues for Discussion',: Hyderabad: NIRD, October 20-21, 2003.
9. India (Ministry of Urban Development), *National Commission on Urbanisation*: Interim Report, p. 71, New Delhi, 1987.
10. Arora, Vivek B, and John Norregaard, (Intergovernmental Fiscal Relations: The Chinese System in Perspective), I.M.F. Working Paper, Washington D.C.: IMF, 1997.
11. *Report of the Eleventh Finance Commission, op. cit.*, Para 8.22.
12. Rajaraman, Indira. (Growth-Accelerating Fiscal Devolution to the Third Tier), New Delhi: NIPFP, April 2001.
13. South Africa (Department of Finance), (*A Short Guide to the Equitable Share of Nationally Raised Revenue for Local Government*), *op. cit.*
14. Oommen, M.A. *Devolution of Resources from the State to the Panchayati Raj Institutions: Seach for a Normative Approach*, New Delhi: ISS, 1995, p. 25
15. India (Ministry of Law and Justice), *Report of the National Commission to Review the Working of the Constitution*, (Chairman: Justice M.N. Venkatachaliah), Vol. I, New Delhi: GoI Press, 2002 Para 9.8.2
16. *Report of the National Commission to Review the Working of the Constitution*, Vol. II, *op. cit.*
17. Datta, Abhijit, (Constitutional Listing of Local Taxes in India), paper submitted at the National Workshop on Implementation of SFC Recommendations and EFC Grants for Panchayati Raj, *op. cit.*
18. Sivaramakrishnan, K.C. *Power to the People: The Politics and Progress of Decentralisation*, New Delhi: Konark Pubs., 2000. p. 133.
19. Datta Abhijit. (Constitutional Status of Local Government in India), *Indian Journal of Public Administration*, New Delhi: IIPA, April-June, 1987.

COMMENTS

AMARESH BAGCHI: Following the passing of the Seventy-Third and Seventy-Fourth Amendments to the Constitution, the Central Finance Commission now has the additional task of making recommendations, regarding the measures needed to augment and consolidate the funds of the states, to supplement the resources of the panchayats and municipalities. This requirement has been incorporated in the Constitution itself, by inserting new sub-clause (C) in clause (3) of article 280. Beginning with the Eleventh Finance Commission (EFS), the terms of reference of the Finance Commission now include this requirement specifically among the matters referred to the Commission by the Presidential Order.

Though not required by the Terms of Reference, the Tenth Finance Commission took note of the reality of constitutionally recognized local bodies and made some *ad hoc* recommendations to supplement their resources. The Eleventh Finance Commission has dealt with it more extensively and made recommendations, not only to augment the revenues of the states to help supplement the resources of the panchayats and municipalities, but also to design the transfers intended for the purpose in such a way that the objectives of the Seventy-Third and Seventy-Fourth Amendments are regarded.

Taking note of the fact that progress in transforming panchayats and municipalities into efficient institutions of local government have been tardy, the Eleventh Finance Commission, while deciding on inter State allocation of funds earmarked for the local bodies, attached weight for factors like decentralization and their own effort in that, in addition to population and other factors.

The recommendations have come in for considerable criticism, mainly on the grounds (1) that the grants provided are too small to make any difference to the functioning of local bodies and (2) the formulae used for the allocation of the amount set apart for the grants among the states are needlessly complicated and quite often are not likely to be of much help in promoting the cause of decentralized government, which motivated the amendments made in 1993.

Prof. Abhijit Datta's paper also reflects this concern and makes wide ranging suggestions for guiding the course of the Twelfth Finance Commission. The paper brings to bear Prof. Datta's concern for empowerment of local bodies, to enable them to function as efficient institutions for local self-government.

He has also drawn on international practices, particularly of Australia and South Africa, in support of his observations and suggestions. Some of these suggestions, if implemented, will have a profound impact even on the federal structure of the Constitution.

Firstly, the approach of the Twelfth Finance Commission in deciding the amounts to be given as grants to augment the resources of the local bodies has to be broad-minded and liberal. The Eleventh Finance Commission had recommended a total grant of Rs. 16,000 crores for panchayats and Rs. 400 crores for municipalities for each of the five years of the award period. They have done it, keeping in view the availability of resources and the overall limits set for the flow of funds from the Centre to the states. Prof. Datta asks, how does one decide what is the appropriate level of Central Government allocation to the local bodies, without increasing the size of the local government expenditure as percentage of total government expenditure? Then he asks, how can the overall limit of substantial fiscal transfer to the states be decided without providing for similar transfer to the local bodies at the same time?

Secondly, the formula devised by the Eleventh Finance Commission in distributing local grants among the states is inappropriate. Referring to the indices of decentralization and local revenue effort, Prof. Datta argues from the angle of fiscal transfers, it is the normative target of expenditure on decentralization, and not institutional decentralization, that should be of primary concern to the Finance Commission.

Thirdly, in terms of vertical gap of local bodies, Prof. Datta suggests target in terms of level of government expenditure, as proportion of total government expenditure, should be set first. In the medium term, he goes on to suggest that the target should be 10 per cent and in the long term 20 per cent.

Fourthly, as regards horizontal equalization in the medium term, a minimum per capita grant from the Finance Commission for local bodies would be helpful for panchayats as well as urban local bodies. In the long term, it is for the State Finance Commissions to see that horizontal fiscal equalization is achieved among all the local bodies.

There are a number of other suggestions in the paper, such as for institution strengthening in national cities, as in China. To ensure that the functional and financial domain of the local bodies is guaranteed, it is suggested that the Seventh Schedule to the Constitution should be amended to create a separate a local list. Prof. Datta argues that the transfer of local government from the State List to the Concurrent List alone, as has been mooted recently, will not do. There are several suggestions for constitutional amendment for strengthening the local bodies in our country.

No doubt the task which the Finance Commission is enjoined under the Terms of Reference, requires making an assessment of the revenue gap of the local bodies and see how far and how best the gaps can be filled up. Assessing the revenue gap of the local governments separately, over and above the gap of the State Government, is a Herculean task for the Twelfth Finance Commission, given the time and resources at its disposal. That apart, given the acute resource constraint at all levels of government, some form of top down budgeting cannot possibly be avoided. Hence, some idea of the overall amount that can be devolved from the Centre is essential.

At the same time, it is also necessary to form an idea of the likely order of the revenue gap that the local bodies face, if they were to perform their basic functions and provide the core services, such as providing the core services at acceptable level and also make an average revenue effort within the powers of revenue raising that can be exercised. Going by absolute standards, it is not going to be helpful and it would end up with impossible targets, as it happened in the past with Sarkaria Commission, and more recently with Rakesh Mohan norms.

Only the average of some of the well-done local bodies should be taken. Given the enormous heterogeneity of the country and the diversities in local conditions even within a state, one has to be cautious in applying the averages. After all, even within the state, there will be municipalities of various categories, which have varying revenue-earning capacity and needs. In this sitution, even the averages also are difficult to work out, especially with the limited time and resources at its disposal. So, it is almost an impossible task for the National Finance Commission to work this out. At best, some state-wise averages can be taken, leaving it to the SFCs to vary them suitably to meet the local requirements. As for the revenue potential, since very little tax powers have been transferred to the local bodies, their revenue potential has to be assessed as part of the exercise for the normative assistance to the revenue gap of the individual states.

This will get around the problem of varying state practices. In the matter of evolution of functions performed at the local level by the local governments, different states have different practices. In this situation, how does the Finance Commission go about working out what is the need of particular states, or local bodies in particular states? It may vary from one state to another in a big way, simply because the functions are not transferred.

Now the grants to the local bodies may be earmarked as a part. So, there is no alternative but to work out the revenue gap normatively for the states as a whole, including their requirement for local bodies. But grants to the local bodies may be earmarked as part of the revenue gap grants recommended for the individual states, with suitable variation to take account of their specific situation, such as the needs of mega cities. Out of the total revenue grants, which are determined normatively by the Finance Commission, a portion may be earmarked for local bodies. That percentage may vary from state to state, depending on the importance of the urban local bodies and so on. But it has to be done, taking into account some transparent criterion.

Some amount out of this may again be earmarked for specific purposes, like capacity building, or for equalizing the basic services, or equalizing certain core services – it is possible to do that – but all within the overall equalization grant worked out normatively.

This is what the Commonwealth Grants Commission does in Australia. Assessing the needs of local government based on some absolute norms and then deciding a share of Central revenues to be devolved to the government below is not practicable. In Australia, having normatively determined the equalization grant, out of that they had proposed some specific purpose grant, which is deducted from the overall amount. Nothing passes from the federal government to the state government, or the government below, except through the Commonwealth Grant Commission. Out of that they decide it. So, some overall ceiling has to be there. Without that, you lose your balance and your bearing is lost. So, within that ceiling, certainly the Finance Commission can earmark a part to be given for local bodies, which may vary from state to state. But it would be deducted, set off against the overall normative gap grants.

Assessing the needs of local governments based on some absolute amount and then deciding the share is not practical. If the budgets of the governments are to be kept in balance, the top down approach is imperative. However, consideration may be given to the suggestions made by Prof. Datta for fixing the target of local government expenditure as a proportion of total government expenditure.

The available information suggests that, so far as urban local bodies are concerned, the revenue expenditure form only less than 5 per cent. Prof. Om Mathur notes that it may be about 3 to 4 per cent, or may be less. Whether they include the transfers made in the form of payment of salaries to staff etc., we do not know. Assuming that it is not more than 5 per cent, it is small. Now the share of rural local bodies is even less. They have very little discretion in spending their amount, for the expenditure that is given to them. Actually, what happens is, particularly if it is a rural economy, 95 to 99 per cent of the total amount spent comes from the grant from the Centre to the states for specific purposes, specific schemes, Centrally sponsored schemes and so on. A survey conducted by Govinda Rao-Vasant Rao in Karnataka showed that they have autonomy and flexibility in respect of only 2 per cent or 3 per cent, which is far removed from what you expect from a vibrant local government system.

In terms of revenue collections, the urban local bodies collect more; the rural local bodies collect very little. The situation is very different for urban local bodies. They collect about 70 per cent of their revenue from their own resources and transfer on account is 30 per cent. However, the proportion of transfer is very widely different across the states, among the municipalities within the state. Incidentally, in South Africa, which Prof. Datta quoted, in the white local bodies in the state, which constituted the main big cities, 98 per cent of their total expenditure is financed out of their revenue. They depend very little on grants or transfer of power. It is far removed from the situation prevailing in India. According to the latest figures, 98 per cent of the expenditure is met out of their own revenue.

Out of the total revenue 70 per cent they collect and 30 per cent is grant. But in some states it is very little. Urban local bodies do not collect more than 30 per cent of their revenue. The share in total government expenditure is small, perhaps not more than 5 per cent. This 5 per cent of the total government expenditure may be 8 to 10 per cent of the State Government expenditure.

Obviously, the country has to go a long way in establishing truly autonomous institutions of local self-government. It is futile to expect the Finance Commission to provide a panacea for all the ills of our body politics. Many of the recommendations of the EFC which could have led to improving things, are still languishing.

The reluctance of the State Governments to transfer power to the government below has something to do with their share of the political power. It is politics. Democratically elected local bodies are routinely by-passed by many state Governments, by creating parallel institutions. The problem has to be dealt with politically.

Nevertheless, it should be recognized also that the level of literacy and administrative competence being what they are, some control and supervision of the local governments from above is unavoidable. So, whether you like it or not, the State Governments will have to exercise some control over power because simply many of the local self-governments do not have the capacity to administer of their own. The nearness of the government to the local people also stands in the way of their exercising any of the powers of taxation. Now we are getting rid of our hands an important and effective tax power to the local governments.

While the Finance Commission cannot remedy all the ills, it can help in the following ways. In assessing the revenue gap of the states, the revenue needs of the States should be given more attention than before. I make a simple point. The assistance should form part of the normative exercise on the basis of principles to be applied uniformly. This assessment should form part of the exercise to find out the revenue gap of the state, which includes the requirements of the local bodies.

If you take some local urban bodies in the States, which are urbanized, their requirements would be more than in some other states, which are not urbanized. They may fell that just because they are urbanized, they require more. They have also got higher taxing capacity. That should be upset. Now once the revenue gap grants are determined normatively, including revenue needs and capacity building needs, a part of the grant may be earmarked as meant for local body affairs. The fraction of the earmark is not uniform for all the states. It may be determined locally.

This approach will leave it to the States to decide what powers and functions should devolve. In the interest of promoting decentralization it would be desirable. But to tie grants to the local bodies to the degree of decentralization, to use the Finance Commission grant for this purpose does not seem to be the best way. It is necessary for us to see that the transfer system does not create a part of the incentive fiscal discipline, which is very common among lower level governments in our country, and many other countries also. From this angle, the normative approach is imperative. That should create the necessary incentive for discipline.

Experience shows that allocating grants on the basis of competitive formula is not very helpful. Besides, it should be left ultimately to the states to decide how much to devolve. However, considering the reluctance of political masters at higher levels to part with power, the minimum set of functions and powers may be laid down, which should be devolved to the local level government. In view of the diversity of capacity of the ULBs, it may not be appropriate to lay down any compulsion in this regard. They vary from state to state. One set of prescriptions may not suit all. Besides, prescribing conditions on what would come under the umbrella of article 275 grants would not be proper.

Perhaps, the only requirement that can be attached to that part of article 275 grants. Which would be earmarked to local bodies, is the fulfillment of constitutional obligations imposed under the Seventy-Third and Seventy-Fourth Amendments, such as holding the elections periodically, payment to.. and so on. The grants meant for local governments cannot be withheld if the obligations, the constitutional obligations under Part IX and IX-A are fulfilled. These are basic conditions flowing from the Constitution. If any of them are not satisfied, the amount meant for local bodies could be withheld.

There should be no objection to imposing conditionalities to article 275 grants, so long as they flow from the Constitution and are not coming from other directions. The Finance Commission may perhaps set these obligations as required to put at least the minimum pressure on the government at the local level. This should meet Prof. Datta's concern. Allocation of grants meant for local bodies under this category should be left to the SFCs, and they can in turn use the normative approach.

The normative assessment of state revenue needs, if you take full account of the responsibility, may yield larger revenue gap than can be met out of the existing pattern of devolution through SFC, especially if you take the equalization grant.

For that the answer is to cut down Centrally sponsored schemes drastically and transfer the amount so released to be given to SFC as Finance Commission grant. The lead way that we have left of 37.5 per cent overall limit to SSFC, within that, if you enlarge the grants to the Finance Commission, it can well go beyond that. At the moment, it is talking about 21 per cent taxable devolution roughly and about 4 to 5 per cent grants. It can be enlarged to 11 to 12 per cent out of 37 per cent, which is given as grants by the Planning Commission. That can be used by the Finance Commission to make the equalization grant.

The creation of a separate Local List in the Constitution does not seem to be a good idea, or the suggestion to bring local government in the Concurrent List. This will undermine the authority of the State Government. Even in Canada, where federalism is flowering in an exemplary way, the local governments are directly under the control of the provinces. The suggestion to bring the local government in the Concurrent List smacks an attempt to micro manage the planning of the government at the local level from Delhi. The baneful results of micro management of the economy from the Centre, practiced in the hey days of planning, by-passing the states, should warn us of any such move.

Keeping a democratic responsive government firmly established at the local level, as much as at the state level, presupposes a truly democratic culture with appropriate institutions above.

JUNAID AHMED: In South Africa, the city of Johannesburg, which is the main city of the country and indeed the richest city in Africa, went bankrupt in 1996-97. They went to the Central Government to ask for money to bail themselves out. The Central Government at that point said, "absolutely not. You have full authority to raise your money, full authority to spend your money. You have full authority to get yourself bankrupt and we have full authority to say no". This bankruptcy plea went on and the Central Government kept on saying "no".

Eventually, in 1999, the political leadership of Johannesburg put together a new leadership to change the city. The order that it gave to the city was "do not fix the lights; fix the institutions that fix lights", with a very clear mandate that we are not going to give you a bail out, nor fixing the bankruptcy problems of the city. It is not just a question of raising new resources, it is completely changing the institutions of service delivery.

Two years later, Johannesburg has gone into the capital market with an investment grade rating, to raise capital resources for expenditure based on a completely new city. The new city has not only coalesced the black and white cities together, but it has taken service delivery and made them into corporations. Some of them are public corporations; others are private corporations, all owned by the city, but very much incentivized to raise user charges and to be held accountable for what they do and what they do not. It was a massive institutional change that led to better service delivery. Now, why was it possible for Johannesburg to actually go that way?

First of all, the rules of decentralization were very firmly imbedded in the Constitution and in the new laws, with three tiers of government, so completely autonomous from the other two tiers, and were actually accountable to the citizens.

Secondly, the transfers from the Central Government and State Governments are formula-driven and very clear. There are no deliveries of Centrally sponsored schemes that can actually be through backdoor, but actual hard budget constraints. So, it was very hard budget constraint on the city itself.

Finally, what is very interesting in the case of South Africa is that its Constitution has been written in the modern era. It was enacted in 1995 and it reflects the reality of the modern era where city matters. In a country where 80 per cent of the GDP comes from urban local bodies and 60 per cent of the population are in cities, it is cities and local goods at the city level that matter. The regions that mattered when it was an agrarian country no longer mattered. So, their government in 1995 decided to make three independent spheres of government rather than tiers of government.

What really matters? Is it national public goods, regional public goods or local public goods? With the way urbanization is going to take off in the next 20 years, increasingly it is the local public goods that will matter, not regional public goods, and certainly not the Central public goods that will matter. In that context, as it has come out very clearly in Prof. Datta's paper, the Twelfth Finance Commission has to come out with a clear message of the direction of giving greater support to the Seventy-Fourth Amendment and its real implementation as essential for the economic growth and the poverty alleviation goals of the Government of India. Unless the Seventy-Fourth Amendment is implemented correctly in the next 10 years. This country will not be able to sustain its euphoria of trying to reach 7 per cent or 8 per cent growth rate, and this is the stake under which Prof. Datta suggested more money to local governments, and in particular to urban local governments.

Delhi today receives 270 litres of water per capita per day. There are countries in Africa, certainly countries in Latin America, and almost all cities in Europe that supply 24 hour water a day, 7 days a week at full pressure at 140 to 150 litres per capita. Delhi gets 270 per capita but 5 to 6 hours of water a day. The difference is not a question of more money for equalization between the rich and the poor, the difference is the whole management of Delhi Jal Board. Unless the institutional incentive to actually deliver the services in a more accountable way is incremental in the inter-governmental fiscal system, equalization will not serve the purpose that we think or we hope that it would serve.

If the argument is that institutional changes and incentives for institutional changes are a prerequisite to have equalization make an impact, how does the Twelfth Finance Commission position itself to actually promote the institutional change? I think that was the question raised by the Chairman in his presentation.

There are at least three vehicles that would be worthwhile for the Finance Commission to look at. The first is that in the Central Government there is a shift now from the traditional Centrally sponsored schemes to a new generation of incentive based schemes, like City Challenge Fund and URIF or the State fiscal reform facility. Though incentive based, none of these schemes is perfect. A lot can be done to improve them. But, certainly, if the Finance Commission were to put some of its money behind these incentive-based grants from the Centre to the local bodies, to State Governments, it would send a major signal as to what the Twelfth Finance Commission was saying about change in the future.

The work that needs to be done for the Finance Commission is to actually analyze these incentive grants, to look at their strengths and weaknesses. For instance, the CCF and the URIF, the two instruments of the Ministry of Rural Development, are run by two different wings of the Ministry of Urban Development but are not dovetailed. If they were dovetailed, we could actually see the state incentive and city incentive are well coordinated.

There is a second element of supporting this institutional change. If you take all the Centrally sponsored schemes and if you take all the incentive reform schemes, you will find that the Centrally sponsored schemes, which in many ways are not incentives, substantially outweigh the amount of money in URIF of CCF or other incentive grants. So, you are either pumping in more money to outspend the bad, or begin to align the bad into the good. The Finance Commission can make a major statement as to what are the principles of alignment of Centrally sponsored schemes with the incentive reform schemes.

That itself would be a major statement of this Commission, trying to incentivize and Central alignment is treated to do that. I believe that putting something behind the Centrally sponsored schemes that are incentive oriented, while coming out very strongly about the principles of alignment itself, will become a very power statement.

Then comes the third instrument. It is not an instrument that the Finance Commission can finance. It is moral persuasion and here the power of the pulpit is very important. I am referring to the soft budget constraint that is not only implicit in the fiscal flows, but also implicit in the financial access to resources. For example, you have many financial parastatals, implicitly or explicitly, by the Central Government, that actually create soft budget constraint on cities. I wish there are statements by the Finance Commission, which begin to say that fiscal instrument and financial instrument need to be separated in the instruments of the Government of India. That will make a major difference on whether the hard budget constraints will be applied or not.

We need a balanced recommendation on greater resources to local governments. The direction of more and more money towards local governments has to be balanced by a statement as to how to strengthen institutional incentives for service delivery change. I would pick up water and sanitation and rural roads as the two major services in which we have this issue of alignment of Centrally sponsored grants into incentive reforms and funding incentive reforms, because this is a powerful mechanism for the Twelfth Finance Commission. It also goes around the question that the Twelfth Finance Commission is not the implementing body. You need to piggyback the implementation on others. Therefore, piggybacking of Central incentive schemes, which are reform oriented, is one mechanism.

Let me just conclude by making two separate points. One is on capacity and the other is on rural-urban divide. We have often entered the capacity game in a supply driven way. We have said, more training, more money. But what we have discovered is that this supply driven approach to capacity building, when local bodies themselves have no incentive to actually face the hard budget constraints, does not really make any impact.

But once decentralization in its real nature begins to get implemented, the Seventy-Third and Seventy-Fourth Amendments, we have discovered around the world that local governments themselves have incentives to seek out capacity and they themselves begin to actually articulate what kind of capacity they need and they begin to seek it out. In that case, building resources and technical assistance in the context of right incentives actually makes a huge difference in capacity building. Prof. Datta's recommendation that there is a need for resources to be put on capacity building, especially in big cities, has to be linked to the incentives of decentralization. Otherwise, you will find yourself in a supply driven mode.

A final comment on the rural urban divide. It is fascinating that the new generation of inter-governmental reforms or local government reforms that are happening, whether they are happening under democracy or under more authoritarian regime, whether it is in South Africa or Uganda, or whether in Pakistan, the boundaries of local governments are being reshaped, that the rural urban divide is actually being thrown out. We discover that towns and their linkages with panchayats or rural areas are quite strong and that it is better off to look at local government boundaries across settlement rather than, say, settlement of towns and rural panchayats should be kept different. This is something that is emerging more and more in service delivery. A concrete example is in the case of some of the African countries, where you have regional water utilities that are anchored to small towns, which also deliver to rural areas. That has happened only because you have redrawn the boundaries of the local governments.

At the same time, what is also interesting in all these new coming decentralization is the drawing of the city districts. While on the one hand you are throwing away rural urban divide, on the other hand, there is recognition of cities as fundamental economic modes, and that has led to the redrawing and decentralization of powers to create city districts. I think that is going to be a major issue in the coming ten years, in the context of South Asia, not only India but also South Asia. In fact, what is interesting is that South Asia is the region in the world, which is about to enter into the real urbanization demographic phase. Even with its low levels of urbanization, it is already the world's second largest urban system.

The future of South Asia is urban, not rural. Therefore, the inter-governmental system that supports urban local governments in a true way is indeed the future, in terms of delivery and economic growth of South Asian countries, in which of course India is primary. It is in that tone that I would argue that the Twelfth Finance Commission statement about institutional changes and service delivery at the local government might be an even more important statement than the one on equalization.

T.N. DHAR: The Prime Minister made a speech in March this year about the local body institutions, "jeb kali hai, jimmedari nahi kar sakte", meaning when their pockets are empty, they cannot discharge their responsibility. This was announced at a meeting where the Leader of the Opposition in Parliament was present, where he said that the constitutional amendment would be brought forward to make Schedules XI and XII mandatory, and not enabling as at present.

We need a National Bank for Urban Development, like the National Bank for Rural Development, to enable the urban local government to leverage easily accessible funds and affordable funds for development.

As for equalization, there are two approaches that have been made here. One is that we should go for incentives and the other is that we should go for equalization. In the Indian conditions, both processes will be required. You have to have both the processes in the Indian context. You cannot suddenly go to the incentivism system, because a large number of such bodies will not be able to utilize the incentives, as they are placed right now. Until they have come to that level, we have to have both.

All the states should have a stake in urban infrastructure development fund. Some have it already. Half a dozen states have this fund, which they have used very intelligently and effectively. They have leveraged these funds sometimes to the extent of 6 to 10 times, as in Tamil Nadu. Gujarat is another example. One also has to delink elected elements from doing assessment and tax objection decisions. I am saying this because it is happening in some states at present.

Further, HRD is one of the most important things that the institutions should seek out with 4, 800 and odd municipalities and 10,000 towns, which are urban local bodies. Today every state has state level academies for training on rural government, institutions through out the country. But we do not have city managers. While the economy may be producing 60 per cent of the GDP from these cities, we do not have enough of city managers. No staff is being trained at the induction level. There are no educational systems in the universities, which produce city managers, specifically meant for this kind of task, which is much more complex than general administration.

In the Tenth or Eleventh Finance Commission, four assumptions were made by different committees for urban local bodies, varying form Rs. 18,000 crores to Rs. 1,25,000 crores. Then we came up with what you call Rs. 2,000 crores, at the rate of Rs. 400 crores a year for urban local bodies. But what is the total budget of the urban local bodies in the country? It would be anywhere between Rs. 20,000 crores to Rs. 25,000 crores. So, you can see what Rs.400 crores would mean in that kind of light.

Parastatals is a mechanism used by State Governments to undermine local bodies. More and more encroachment is taking place. It is true that very large projects have to be done by parastalas. We concede the construction may be done by specialized agencies. Once the construction is done, it should be handed over to the local governments for maintenance and running with their own O and M cost. There is multiplication of parastatals and this is happening all the time. The State Governments are using this method to reduce the functional autonomy of urban local bodies.

The other issue is synchronization. It has not occurred between Central Finance Commission and SFC. Some kind of synchronization must occur so that the Central Finance Commission have the SFC Report for taking a more pragmatic and practical view of the needs of these bodies.

A great deal of outsourcing and participatory management to reduce costs can be suggested strongly, if we want to make it succeed, because purely devolution or raising their own revenues will not by itself do much, will not be enough, I should say. Lastly, coming to urban rural divide, the district planning committee had been mandated by the Constitution. I am sorry to say these are not operational in most of the states. Some of the states have even passed Acts, but they are not operational. District planning is not an integral part of planning for urban and local bodies, which it ought to be.

RAVI KANT JOSHI: It is not a fiscal issue, it is a systemic issue. Today, municipal bodies are not delivering what they should deliver. But the question is, are they having the capacity or the authority to do that? We are discussing the Constitution Seventy-fourth Amendment. But at the ground level, nothing has happened.

For 10 years, an NGO called Yuva has been pleading in the Bombay High Court, praying to kindly instruct the State Government to have democratic decentralization, which is the principle of the Seventy-Fourth Constitutional Amendment, by creating ward committees and similarly DPCs and MPCs.

In Gujrat, the Second State Finance Commission has not yet been established. Take the Tenth and Eleventh Finance Commission. When their grants come down to the local level, when 80 per cent comes from the State Government, most of the municipal bodies were not able to utilize those grants, because they do not have the equalizing share with them, as their resources are only 10 or 15 per cent.

The money came to the state level, but the decision making power is with the State Government. It took 2-1/2 years for the Baroda Municipal Corporation to utilize the Eleventh Finance Commission grant, because Baroda being comfortable in water supply, we proposed that we may be allowed to go for sewerage. But the DMA authority was not able to sanction it, because the list says that water supply is first and sewerage is second.

The kind of institutional reforms which need to take place is not happening. In fact, some sort of political decentralization has taken place but in the last 10 years there is financial centralization. The municipal bodies have become more dependent on the State Governments and the assistance has to come through this supply driven approach.

The Twelfth Finance Commission can pave the way for the Thirteenth Finance Commission by creating the urban infrastructure data information system, so that we will have the correct data to decide the devolution of resources to the municipal bodies.

The problem at the municipal level is that they are dependent on outside sources for 85 per cent of their resources. We are saying that they are not using taxation to raise their own resources. But the tax rates are decided by the State Governments. No doubt, there are systemic deficiencies, rent seeking approach, assessment problems and all that. Even the rates and exemptions are decided by the State Governments.

D.K. GUPTA: Uttaranchal, is a hilly area, where the density of population is very thin. The taxes that we have imposed are already quite high. For the time being, the total taxation in the municipal bodies is about 25 per cent of the annual value or annual rent. It is already too high and I do not think that the local population can pay anything beyond that. The major tax has to come from the tourists and pilgrims, who are visiting Gangotri, Yamunotri, all the holy places and places of tourist interest in the hilly areas. But they hardly contribute anything to the municipal income. This is a special case for Uttaranchal, because the generation of resources by the local people is not possible beyond this point. Further, there is no entry tax on the tourists and pilgrims, who travel through the state. Ten years back, there was an entry tax. Because of the opposition on the ground of safety in the national highway and other grounds, this entry tad was scrapped. We spent our resources on these users, who are travellers. We provide them these services but we do not get anything by way of return. This problem of Uttaranchal needs special consideration by the National Commission while looking at devolution of funds to states.

C. RANGARAJAN: In some ways, the work of the Twelfth Finance Commission, or any National Finance Commission, would have been easier if the State Finance Commissions had taken the same approach, which the National Finance Commission takes, namely, that in trying to decide on the resource transfer to the states, they look at the tax devolution, they look at what the emerging gaps could be on normative basis, fill them as much as possible on a normative basis and also provide certain other kinds of observation grants and so on. If the State Finance Commissions had done this work, then a view could emerge as to what is the available gap, which can be filled in by the National Finance Commission. That work has not been done by the State Finance Commissions. If the National Finance Commission has to work and find out what the gap is, it is going to be a very very difficult task. I think this is a task that cannot be easily accomplished within a matter of 6 or 12 months, which is all that is available to the Commission. After all the initial steps are taken, there are only 12 or 15 months available and it cannot be done in that period. If all the State Finance Commissions had done it systemically, we would have had some idea of the gap that is emerging and we could make some recommendations on how they could be filled.

A suggestion was made regarding the revenue deficit grant, how a portion of it can be earmarked. Fine. It can be done. But the problem is this. As we know, many of the states do not come under the category of revenue deficit grants. Except for the Special Category States and one or two non-Special Category States for the first period, the rest are out. Therefore, building gap into this might give some kind of a result regarding what the revenue deficit can be, but it may not necessarily be the instrument through which some of the things that have been sought could be accomplished.

Ultimately, two questions have been raised. One is on incentive based grants. I think there is a certain history to it. If you follow the history, let me say "as is where is situation", there is very little that can be done. But if you fundamentally modify the rules of grants versus tax devolution, perhaps it is a possibility.

Therefore, there are two things. One is incentive based grant versus (not versus but cum) equalization principle. I think equalization principle is not simply supply driven. I do not think we should really take the equalization principle as supply driven. In a sense what we are essentially saying is that if the municipal authorities and others are required to perform certain services, one must take a view whether these services are adequately provided. If they are not adequately provided for reasons, which are beyond their control then that gap should be filled in by somebody, either the state government or the national government. It is also possible that you can build some incentives into it. The only thing is what you call conditionality should not degenerate into taking away powers. I think this is the most important point. The conditionalities vary in quality, vary in typology and so on. But I do not want to enter into a situation in which the conditionality becomes something, which ultimately takes away the autonomy, which we are talking about all the time. Therefore, the conditionalities will have to be of some general nature, like when the funds are made available for purpose X, it should be utilized for the purpose of X. That is the extent to which one could go.

A point was made about city districts and so on. This raises a further fundamental question. While we are all very much desirous of saying that the urban village bodies and village panchayats should become very important, we have also to recognize the fact that many of their problems transcend the village and city level.

For example, the question of water supply to the city of Chennai is not the problem of the city of Chennai alone. I think the city of Chennai will not be able to handle it. If we have to get the water from the Krishna River, or if we have to get the water from Veeranam or some other places, then the task is not simply that of the Corporation of Chennai alone. Therefore, we must recognize that some of these problems transcend the boundaries, if you want to use that word, of the cities and villages, and will require financial resources far beyond the capability of that particular city.

This is not an argument to take away everything from the city. But we must also recognize that the cities are autonomous in certain areas, but the cities also rely and depend upon others in order to fulfill some of their own basic services. There are advantages in linked cities; there are advantages in doing a sewerage system, which includes not only one town but also a number of towns. It depends upon the topography and so on and so forth. Therefore, many of what we call civic problems cannot be resoled within the boundary of a particular village or a particular city and will require extra support, which has to come from the state.

I do not think, we can envisage a system in which there will be a Central Government, powerful local bodies and a state which is not powerful enough. I still see a strong Center, a strong State and then the third tier. I think we must recognize where the limits of the powers lie.

We will try to see the best way to combine the incentives in the broad sense of the term with the equalization principle and also include all those kinds of institutional changes, which may be required not only for the delivery of the services, but also in enabling them to augment better and raise better resource.

4

Powers and Functional Responsibilities of ULBs: Potential for Tax and Non-Tax Revenues Commensurate with Services Expected

–M. Nageswara Rao

In the past one century, starting with Lord Rippon's Resolution (1882) on municipal committees, Royal Commission on Decentralisation (1906) that resulted in the Act of 1919, and the Government of India Act 1935 a significant beginning of urban local self government was made, the financial powers and functional responsibilities were the topics for discussions, deleberations and debates. The situation continued even after independence. Many Committees have been constituted by Centre and States to study the same area and recommend measures to strengthen the urban local bodies (ULBs). Notable among such committees are Local Finance Enquiry Committee (1951), The Taxation Enquiry Committee (1953), Rural-Urban Relationship Committee (1963), Committee on the Augmentation of Financial Resources of ULBs (1963). In addition, recent Central Finance Commissions have been added in the list. For example referring with the 11th Finance Commission (EFC) recommendations, one can find that the recommendations of EFC with respect to ULBs are also similar to earlier Enquiry Committees and Commissions except change in language. In own tax resources of ULBs, the EFC has recommended with an observation that the "Property tax/House tax has not been exploited to its full potential. The relevant tax legislation should be suitably modified to delink this tax from rent control laws ....." (P. 114). In the case of non-tax sources the EFC recommended that "the rate structure of user charges levied by the local bodies should be revised regularly to keep pace with inflation and to recover atleast, as far as possible, the full O & M cost. Local bodies should have the power to fix rates of taxes and user charges " (P. 114).

After the 74th CAA, most of the State Governments have constituted State Finance Commissions, with some resemblances to Central Finance Commissions.

These State Finances Commissions too have examined their own municipal structures, powers, finances, functions etc. and have made recommendations that once again resemble the earlier committee and commission reports.

Under these circumstances, the preparatory work of 12th Finance Commission has to some extent deviated from the conventional approach and exploring some new and innovative strategies - as seen from the initiatives taken to examine the gamut of issues related to ULBs.

One of the inputs that has been asked to examine is whether the potential for tax and non-tax revenues commensurate with the services expected from the ULBs given the powers and functional, responsibilities ? However , the question appears to be incomplete. Having examined the question, it should also ask for the possible solutions – in the changing public sector environment – most appropriately the avenues of new and innovative strategies. This is exactly what is attempted in this paper in the following order :

- An introductory review and recap of the relevant reports and their recommendations in the past one century in the first section ;
- A case of one State, taking Tamil Nadu as an illustration to answer the title and theme question in sections 2 to 6.
- A descriptive presentation of the silent revolution that is going on in Tamil Nadu to break away from the traditional approach to more meaningful, scientific, explorative and innovative strategies that are resulting in significant results in urban sector - specifically among ULBs in the last two sections.

Tamil Nadu – Municipal Sector

In the State of Tamilnadu, there are six city Municipal Corporations, 102 Municipalities and 611 Town Panchayats with a total population of 27 million. The State is the most urbanised State in the Country, with an additional 111 Towns which are non-statutory and 2 Cantonments classified as Urban as per 2001 census. The ULBs are presently governed by seven Acts, one each for six city Municipal Corporations and one for Municipalities and Town Panchayats. The Town Panchayats which were earlier governed by the Tamilnadu Panchayats Act, 1958 were brought under Tamilnadu District Municipalities Act, 1920 consequent on the historic 74th Constitutional Amendment Act (74th CAA) and on the basis of conformity legislations adopted by the State Legislature from 1st June 1994.

Tamilnadu has a long and chequered history of local self government for several centuries undisturbed by Kings and rulers. In modern times, the enactment of Town improvements Act 1850 and the District Municipalities Act, 1884 consequent on Ripon's Resolution paved way for establishing town administration with a proper organisational and functional setup. Later on with improved resource mobilising capacity, additional functional responsibilities were entrusted with ULBs.

Functions and Responsibilities

The earliest local institutions of 1730's were managed wholly by officials with no role for public. The town constabulary was the major responsibility and its maintenance was the first charge on Municipal Funds and the remaining limited functions then entrusted viz. sanitation and market places took second priority.

The Improvements in Town Act of 1850 (India Act XXVI of 1850), authorised Government to introduce Local Administration in any town, where people want to make better provision for "Constructing, Repairing, Cleaning, Lighting any Public Streets, Roads, Lanes, Drains or Tanks for preventing nuisance or improving the towns".

The Town Improvements Act 1865 (Act X of 1865) entrusted with the Local Bodies these responsibilities and empowered them to levy taxes. Not less than five inhabitants of the town were made councillors by Government with the District Magistrate as Ex-Officio President. The Town Improvement Act of 1871 gave additional functions such as maintenance of Schools, Hospitals, Dispensaries, Birth and Death registration and vaccination. After Ripon's resolution, the Madras District Municipalities Act, 1884 was enacted and this gave few additional responsibilities with the aim of lesser external control for the local bodies to fulfill the aspirations of the people apart from some major structural changes.

Finally, the Madras (Chennai) City Municipal Corporation Act 1919 for Chennai City Municipal Corporation and the Madras (Tamilnadu) District Municipalities Act, 1920 (Act 1920) for Mofussil towns were enacted and these two Acts have stood the test of time for over eight decades. One significant feature of these two Acts for the purpose on hand is that it has listed out the functions and responsibilities of the Municipalities in an elaborate manner. These functions and responsibilities have been classified as 'Obligatory' and 'Discretionary' to prioritise their responsibilities depending on their resource availability.

It is necessary to dwell upon briefly on fare furl expenditures of ULBs. The expenditure on the following purposes is listed as **"authorised expenditure"**. They are generally classified as `public safety, health, convenience, education and everything incidental to administration.'

(i) **Public Safety** includes :

Lighting of public or private streets, places and buildings,
Extinction of fires,
Regulation of traffic,
Control or removal of dangerous structures or trades,
Removal of obstructions in public streets or places and
Famine relief/scarcity relief.

(ii) **Public Health** includes:

Hospitals and dispensaries and treatment of infectious diseases,
Vaccination and training of medical practitioners and others,
Registration of births and deaths,
Lunatic asylums,
Markets, slaughter houses, latrines, sewage farms, removal and disposal of wastes,
Water works, drinking fountains, tanks, wells,
Wash houses, parks, squares, gardens,

Street cleaning and other sanitary measures,
Burial and burning grounds and crematoria and
Acquisition of land for the above purposes.

(iii) **Public convenience, education and amenities** include

Construction and maintenance of streets, bridges,
Regulation of building, removal of encroachments,
Planting and preservation of trees,
Maintenance of schools, public libraries, reading rooms, gymnasium,
Maintenance of public halls, theatres, playing fields,
Prevention of diseases of animals,
Construction and maintenance of choultries, poor houses, pounds, and
Public baths, Public clocks, Clock-towers, Music.

Out of the above **authorised items** of expenditure for various functions and activities, the following functions are **mandated as obligatory** functions in the Tamil Nadu District Municipalities Act 1920 :

Construction and maintenance of Streets, bridges, Causeways and Culverts.
Maintenance of public property and monuments vested,
Maintenance of Municipal Property,
Waste Management including regular sweeping and cleansing of the streets,
Lighting of public street,
Planting and preservation of trees in public places,
Burial and burning grounds,
Medical Relief,
Diffusion of education,
Registration of births and deaths,
Vaccination,
Slaughter houses,
Maintenance of Schools including Elementary schools,
Water supply and maintenance of public wells, tanks and reservoirs,
Drainage system (Public and Private),
Regulation of building activity,
Provision of public latrines and urinals,
All other objects declared obligatory by law or rule.

The expenditure on other authorised expenditure items is **discretionary**.

Out of the above functions, the following functions and responsibilities, which attract major capital investment are identified as **core functions** in Urban Local Bodies.

1. Water supply
2. Waste Management & Sanitation
3. Roads
4. Drains
5. Street Lights
6. Public Health.

Annual Finances of ULBs in Tamil Nadu

A glance through the Table I gives the indication that the establishment cost constitutes 34 per cent in 1995-96 to 31 per cent in 2002-03. On the otherhand if we add O & M expenditure on services to establishment expenditures, they exceed the own revenue. The situation is appropriately summarised and concluded by the Second State Finance Commission stating that " the resource base of local bodies is not elastic (particularly with respect to tax bases like property tax) and non-tax items are not significant " (SSFC, P. 16). Also noted that, in addition to the base being small, it has all along been subjected to ceiling and other Government controls with the result that the local bodies are unable to bear the annual increase in expenditure without matching income (SSFC, P. 16).

The situation is similar even at the national level.

Table-1 gives the summary of finances (Revenue and Expenditure) of ULBs in Tamil Nadu.

Investment Needs

Even though the First State Finance Commission has identified the minimum requirement of funds for maintaining the **core services** and for filling up the gaps in the level of Civic services expected from ULBs and those actually provided, for the dispensation period of First State Finance Commission (FSFC) for five years starting from 1997-98, neither the ULBs could generate sufficient revenue surplus for the same, nor the Central or State Government could transfer funds to the required level. The estimation of funds for the five years 1997-1998 to 2001-02 was as given in Table-2:

Table-1

Finances of All Urban Local Bodies in Tamil Nadu

(Rs. Crores)

Budget Components	*Year*		
	1995-96	*1999-2000*	*2002-03(BE)*
A. *Revenue Receipts*			
1. Tax	49.22	490.58	585.37
2. Non-Tax	115.24	233.22	327.22
3. Own Revenue (1 + 2)	364.46	723.80	912.59
4. Assigned Revenue	243.71	283.91	404.42
5. Grants	21.22	338.78	449.77
6. Others (Water Supply etc.)	40.56	88.42	111.68
Total – A	*1034.41*	*2158.71*	*2791.05*
	(798.95)	*(1681.00)*	*2194.96*
B. *Capital Receipts*			
Loans and Grants			
Total - B	*62.70*	*331.71*	*566.68*
Total Revenue (A + B)	*1097.11*	*2490.42*	*3357.73*
C. *Revenue Expenditure*			
1. Establishment	248.55	472.84	665.97
2. O & M of Services	190.93	411.44	639.28
3. Water Supply	55.35	126.87	163.19
4. Debt Servicing	19.43	146.46	151.29
Total - C	514.26	1157.61	1619.73
D. *Capital Expenditure*			
Total – D	*207.32*	*633.70*	*670.02*
Total Expenditure (C + D)	*721.58*	*1791.31*	*2289.75*
1. Revenue Account Status (+/-)	+ 520.15	+ 1001.10	+ 1171.32
2. Capital Account Status (+/-)	- 144.62	- 301.99	- 103.34
3. Overall Budget Status (+/-)	+ 375.53	+699.11	+ 1067.98

Notes: Figures in brackets are as given in the Report

Source: Compiled from Report and Recommendations of Second State Finance Commission – Tamil Nadu 2002-2007, May 2001, Volume-II.

Table-2
Capital Investment Required (95-96 Price Level)

(Rs. in Crores)

Service	*6 Corporations*	*102 Municipalities*	*611 Town Panchayats*	*All ULBs*
Water supply	416.23	168.76	133.39	718.38
Severage and Sanitation	697.26	414.74	100.97	1212.97
Solid Waste Management	32.31	25.91	18.75	76.97
Roads	229.23	99.43	153.34	482.00
Storm Water Drains	268.55	157.28	49.12	474.75
Street Lighting	20.96	16.82	49.90	87.68
Total	*1664.54*	*882.96*	*505.47*	*3052.97*

Source: Compiled from Report and Recommendations of Second State Finance
Commission – Tamil Nadu 2002-2007, May 2001, Volume-II.

Since the investment was required for creating new assets to fillup the physical gaps, and as one of the Terms of reference to the FSFC

Table-3
Capital Investment Pattern : Pre and Post Devolution Period

(Rs. in Crores)

ULBs	*Pre-Devolution*			*Post Devolution*	
	1995-96	*1996-97*	*1997-98*	*1998-99*	*1999-2000*
Town Panchayats (611)	42.43	59.12	118.40	191.39	209.22
Municipalities (102)	37.16	48.48	87.79	117.38	147.84
Corporations (6)	127.73	130.42	194.40	248.18	276.64

Source: Compiled from Report and Recommendations of Second State Finance
Commission – Tamil Nadu 2002-2007, May 2001, Volume-II.

was to study 'the requirements of the Local Bodies for meeting revenue expenditure including maintenance of capital assets', the stress was only on the need to meet revenue expenditure (O & M) and recommendations were made accordingly. The capital investment needed was suggested to be tackled by way of accessing open market through bonds etc. and by attempts for partial privatisation efforts.

However, compared to pre-devolution era, in the post devolution period, there has been substantial increase in the capital investment actually made. The pattern is presented in Table 3.

The FSFC has, estimated the O & M requirement for 1997-2002 for Core Service Sectors as indicated in Table 4.

Table -4

Expenditure Pattern on Core Services in ULBs (Rs. in Crores)

Local Body	*Corporations*	*Municipalities*	*Town Panchayats*	*Addl. Investment for New Assets*	*Total*
1. Water Supply	339.07	215.40	167.53	41.45	763.35
2. Sewerage & Sanitation	425.80	160.45	52.52	77.44	716.21
3. Solid Waste Managemnt	444.32	397.52	102.55	64.23	1008.62
4. Roads	209.34	248.34	655.27	45.19	1158.14
5. Storm Water Drains	7.49	11.61	12.56	3.71	35.37
6. Street Lights	104.06	86.10	82.23	50.28	322.67
					4004.36

Source: Compiled from Report and Recommendations of Second State Finance Commission – Tamil Nadu 2002-2007, May 2001, Volume-II.

The O & M requirement was fairly met with FSFC devolution and own funds of the ULBs in the initial years. The demand outgrow the supply later on, due to various factors including the steep rise in the establishment and pension costs consequent on the Recommendations of Pay Commission Report which was given effect two years retrospectively from 01.01.96 during 1998, making it impossible to meet. Consequently the deficit in capital and O & M requirement has remained at a substantial level.

The Second State Finance Commission (SSFC) has assessed the sectorwise capital needs of ULBs for the next five years viz 2002-2007 as follows.

Table-5
Sectorwise Capital Needs Of ULBs
For 10th Five Year Plan Period (2002-2007) (Rs. In Crores)

Service	*Corporations*	*Municipalities*	*Town Panchayats*	*All ULBs*
Water supply	506.20	673.38	1409.41	2588.99
Sewerage/ Sanitation	409.34	391.28	41.67	842.29
Roads	310.81	204.37	406.51	921.69
Storm Water Drains	747.94	1101.63	684.47	2534.04
Street lighting	43.19	43.58	125.30	212.07
Solid waste management	115.95	33.75	20.48	170.18
Others	341.68	231.03	282.91	855.62
Total	*2475.11*	*2679.02*	*2970.75*	*8124.88*

Source: Compiled from Report and Recommendations of Second State Finance
Commission – Tamil Nadu 2002-2007, May 2001, Volume-II.

Similarly, the SSFC has assessed the O & M needs of the ULBs as shown in Table-6.

Having known the capital and O & M needs of the ULBs based on set reasonable norms for the identified core civic services, as set forth above we **may examine the resources at the command of these ULBs.** We should also give due regard to the left out responsibilities and functions listed out in the Twelfth Schedule of the Constitution of India.

The following functions under Twelfth Schedule of Constitution of India for which capital and O & M need to be assessed separately.

1. Urban Planning
2. Regulation of land use
3. Planning for economic and social development
4. Fire services
5. Urban forestry, protection of environment and promotion of ecological aspects

Table-6

O & M of Sources : Financial Needs of ULBs

(Rs. in Crores)

Sector	*Corporations*	*Municipalities*	*Town Panchayats*
General Admn - Taxes	366.27	374.28	206.88
Public Works Road	761.47	329.75	123.01
Public Health Conservancy	264.02	202.80	133.50
Sanitation & Drains	179.96	51.81	-
Street lighting	271.90	221.70	210.89
Water	218.40	289.27	239.96
Miscellaneous	97.36	82.34	155.41
Addl O & M for new cap. investment	122.73	107.55	144.91
Town Planning	4.64	3.65	-
Education	61.91	14.64	-
	2348.66	*1677.81*	*1214.56*

Source: Compiled from Report and Recommendations of Second State Finance Commission – Tamil Nadu 2002-2007, May 2001, Volume-II.

6. Safeguarding the interests of weaker sections of society including the handicapped and mentally retarded.
7. Slum improvement and upgradation
8. Urban poverty alleviation
9. Parks, Garden and Playgrounds
10. Promotion of cultural, educational and aesthetic aspects
11. Cattle pounds

Some of the functions are yet to be devolved on ULBs and the investment needs of some of the other functions could not be immediately and accurately assessed as standard norms are yet to be fixed on such functions and services. Even without these functions, the investment needs are enormous and with the resource availability, the demand under the identified few core services could be met only partially.

With this we may examine whether the tax and non tax resources of ULBs are commensurate with the service expected from ULBs.

Revenue Sources

The ULBs in Tamil Nadu are empowered under the statutes to levy the following taxes and non taxes.

Taxes:

(1) Property tax including vacant land tax
(2) Profession Tax
(3) Advertisement Tax
(4) Vehicle and Animal Tax
(5) Pilgrim Tax
(Octroi is not levied in Tamilnadu)

Non-Taxes:

(1) Water charges
(2) License fees on trades
(3) Rent on lands and buildings
(4) Building license fees
(5) Income from Markets, Shandies
(6) Bus stand and parking fees
(7) Encroachment fees and other misc. items.

In addition to these, State Government is collecting and sharing with the ULBs, 95% of Surcharge on Stamp duty collected on five instruments of title transfer and 90% Entertainment Tax. The power to levy Cable TV Tax, which was entrusted with the ULBs three years back has been withdrawn from them and Government have agreed to compensate the loss of income, actually realised by the ULBs during the previous year.

Tax Revenue

The major tax revenue to ULBs comes from Property Tax, the income from Advertisement Tax, Vehicle and Animals Tax and Pilgrim tax is insignificant. At present it is less buoyant. It is a typical case reflecting the national pattern. The receipts under property tax during the past few years are as given in Table-7:

The sudden upward trend during 1998-99 was due to quinquennial revision after a long period of stagnation in property taxation. Though the collection performance may be a factor, the general position in the contribution of property tax to total revenue is around one third in Corporations and Municipalities and less

Table-7

Property Tax-Receipts (Rs. in Crores)

ULBs	*1995-96*	*1996-97*	*1997-98*	*1998-99*	*1999-2000*
1. Corporations	109.15	117.47	154.41	172.58	214.65
	(31.7)	(30.3)	(31.0)	(29.4)	(31.8)
2. Municipalities	77.52	79.30	81.53	70.02	153.15
	(35.9)	(30.5)	(22.8)	(18.8)	(34.2)
3. Town Panchayat	18.99	18.08	18.97	17.25	53.41
	(17.3)	(14.4)	(7.7)	(6.5)	(17.0)

Source: Compiled from Report and Recommendations of Second State Finance
Commission – Tamil Nadu 2002-2007, May 2001, Volume-II.

Note: *N After Quinquennial revision from 1.10.1998
(Figures in brackets are per cent to total Revenue)

than 20% in Town Panchayats. The next major tax revenue is from Profession Tax. The revenue earned from profession tax by ULBs is indicated in table - 8

Table-8

Receipts from Profession Tax

(Rs. in Crores)

ULBs	*1998-99*	*1999-2000*
1. Corporations	28.26	30.74
2. Municipalities	12.93	12.89
3. Town Panchayat	9.32	10.17

Source: Compiled from Report and Recommendations of Second State Finance Commission–Tamil Nadu 2002-2007, May 2001, Volume-II.

The poor compliance from trading community is the main reason for less revenue from this source.

Non Tax Revenue

The non tax revenue mainly consists of water charges, rent from lands and buildings and fees collected for various services and licenses. The income from non tax resources for the ULBs for a period of five years is presented in Table-9 :

Table-9

Receipts from Non Tax - Resources

(Rs. in Crores)

ULBs	*1995-96*	*1996-97*	*1997-98*	*1998-99*	*1999-2000*
1. Corporations	46.37	80.93	93.62	124.59	112.43
2. Municipalities	44.21	51.42	70.57	79.42	72.41
3. Town Panchayat	24.68	27.52	34.88	40.43	48.39
	115.26	*159.87*	*199.07*	*244.44*	*233.23*

Source: Compiled from Report and Recommendations of Second State Finance Commission – Tamil Nadu 2002-2007, May 2001, Volume-II.

Compared to the total revenue income, the non tax revenue represents roughly 20-25%. Inview of the poor supply position and restricted hours of supply, the water charges are not increased by the local bodies to the desired level. The huge loan borrowed by the local bodies for water supply systems has become a great burden. The water supply account is therefore heavily subsidised. There are problems in leasing out municipal properties including commercial complexes, shops, stalls, etc. because of litigations seeking renewal without public auction. The rates of license fees remain the same for quite a long time in a few municipalities and there is reluctance on the part of the councils to increase the rate of fees periodically.

In view of the above circumstances, due to inelastic resource base, the fiscal management problems and financial short falls to deliver efficient services in ULBs are compounded daily. The basic problem of municipal finance is reflected in the large and growing gap between municipal financial resources and expenditure. The revenue gap of all ULBs in O & M and capital requirements is furnished in Table-10 :

Table-10

Revenue gap for O & M and Capital Requirements for 2002 - 2007

(Rs. in Crores)

ULBs	*O & M*	*Capital*	*Total*
1. Corporations	2974.12	1284.77	4258.89
2. Municipalities	2475.52	823.40	3298.92
3. Town Panchayat	1476.61	958.31	2434.92
	6926.25	*3066.48*	*9992.73*

Source: Compiled from Report and Recommendations of Second State Finance Commission – Tamil Nadu 2002-2007, May 2001, Volume-II.

It has to be borne in mind that this gap is only in respect of the needs under core services and O & M. There are civic services other than core services and there are still many functions yet to be actually devolved on ULBs for which the requirement of funds has to be worked out and added to the above estimates.

Identifying Problem Areas

The growth of municipal revenue does not match the increased demand for urban services both in terms of quality and quantity. Property value is revised once in every five years - not annual - for levy of property tax. The collection performance has to improve especially under vacant land tax. Other local taxes lack buoyancy. The ULBs also lack the autonomy to establish their own tax base. The extent of control over municipal income varies. Only few items are under the control of ULBs. The State Government suddenly reduced the rate of surcharge on stamp duty from 5% to 2%. They have also withdrawn the power of levy of advertisement tax on hoardings and also cable TV Tax and have announced liberal concessions under Entertainment Tax affecting the resources of the local bodies.

The present "**Self Reliance**" indices of ULBs including own taxes and assigned revenue as calculated by SSFC (average self reliance index 2001) are :

1. Corporations	54.7%
2. Municipalities	52.57%
3. Town Panchayat	39.86%

The other sources of revenue are through inter-governmental transfers or revenue sharing and through borrowings for projects. Land development charges and settlement fees are taken away by the development authorities like LPA and the local bodies could not use this fund.

Apart from own resources, the ULBs get share as 'Assigned Revenues' from State Government such as Entertainment Tax and surcharge on stamp duty. Even though these are local taxes / duties, the State Government is collecting them on behalf of the Local Bodies. In addition to this, financial transfer by way of devolution from State are also provided after 74th CAA. But these financial transfers, though reasonably predictable, are not enough for the ULBs. Most of the times, there are large scale deductions towards Government dues like debt and non-debt liabilities. The Central and State Governments, themselves, are not in a position to be more liberal in the matter as their own financial position is not better as reported in a couple of documents.

As pointed out earlier, the Tax and non-tax revenues of ULBs represent less than 50% of their total income and are not sufficient even for their O & M requirement. In a traditional and conventional language, we have to say that there is (definitely) no alternative (TINA factor) or scope for creating revenue surplus to meet their capital needs.

In the present changing environment we have to explore with an optimistic hope that there are number of alternatives approaches (TANA Venture). The alternatives available to us are new and innovative solutions to the problems of Urban Finances infrastructure development as it has become a great challenge.

Innovative Approaches

Among other recommendations on tax, non-tax and transfers from State to ULBs, a notable feature of T.N. SSFC is its focus on " better fiscal management " of local bodies. The SFC specifically advocated innovative approaches to –

(*i*) augment income mobilising additional resources under tax and non-tax domain;
(*ii*) containing expenditure of ULBs;
(*iii*) accounting reforms;
(*iv*) zero-base budgetting;
(*v*) privatisation of core civic services;
(*vi*) fixing fiscal responsibility;
(*vii*) cost-effective and vigil over expenditure ;
(*viii*) asset management;
(*ix*) productivity norms;
(*x*) constitution of Local Body Tribunal;
(*xi*) mechanism to collect arrears of taxes and non-taxes;
(*xii*) remunerative enterprises; and
(*xiii*) generating wealth from urban solid waste.

The Tamil Nadu Government have taken most of the suggestions and developed the strategies under the following direction. During the past decade, Tamilnadu Government has made financial, legislative and administrative reforms in the Urban Sector, for which

74th CAA has also played a vital role. Some of the major reforms are indicated below:

1. Enactment of conformity legislation consequent on 74th CAA;
2. Enactment of **common law** for ULBs of Tamilnadu with provisions suited to current urban scenario;
3. **Liberalised Profession Tax Act** to improve compliance level. Collection from Traders to be entrusted to Commercial Taxes Department;
4. Levy of Advertisement Tax - License fee for **hoardings;**
5. **Cable TV Tax** - Compensation equal to the revenue realised;
6. **8% devolution from State's own Tax** Revenue from 1997-98;
7. **Incentive Fund** (@ 7½% of SFC devolution for 5 years and 5% of SFC devolution for next 5 years) for better performance including tax collection/ debt service etc.
8. Preparing **'Performance Indicators'** to introduce **'Score Cards'** to reward better performing local body.
9. **Computerisation** of Municipal activities, e-mail and website for improved information network;
10. **On-line services** including payment of taxes.
11. Introduction of **Accrual based accounting system.**
12. **Privatisation** policy to encourage private sector participation.
13. Enhanced share from entertainment tax from 65% to 90%.
14. Enhanced share from surcharge on stamp duty.
15. Preparation of **City Corporate Plan** to involve other stake holders for improved capital in put for infrastructure.
16. Encouraging **public participation** in major municipal service projects.
17. Introduction of **Property Tax Reforms:-**
    - (*i*) Area based property tax and vacant land tax;
    - (*ii*) Self assessment return and self assessment tax;
    - (*iii*) Uniform tax for similar buildings;
    - (*iv*) Elimination of discretion;
    - (*v*) Separate tax for water supply, sewerage, education;
    - (*vi*) Service charges for exempted buildings;
    - (*vii*) Minimum Tax for huts;
    - (*viii*) Interest for belated payment, penalty for failure to submit self assessment return and for filing wrong return;
    - (*ix*) Counter collection, bank collection, on line collection facilities. Computerised receipts;
    - (*x*) Improved accounting procedures;

(*xi*) Separate tribunals for tax disputes;
(*xii*) Bar on lower courts regarding tax disputes;
(*xiii*) Systematic periodic revision and budget linked enhancements;
(*xiv*) Improved collection performance;

19. **Compulsory revision of fee structure once in 3 years**
20. **Costing of services** to levy appropriate user charges

In most of such new and innovative attempts, a major constraint has been the resistance from certain sections of municipal staff, elected representatives and general public as well. Such minor hurdles have also been overcome by some corporations and municipalities through proper motivational and training course strategies.

With the encouragement and due support from the State Government, some Corporations and municipalities have infact started introducing such strategies. The results, though not fully tested, are very encouraging and are being introduced in many other ULBs, some such strategies are :

(*i*) Computerisation;
(*ii*) Privatisation of O&M of street lighting and bus stands,
(*iii*) Community participation in door to door collection of garbage and seggregation;
(*iv*) Public-Private Partnership;
(*v*) Introducing transferancy in public works and tender proceedures;
(*vi*) Compliance to the Municipal Solid Waste Management Rules 2000 for urban environment protection, clean city concept and eco-friendly conversion of garbage to manure, and so on.

Similar to the Central Government strategy, introduction of the concept of "Fiscal Responsibility" and Budget Management", the SSFC also suggested to the Tamil Nadu Government to follow such strategy. Accordingly the commission has identified major areas and parameters of fiscal responsibility as applicable to ULBs. Here again among others:

- Levy of right level of user changes;
- Fix target for collection :

(*i*) current demand at 95%
(*ii*) arrears demand at 75%

After due processing and vetted by Law Department, suitable provisions need to be made in the common ULB Act 1998.

Conclusion

Even with all the reforms undertaken and proposed, it may take some years for the local bodies to reach their full potential in tax and non tax resource mobilisation and even then they will feel the shortage of funds, because by that time the demand for services would have also grown due to rapid urbanisation.

The Centre and State should come to their rescue by way of appropriate transfers, which should be transparent and predictable. Better performances should be rewarded with additional transfer to encourage, improved self - reliance. Share from some of the byouant central income to ULBs should be given due consideration as the economy of the country depends more and more on urban sector.

While these are routine suggestions, the approaches, that have been suggested by Tamil Nadu SSFC through new and innovative strategies appears to be worth testing.

COMMENTS

P.K. SRIHARI: All along we have been discussing about the distribution of resources, pattern of distribution of resources, whether it is revenue deficit approach or gap filling approach, share of resource transfer, devolution and so on. However, improving organizational capacity is also very important.

Recently I was browsing through IBM Website, where it has given a strategy to US Administration. It talks about three phrases. Any information system should have three qualities. It should be accurate; it should be timely and it should be analytical. This is what we have done. When we started doing some reforms in Bangalore City Corporation, we found that finance has just no limit when we have a good information system.

These are points that are very well known – weak financial position of BMP, inadequate resources, correct fund position not known, status of assets and liabilities of BMP not fully known, liabilities on account of on going work not fully known, ability to measure up service cost not available, manual posting by entire accounting staff wasting their time only on pay roll, timely, structured and accurate information for making management decision not available—and the list is endless. Our decision-making is not based on any information that is given to us.

There is no computerization in the Finance Department. The manual system is labour intensive, inadequate in many respects and not available on time. We would take 48 days to make an assessment of the financial position of the ULB. Before you think of taking any corrective measures, you would have lost 48 days. So, we just could not have done anything without correcting this kind of system. It was absolutely opaque. There was no transparency in accounting. I am not talking in terms of the accountability of the organization to the citizen. I am talking about the accountability of various levels of staff to the top management. Even that was not available or was obsolete. For example, the Commissioner would not know what the Revenue Inspector is doing on a given day. The motivation that we had was that there was increasing pressure on infrastructure, because the new government said that Bangalore should become a global city.

We had all these objectives that you see on the transparency coming out of that. First we are talking about reforms within the organization. Within the organization, the reform has to happen in resource mobilization. But the other part is normally forgotten. How could we have a good tool, which ensures that the expenditure that is going into the field, every rupee spent in every budget, either creates that kind of an asset or delivers an equal amount of service? So, on one side there is resource mobilization. On the other side, the expenditure sector is covered by accounting and budgeting exercise and the reforms thereof. These are internal reforms within the organization. If you speak of external reforms, it should have citizen-centric measures, because the moment the confidence of the citizen improves with the performance of the ULBs, the more tax revenue the ULB would get.

We had the self-assessment scheme (SAS), which is incorporated in the procedure for giving title to urban properties, so that immediately the owner of the property starts paying.

As an additional way of mobilizing non-tax resources, we had a MOU with the State Government, the first of it kind, saying "for the next three years, we are going to have reforms ourselves in 33 sectors. So, please give us some grants in assistance to satisfy the immediate capital requirements". The State Government readily agreed. They signed the agreement on the 12th July 2001, under which we have received almost Rs. 120 crores as additional grant.

We also requested the Government to pass amendments to the Karnataka Municipal Corporation Act to facilitate us to reform some user charges, predominantly in the collection of garbage, what is called solid waste management cess being levied shortly. The other tax we proposed is on vehicles as infrastructure cess. Both the amendments have been carried out and are in the final stage of implementation.

On the expenditure side, we have introduced fund based accounting system. It came out on the initiative of "Bangalore Agenda Task Force", which is an entity created by issuing a Government Order at the end of 1999, when the new government took over. The Chairman of the Bangalore Agenda Task Force is Shri Nandan Nilakeni, who is the CEO of Infosys. This is a body created by professionals and other businessmen, who actually bring in their own money. Government does not give them any money. They pool in their own money and try to take up some projects, intellectual projects, which are required for bringing about reforms within the city.

One such project was the introduction of the fund based accounting system. It cost about Rs. 2. crores. It was entirely funded by Shri Nandan Nilakeni. He started with passing some accounts regulation, which were provided in the Karnataka Municipal Corporation Act. It was already facilitated. What we went and did was that we chose to use it, exploit that provision in the Act. In the budget regulation, we made a zero-based approach. This is now before the Council for approval.

The significant accounting policy is also before the Council for approval. There is a scientific approach in the preparation of the budget. We have implemented certain key elements of the zero-based budget, what we call BIDS. It actually means Budget Information Data Store. We have about 20 departments. The head of each department has to really bid for his expenditure allocation. Then only it is given to him. So, when we allocate that expenditure to him, he is not only accountable, he is also responsible to carry out and achieve the results, which he wants to do out of that expenditure.

There are citizen-concentric measures like the self-observance scheme, where the assessment powers are given to the citizens themselves. We have simplified the trade licence scheme. We have simplified the sanction of building plans.

We released several manuals for different schemes to the citizens. There is an organization called public Record of Operation Finance (PROOF). They organize quarterly debates on BMP performance and its financial results the way the corporate sector does. We have started doing it. Last year we had four such quarterly debates. This year we did just one half yearly debate. In that debate, some selected citizens, almost 60 to 70 persons, assemble and question us on each and every aspect of the work of the BMC and what it has achieved in the last 3 to 4 months.

There is a small expansion of the fund based accounting system. It is actually a kind of enterprise resource planning approach, which you normally find in private or corporate sector, where finance and administration is made the center of different activities, so that all the departments get closely knit with finance and administration. Finance becomes an active department, not just a passive department for maintaining records. So, you have state Governments, lenders, elected representatives and citizens get benefit out of this. This is the CRP model, which is very widely used in the private sector.

The existing system had very limited capacity to generate information. The new system actually moves out and enters into different departments. If you take the Revenue Department, it actually gets on to the demand collection book of property tax, fix up that demand and put that information together so that the top management will know what actually is the balance to be collected, how much is collected, how much more he can commit.

Similarly, on engineering department, not just data on what is paid, but even committed payments or works on the field with liability. That is also counted, so that you do not end up having too much of work and the payment gets delayed, which affects the political work. So, you can always have a proper management control on works also, using this kind of information, which is available to you on a daily basis. Earlier, it was available 48 days later. Now it is available on line any time of the day on a daily basis.

Then we have fund based accounting system and double entry system of accounting. What it does is, it actually recognizes the complexities of running the government. Government has different kinds of activities. Some of them really cannot be brought under any costing or working out returns, that kind of methodology. So, we have those kinds of activities. For example, the Bangalore City Corporation runs schools and colleges, it maintains stores, and it lifts garbage. Those kinds of activities, from which there is no immediate return, those kinds of activities are budgeted as governmental activity, where typically it is taxed basket. Coming to other kinds of activities, the Bangalore city Corporation also runs commercial complexes and it runs film theatres. This kind of activities can be classified as enterprise fund, where you can apply typically the corporate sector guidelines to administer those funds.

You have a third category called tertiary activities, where you take up some of the projects on behalf of the World Bank, for example, the Indian Population Project. At the end of the project, you get some asset, like hospitals. You are not incurring any cost on that asset at the ULB level, as the repayment is done at the Central level. So, those kinds of activities are also taken care of. The new system produces an important sheet, called balance sheet, which shows what it owns and what it owes. It also produces another statement called revenue and expenditure statement, which is actually expanded receipt and payment statement. Which gives the total financial position of the organization.

So, under the SAS scheme, out of 4-lakh properties, 2.3 lakh opted for it. In 1998-99 we had collected Rs. 94 crores. In 2002-03, we achieved Rs. 195 crores. The citizens are happy because we are able to give any information on BMP any time they want. The corporators wanted to know what is happening in each of their wards. We had 100 wards. Each corporator wanted to know what are the different development activities and the status of those development activities. We are able to give that. We are able to give any kind of information for the public administrator. So, decision making becomes more informed decision-making. Thus, it is able to achieve a kind of improved overall governance year after year. Timely payment to the contractors actually improves the quality of work by the contractors.

The self-assessment scheme was a kind of transition between ARV and the capital value. The self-assessment scheme or area based valuation guidelines fixed in that format is supplied to the citizens. For the capital value system, the amendment has come through last year itself. The rules have been framed, because this capital value system is now being adopted across all ULBs in the state. We have 226 ULBs and 6 municipal corporations. The case of Bangalore is very unusual. It is far ahead of the 5 corporations and 220 plus ULBs. Since the provision was made common for all, we requested the government that they should facilitate us more by providing special provision for BMP. That is given in the format. A separate set of rules for the Bangalore City Corporation is in the advanced stage. We are likely to implement it in the next fiscal year.

These are some of the specific impacts. We have up-dated the cash position. We have real time knowledge of the revenue position, review of collections and the target is made easy.

For controlling the works, we have devised what is known as work storing system, where even the smallest work costing about Rs. 10,000 is stored properly, along with works costing over Rs. 10 crores, so that these works can be tracked at any point of time. There is no duplication of work, which was basically allowing the system to get into corruption.

The Bangalore City Corporation had something like Rs. 40 crores of its money lying in various bank accounts, which was not known. We called the banks said, Every week you are supposed to give us the money. If you return it later than that, you are supposed to give us interest". Though the accounts people earn their salary, they are supposed to be non-revenue yielding staff. Now we have a totally new model of asset management, where the assets have been transferred properly and in a transparent manner.

We have something like 2,600 landed assets and 22,000 buildings. We have valued them. It does not include roads, rails etc.

Coming to overall administration, the decision making in the BMP is supported through the MIS reports. We have decentralized the vehicle maintenance. Now each officer is maintaining his own vehicle. We have brought down the inventory to zero. Even in small municipalities this kind of innovations can be made very easily.

'Artika Darpan' is one handout we have made out only for the corporators, where we do give details of revenue collection, the expression of works, number of works, value of works. It has become a very effective tool for every corporator. One particular corporator, one day came to my chamber and said, "Sir, look, there is nothing happening in my ward and no official is listening to my request for information. What should I do?" I gave him a print out of what are the works that are supposed to have been happening in his ward. A month later, in the Council meeting, he stood up with the print out I gave him and said, "I went on inspection of these works. I found that out of these 10, three have not started and for three nobody knows what is the position." So, this information has transformed him into a true elected representative.

We have published our financial results. We are the first to do it. For the year 2002-03, we published our financial results in The Financial Express and the Economic Times of 23rd May 2003. So, nothing is secret, everything is transparent.

We borrow and invest in building commercial complexes and multi-storey car parks. Because we are transparent and we are forthcoming, there is private equity coming up. So. I need not borrow money or invest out of my own funds.

Earlier we were building bus shelters, developing road mediums and doing traffic junctions. Now people are coming and investing in them.

Coming to staff behaviour in BMP, there is one NGO called Public Affairs Centre for Bangalore, who do a report card. They did one report card in 1993, the second on in 1999 and the third in 2003. The reforms have taken place between 1993 and 2003. So, these cards reflect the effectiveness of the reforms that have taken place. In the Bangalore Mahanagar Palika the staff behaviour with general household has improved from 26 per cent in 1999 to 89 per cent in 2003.

On the corruption level, in 1994 it was 14 per cent, it went up to 22 per cent in 1999 and now because of the reforms it has been brought down to 9 per cent. This actually reflects the overall success of the internal reforms that have been carried out, specifically in the financial sector to start with.

We have just followed the mandate that the municipal bodies should adopt a good accounting system. Having seen that the system change within the corporation can give us every good results in terms of total governance.

RAVIKANT JOSHI: Turn-around is possible, but not for every municipality. This is possible, if it is linked with the system, which is an enabling one.

The case study in Tamil Nadu clearly shows that the State Government has removed those reform obstacles by coming out with enabling orders. Karnataka Government brought out certain changes, particularly removing the obstacles and allowing or giving a free hand to the municipal bodies, to carry out the reforms. Here everything depends on systemic improvement. As Shri Prasad said in the morning, it is not a fiscal issue. I know that this may not be within the purview of the Finance Commission, but they can definitely come up with a statement, because everybody is requesting for some kind of incentive grant for such kind of incentivized reforms.

I have seen so many case studies, where turn-round is possible. There are good case studies in Andhra Pradesh and Maharashtra. Indore in Madhya Pradesh has almost doubled its property tax revenue. So, there is huge untapped reform potential. What is required is an enabling system. No doubt, certain municipalities, may be 50 per cent may not be delivering; but 50 per cent would definitely be delivering and coming out with flying colours, if provided with a system solution.

K. K. PANDEY: Tamil Nadu is in a way a model for us. I will substantiate and support this argument.

Tamil Nadu has done many things for the first time in the country, like bringing out a bond issue, refinance of Madurai by-pass, toll bridge of Karur, Alandur community contribution and BOT project at Tiruppur. There are a number of initiatives, like double entry accounting system. For the first time in the whole State it has been done in Timil Nadu.

What the driving force? That is the institutional mechanism, which is in place in Tamil Nadu. Here a special mention is needed of the Tamil Nadu Urban Development Fund (TNUDF), which is taking a lot of initiatives, along with Timil Nadu Urban Development Project (TNUDP). Then there is a very pro-active role of the Directorate of Municipal Administration and the Rural Director of Municipal Administration (RDMA).

This institutional mechanism has helped the town to prepare detailed project reports for specific tasks. They have come up with guidelines, check lists and other basic modalities, which are needed to take up reforms. They have also been providing financing and monitoring support to take up these reforms. Provision of the institutional set up at the State level can support these initiatives.

DR. Rao mentioned about convergence. Many of the steps that Dr. Rao suggested, which Shri Joshi also mentioned, are part of other initiatives taken by the Central Government, particularly under the Urban Reforms and Incentive Fund (URIF), which cover property tax, enhanced taxation, cost recovery, computerization and provision of Rs. 500 crores per annum. So, there is need to converge the Central

Government resources. While making recommendations, these funds should also be taken into account."

M.C. GUPTA: When Mr. Gorbachov was embarking on the road to opening up, Perestroika and Glasnost, he said "You can have total freedom of action and you can take decisions. For yourself, provided you raise your resources."

Rather than the urban local bodies and the panchayati raj institutions insisting on what the State Governments should give to them, and taking note of the recommendations of the State Finance Commission, what the National Finance Commission or the Twelfth Finance Commission should be giving to the states, or through the states to the urban local bodies, the more sane approach would be first to look at what the urban local bodies can do for themselves and even the panchayati raj institutions can do for themselves.

We should first look at the structure of the Constitution, what taxing powers the Union Government have, what taxing power the States have and what taxing powers the urban local bodies and panchayati raj institutions have, not only taxing powers but also powers to raise resources in the nature of non-tax revenues, and insist that these powers are exercised. The abandonment of this resource raising capacity has gone on for a very long time. The new innovations are very very impressive, both in terms of new resources and in terms of how you really harness them. What we should look at is what all is possible and also look at the possibility of transferring some of these tax raising measures or taxes from the Union to the States and from the States to the urban local bodies and the panchayati raj institutions.

One is the entertainment tax. It used to be one of the major resources of the States at one time. Unfortunately, with so many channels of television and video, entertainment tax is not having the same eminence as it used to have. But, even then, some of the states have a large number of cinema theatres and sometimes you do get films, which run for six months on end. The box office collection is huge, which means the cinema is not really becoming unpopular. The entertainment tax by and large is with the state Governments. I see no reason why it should not be transferred to the urban local bodies.

Similar is the case with professional tax, which some states have abandoned. They are not insisting on that. Some have retained the powers with themselves, excepting a couple of states. I think this is a measure, which is eminently suitable to the urban local bodies.

The other thing I would like to say is to look at the GDP in terms of what the economists call "factor contribution", If you look at the primary sector, it is contributing only 24 to 25 per cent. And the primary sector in India does not include mining, because mining is reflected in the secondary sector or industry sector. So, agriculture and related services contribute only 25.5 per cent or so and the industries around 25.5 per cent. So, the two make only about 50 per cent. The service sector has now risen to 49.5 per cent or so, but the tax realization from the service sector is very low.

We should look at a comprehensive value added tax, as is the case in UK, as is the case in Italy or Germany, except in USA. There even the services are subject to value added tax. It is virtually a uniform rate of tax. I think in England it is 17.5 per cent and in Italy it is 18 per cent. In Germany they have two rates. I think most of you know these details more than I do. So, 49 or 49.5 per cent or almost 50 per cent of the GDP is coming through the service sector and very little has been captured in the tax net, as far as this sector is concerned. When you come to have a comprehensive value added tax system, which would subsume Central excise – it should subsume Central excise, state sales tax and octroi and other local taxes – then you can decide as to what percentage should really go to the Union Government, what should go to the States and what should be given to the urban local bodies.

It would be unwise to work only on the basis of the Union Government or the State Government levying or collecting the taxes and then transferring them to the urban local bodies, because I quoted Mr. Gorbachov. I think the maturity of management of any administrative unit also lies in raising your own resources. Just getting grants, subsidies or subventions from the higher body, in the case of ULBs and the panchayati raj institutions, from the State Government and for the State Government to get the subvention from the Union Government, is not the best thing to happen, and it does not really go down very well with the concept of governance.

For solid waste disposal or garbage collection, the Gurgaon Municipality or the Haryana Urban Development Authority (HUDA) do not charge any tax, fees or levy. Some others also would have also done it, like in Bangalore. They have contracted with certain private parties. The contractor would collect garbage door to door every day, including Saturdays and Sundays, and every household will pay a certain amount. Rs. 50 is paid by each household every month.

Hardly, they would have not showed up 3 or 4 times in the last 20 months. The payment is directly made by the citizens or by the occupiers to the contractor. There is no dumping of the garbage, no pigs and we do not pay anything to the Haryana Urban Development Authority.

The other issue is that of octroi. I have earlier said that I am all for a comprehensive value added tax system. If that happens, octroi will be subsumed into it. I think that octroi has been the mainstay of a very large number of urban local bodies, and those who have abolished it have abolished it at their own cost.

All units of administration should really try to raise their own resources. If you abolish octroi, you will have to give subventions by some other means. Look at the eligibility or the lack of capacity of the State Governments. All of them are running into overdrafts and none of them has a surplus amount in the current account. Almost half the States have not enough even to meet the salaries and wages of their employees. In such a situation, if you abolish octroi and expect the State Government to give them funds every month in lieu of octroi that they have lost, it is a very difficult proposition.

The problem of octroi is not subvention itself, tax or levy. The problem arose because of the way it was collected, because you had all those collection points at all entries and exits of the urban local bodies. These were centers for harassment, corruption and extortion. The Haryana Government at one time had privately contracted out octroi, which again is wrong, because it is a sovereign function.

My suggestion was to abolish all that, do not do any spot collection, do not charge anything on items of personal consumption, confine it only to stock in trade, whether raw material or finished product, and that too through a statement to be filed by every dealer or manufacturer living in the urban local body. Unfortunately, because of pressures of populism, the Haryana Government abolished octroi, and they are regretting it even today. Gujarat and Maharashtra have retained it and they are really doing well. The Southern States have come out with their own formula of sales tax.

The basic need is that the urban local bodies should be encouraged, supported, advised and exhorted to raise their own resources to the extent they can. There are many things, which they cannot do. To that extent, there will have to be subventions from the State Finance Commission and also from the National Finance Commission.

There are two more basic issues. One is that there should be synchronization of the time frame of the State Finance Commissions and the National Finance Commission, and the other is the time frame.

The five-year time frame is a little too short. I do not think the National Finance Commission or the State Finance Commision should be set up once in five years. It should really be once in ten years. This Finance Commission will make recommendations for the period ending 31st March 2010. The State Finance Commissions should also do it in time. The next time frame should be ten years starting from 1st April 2010.

5

ULBs in India:
Focus on Transfer of Functions and Funds

–P.K. Chaubey

India has undergone a silent yet definitely significant political revolution, almost simultaneously with eloquent economic reforms, in the first half of the nineties of the century gone by. Relative rise of market vis-à-vis state and relative importance of local governments vis-à-vis central government may be viewed as extension of the same logic. The import of perpetual existence, ensured with passage of 73rd and 74th Constitution Amendment Acts, 1992 may have yet to be fully realized by over 30 lakh people's representatives, including 73000 in urban areas, of whom over 10 lakh are women, through about 2 lakh rural panchayat bodies and about 3700 urban municipal bodies.

More importantly if quoted Gandhi's talisman of recalling the face of the poorest and the weakest, has any chance of being operational, in terms of realizing the impact of one's action on the poorest of the poor, it is only at the level of local governance where service is delivered to citizens at their doorstep and in their neighbourhood in concrete terms.

The Constitutional directive (Art. 40) to the State (of India, which means the Union and the unit States) to take steps to organize village panchayats and endow them with such powers and authority as may be necessary to enable them to function as units of self-government, was followed more in breach than in observance, notwithstanding that many unit States did good work in many respects. It is a sad story to recount that the Article itself was included as an afterthought[1]. Urban local bodies that way were slightly more fortunate that they were in place and they got mentioned in the State List of the Seventh Schedule as item number 5 which reads: local government, that is to say, the constitution and powers of municipal corporations, improvement trusts, district boards, mining settlement authorities and other local authorities for the purpose of local self-government or village administration.

According to dictionaries, 'self-government' is a government under the control and direction of the inhabitants of a political unit rather than by an outside authority. In fact, the alien rule did think of self-government at local level or sub-provincial level. In different phases, they had different philosophy for promoting it—right from training of politicians to gradual self-government at higher levels[2]. In the present set-up, when the county is self-governed, self-government should mean direct government of public affairs in which elected people have executive powers alongwith deliberative powers if not exactly what may termed as legislative powers.

Yet, it is true world over, under the modern dispensation and under the dominant Dillon philosophy, that the local governments draw/derive their authority from superior legislative bodies and do not have any legislative power but do enjoy considerable decision-making power[3]. While the Legislatures of the unit States are given exclusive power, under Article 246 (3), to legislative items in the State List of the Seventh Schedule and power to legislate on items, with some restrictions, in the Concurrent List of the said schedule, legislation in the matter of local self-government fell in the exclusive jurisdiction of the unit States though Article 40 enjoins all levels of the Government to do their bit in organizing village panchayats and endowing them with such powers as enable them to function as units of self-government.

It was therefore expected of the State Legislatures and the State Governments to constitute and empower by legislation the local bodies so that they could act as the units of self-governments. While municipal acts and municipal bodies were already in existence from the time before independence much in the same way as today with little more autonomy and few more core functions and relatively more funds in the fifties and sixties, the rural local bodies were generally at the district level or at most sub-district level though village panchayats were desired by Royal Commission on Decentralisation (1907-08) and provincial legislations poured in for constitution of village panchayats after Government of India Act 1919. A little before independence, after resumption of power by Indian leadership in 1946, most of the provinces remodelled their village panchayat Acts with a view to conferring more powers and functions. However there was not much concrete until Balvantray Mehta study team (1959), constituted as a part of a larger committee on Community Development and National Extension Service, suggested a democratic structure for people's participation to make the implementation of these programmes more effective.

While many a State Government—both Congress and non-Congress—did tremendously good job of delineating the role of various inter-connected tiers of rural bodies and various levels of independent urban bodies so much so that the Constitutional Amendment Acts themselves drew aspirations on many items from them (Sivaramakrishnan, 2000), it remains a sordid fact that the local bodies were superseded no sooner they were constituted with the change of guards at the State level or they were kept under suspensions for long spells (a mirror image of what the Union governments did with State governments particularly in the seventies and the eighties of the gone by century). As of late the State Governments were short-lived, local bodies had little chance of survival. Worse than that, many public functions—which were genuinely local—were made part of state functions, neither technology nor other forces made this change necessary.

Many State leaders felt that the only solution to this quagmire lay in a Constitutional provision about the establishment and life of the local public representative bodies. Thus, after 40 years, under constitutional directive (Art. 40) did the Republic State of India come forward to constitute the local bodies in terms of broad structure yet left it to the unit States to endow them with powers and authority to enable them function as units of self-government.

The exercise of bringing amendments to the Constitution for giving statutory status to the local elective bodies took about four years in its final attempt. Despite many setbacks and candid admission that these amendments are not a masterpiece of legal drafting (*ibid*, xi), it seems that in each stage of revival of the bills some serious and meaningful suggestions (and a few cumbersome suggestions) were made. In its final leg, the two bills were referred to the two separate Joint Parliamentary Committees. The draft bills had provision for the periodic constitution of State Finance Commission in each State to deal with financial relations between a State and its local bodies. The Joint Parliamentary Committees widened the scope of the Finance Commission through amendment of Art. 280 (inserting clauses (*bb*) and (*c*)) to consider the recommendations of the Finance Commission of a State and suggest measures needed to augment the Consolidated Fund of a State (in order) to supplement the resources of the Panchayats and Municipalities in the State.

Reasoning why (urban) local bodies have become weak and are not able to perform effectively as vibrant democratic units of self-government, the Statement of Objects and Reasons made at the time of introduction of 74th amendment bill, mentions three facts, among a variety of reasons that hold good in case of many states: (*i*) failure to hold regular elections, (*ii*) prolonged supersessions, and (*iii*) inadequate devolution of powers and functions. The amendment sought to (*a*) put on a firmer footing the relationship between the state government and urban local bodies with regard to the functions and taxation powers and arrangement for revenue sharing, (*b*) ensure regular conduct of election and timely elections in case of supersession, and (*c*) provide adequate representation for weaker sections like scheduled castes, scheduled tribes and women. While with initial hitches and hiccups, the latter objectives have by and large been fulfilled almost in all states, the first one and the difficult one when the States are themselves facing the fiscal crisis, has been eluding serious attempt except in a few States. While the State Finance Commissions have been constituted in almost all states, adequate devolution of functions and funds has still to go a long way.

It is in this background that we are supposed to address in this piece on (*i*) functions transferred to Urban Local Bodies in the wake of 74th Amendment of the Constitution and (*ii*) adequacy of resources transferred to perform these functions. While many of the new functions suggested for transfer are regulatory or administrative in nature, adequacy of resources at the disposal of local bodies is a perennial question. Gopal Krishna Gokhale had moved a resolution in the Indian Legislative Council on 13th March 1912, which read:

> That this Council recommends to the Governor General in Council that a Committee of officials and no-officials may be appointed to

> enquire into the adequacy or otherwise of the resources at the disposal of local bodies in the different provinces for the efficient performance of the duties, which have been entrusted to them, and to suggest, if necessary, how the financial position of these bodies may be improved (Manager of Publications, 1951, p. 21).

Partly on assurance from the Finance Member of the Government of India and partly for the fact the resolution was sure to be defeated, Gokhale withdrew the resolution but the fact remains the local bodies, particularly rural ones, hardly had any powers and a huge proportion of whatever proceeds of land cess had to be devolved to them was to be deducted for chowkidari police. Gokhale had pointed out to the (*a*) inadequacy of services, (*b*) inadequacy of taxing powers and (*c*) inadequacy of grants – the matter again and again a subject of discussion.

Straight answers to the issues posed to us by the Finance Commission would have been far more easier but deceptive and therefore a somewhat longish response is being attempted here. As complexity of exercise would hardly permit one to check whether transfer of resources is commensurate with the transfer of additional functions, we shall consider only desired expenditure on the functions traditionally considered 'municipal' – core or otherwise and whether resources available are inadequate and if so, to what extent. I may hasten to add that not all municipalities were always resource-less otherwise they would not have undertaken many functions of non-obligatory character. Needless to mention, they had trust of the people too for carrying out collective functions!

There are three parts in this paper. Part A deals with Basics, Part B with urban local domain, and Part with adequacy of services and resources.

PART A: BASICS OF LOCAL GOVERNANCE

Before proceeding further, we should note that the bodies we are going to deal with have two characteristics 'urban' and 'local' and both have their own peculiarities. We shall primarily be dealing with matter concerning public finance/public economics. However, we do feel that some elements that are not adequately dealt with in fiscal economic domain concerning 'self', 'local', and 'urban' need to be first underlined. We iterate here a set of *panchasheelas* concerning the elements of 'self', 'local', and 'urban', which we try to adhere in our approach to address the issues of devolution of functions, functionaries and funds to the urban local bodies in a multi-layered federal polity, which is India.

Panchasheelas

1. **Principle of Democracy in Structure**: It has been asserted in many committees concerned with local governance that what could be done at a lower level, must not be passed on to any higher level[4]. This suggestion emanates from two different quarters. In India, in reports of various committees and commissions, and of study teams and task forces—at state level and at national level, this is suggested in keeping with political ethos. In the western literature dealing with local public economics, finance and policy, which we increasingly refer to, the suggestion emanates from the consideration of economies of scale and spill-over area of externalities. In other words, in our reports it is giving vent to homo politicus in us while there man is primarily considered as homo economicus (and perhaps consumer qua consumer). That is why in their treatment local governments would compete, as firms do, in the provision of a variety of public goods to allure the citizens and residents would move across the local jurisdictions suiting their tastes[5]. The citizens in the western models, not lands, are passive consumers, not active participants.

   While we do not ignore the basic economic logic, we underline an important axiom that people are not just interested in the product howsoever it is provided, they very much wish to be a part of the process of decision-making. It is not a matter about what is gained but also how what is gained, is gained. The fact that polling percentage in local elections is somewhat (65-70 per cent) higher than that at non-local elections (40-50 per cent) may be taken as an indication of greater interest in local democracy.

   It means the members and chairperson of the local governing bodies should all be elected ones, no matter how the chairperson is elected. The matter whether we should have party-less democracy or party-based democracy should not detain us here.

   But all public bodies catering to local needs or to local areas should be part of the local self-government. If at all it is found desirable that certain functions need specialized knowledge or expertise – which in today's world almost all functions require, then such bodies should be subordinated to the local bodies. In other words, such bodies could assume the role of para-municipals rather than of para-statals.

Similarly, local bodies that have to take care of several bodies and several levels, like district planning committee and metropolitan planning committee have to be as representative as possible. It means that the members of these bodies should be from amongst the elected representatives.

Democracy believes that people have enough common sense to make decisions. Public decisions are too serious a matter to be left with the non-elected experts. One may question if the people commit mistakes. Yes, they can; we all do. Individuals, families, states and nations are all post facto discovered to commit mistakes. Then, I hold a view that 'the right to commit mistake should lie with the people who have to bear the consequences' and 'the people should not be made to suffer for somebody else's mistakes (like BDO Sahib's)'.

2. **Principle of Autonomy in Functioning**: Early scholars, like K.C. Wheare, writing in the area of fiscal federalism suggested that different tiers of government in a federal polity should be coordinate with each other rather than one being subordinate to another. As functional and financial domains could hardly ever match severally, inter-governmental transfers were developed as a means to bring balance between expenditures and receipts at disaggregated level. Later, when it was found, say in the US, that federal government had much more resources than it needed for its traditional functions while its counterpart state and local governments had much less than needed for the functions assigned to them, the former resorted to undertake many local functions under national schemes/ programmes. Many asserted that the essence of federalism is mutual inter-dependence rather than mutual independence, though inter-dependence often turns out to be dependence of so-called lower tier jurisdictions on higher ones (M.J.C. Vile is quoted by Reagan, 1972, p.11).

The existence of horizontal mismatch is the very basis for creation of vertical mismatch under the assumption that lateral transfers would involve heavy transaction costs in terms of processing information and conducting negotiation.

Local governments have been subject to so many restrictions on financial side, world over, if not on functional side. There is mismatch between rights and duties. Duties cast upon them are much larger than rights they have over resources[6]. Even if the gap is bridged through transfers from the higher levels, it is often not as a matter of right but only in terms of grants and loans (entailing burden in future).

Besides fiscal area, there are always some bodies to appraise/approve/ sanction in the beginning, inspection in the middle and audit at the end. Their tax efforts are circumscribed by so many limitations in terms of rates, procedures and ceilings. Government departments determine the rates and the ceilings (and sometimes even the floors) and so is the case with exemptions and concessions. Certain traditional taxes are withdrawn without adequate compensation.

While recent Constitutional amendments have been so good otherwise, they echoed the same archaic state laws on the financial matters except the mandate for constitution of state finance commissions. May be the wisdom lay there: lest the amendments be miscarried. Yet, the point to be emphasized that the derivate governments must have functional autonomy to take initiative and innovate.

However functional autonomy has little meaning if there is not enough financial independence. Said verily the Local Finance Enquiry Committee (Manager of Publications, 1951, p. 1): no system of local self-government can be successful unless it is provided with adequate funds. It quoted from the Presidential Address of Sardar Vallabhbhai Patel, who was incidentally the Chairman of the Ahmedabad Municipality at that time, at the Provincial Local Bodies Conference at Surat in 1935 to have said:

> It is being said that the franchise of the electorate has been enlarged and the local bodies have been given very wide powers. True, I accept it. But what good would come out of it unless and until the question of local finances is settled first. The extension of franchise and widening the scope of duties would be like dressing a dead woman. (*ibid*, p.1)

Taxes, duties tolls, fees and cesses should preferably be devolved through a piece of legislation. If voting by feet is the fear then the rates may be decided by the government but total administration should lie with local elected bodies. If the cost of collection is high, cess imposed by a local body, which is adjunct in nature, can be collected at higher level but the proceeds should be passed on immediately even by the collection office itself. The cardinal principle should be that, in most cases, the local bodies should have enough resources of their own to provide for the core municipal services.

3. **Principle of Fraternal Feeling**: We are discussing the issues of those urban local bodies, which have their rural counterparts and which are saddled in a framework of Union-State federal polity and do not exist in isolation, like Greek cities. They are not constituents of a unitary polity though existence of local governments makes any polity of reasonable size, a federal one in some concrete sense.

When people of different habitations come together to form a multi-habitation political unit on their volition, which rarely happens in real history, it may be conjectured that there are in existence some public goods having spillovers beyond local areas for provision of which they need a larger political area. But why political area?

Of late, we are witnessing common economic unions happening and we have for quite some time been talking of developing a common national market and so on in our own country too, where perhaps unintentionally many barriers got created between states and even between districts because of circumstances. Some cultural affinity and some societal ethos make them form a political union. No two countries are of the same size whether by population or by area or by any other criterion like race or area. We also know that they have come about by historical circumstances and accidents.

Yet there seems to exist, at least in common perception, some commonality, which bind the people together and make others alien. We are then one but not completely so. For example, in a society long nurtured in a tradition of village exogamy, it is not only two families but two habitations too develop some common interest.

The point is that we look forward to cooperate with fraternal units in larger interest of the total community even if we have to suffer temporarily a bit. The question of equity across habitations then assumes significance. If the two units are not having the same capacities but the two units feel that both the units should enjoy the same level of consumption of certain goods, the resources may have to be transferred from the more prosperous to the less prosperous. The limit to transfer is half the difference in the present should it reverse the positions of the two units in question[7].

While redistribution is a major responsibility cast upon the modern government, the units cannot perpetually continue to enjoy transfer of resources. The resentment from the more prosperous is likely to erupt. Some would point out its impact on efficiency too while others would point towards non-fiscal transfer of resources from one unit/area/jurisdictions to another.

We should note that in all multi-habitation polities there will always be need for equity transfers from some units to others though the sets of habitations cannot continue to be the same. While more prosperous ones have been objecting to the redistributive measures undertaken by Planning Commission and Finance Commission, we have started hearing from some no-so-well-off states that they should also be put in the special category states[8].

4. **Principle of Diversity in Preferences**: As human beings, we are very similar and in very broad terms our needs may be quite similar. But our geography, history and culture make us choose some very different goods. This may be true of public goods as well. We have long been suggested a division between national public goods and local public goods. There could be full spectrum of public goods from local to global and no given set will fit all the countries. Yet, it can scarcely be gainsaid that the quantity and intensity, and also priority, of our collective wants for local public goods may differ considerably across habitations in comparison to national public goods or global public goods. This diversity has long been regarded as geographical variation in tastes.

   We may note that many commentators point towards variation or differences in the sets of functions across different states, between rural and urban, and between different levels of municipal governments as if uniformity in itself is a desirable attribute in all cases. This confusion arises because of their impatience for summary statistics. Diversity is too easily confused with disparity.

In view of certain scholars, differences in local aspirations, in provision of public goods and in provision of public utility services are the substantial economic bases for local governance of public affairs of local nature. It is further asserted that local politicians are better informed about local tastes and their choices would better conform to local taste. Voters can be better informed of services and costs thereof, which they can easily relate.

Part of the confusion referred to owes to the emergence of national concern for many local public goods, semi-public goods and merit goods as well as to universal kind of technology. Nevertheless, the regard for diversity should continue to be a cardinal principle.

5. **Principle of Heterogeneity of Units**: Size of our States vary from 6 lakh to 16 crore, that of union territories varies from 70 thousand to 130 lakh and of cities, within the category of urban habitations, the range varies from a few hundreds to several millions. We may have a district of 2 lakh and also of 20 lakh. There are several factors making this to happen, population size is only a proxy and being used for the purpose of illustration. This simply suggests that we should expect not a uniform list of functions across the states or even within the states, as we often do.

Our States had taken due note of such diversity and their acts could be seen as differentiated products. Our politicians and bureaucrats, while drafting and reviewing the amendment bills, had wisdom to take cognizance of the fact and provided a lot of flexibility to the state legislatures in devolving or delegating functions to a particular category in their respective states. And they exercised this option in quite judicious manner. However, researchers in this area do not feel happy with an amazing level of diversity and wish that could there be a uniform list so that their studies could be easily handled.

Therefore, we have to keep this factor in mind so that we are not after simple solutions of fit-all variety.

Another point that deserves mention here is that our megapolises and metropolises are not truly local. They are spread over many districts. The metropolises are local in the sense that they are sub-state entities. This seems to have been in minds of the members of the JPC when they insisted on the provision of metropolitan planning council in the 74th constitutional amendment bill (Sivaramakrishnan, pp. 98-100).

Goods and Bads of Urban Local Habitations

Some public goods and utility services could be provided rather economically if a habitation has sufficient population size and is sufficiently dense. Internal roads could be paved, footpaths could be provided and drainage of wastewater could be arranged. Water supply pipes and sewer pipes underground and electricity wires/ cables and telephone wires/cables, earlier over-ground and now underground could all run in parallel. These networked services would not be cheap in habitations too small in size or too sparsely inhabited. This felicity is considered as the economies of scale. The same logic applies to development of market.

As these features permitted better division of labour, there usually emerged a more diverse pattern of economic activities – one leading to another except in a few specialized towns such as temple towns and cantonment boards. This could be termed as the economies of scope. Most towns are today industrial/commercial in character. Urbanization is found to be associated with industrialization.

These peculiarities put together made urban life different than its rural counterpart. The leisure activities, pastimes and amusement in two types of habitations are markedly different.

However, development in size and density in cities and development of technologies in different fields may turn out to be synchronous or non-synchronous. Some utility services need not be in public domain as they may no longer be natural monopolies. It is just possible that density, a positive idea, may cross a limit and becomes congestion. In North Eastern District of Delhi, density is 30000 persons per sq. km. and there may be still denser pockets in many other cities. Solution to space scarcity in terms of high-rise buildings may pose problems for water supply, drainage and sewerage, making roads porous. Communication means make the roads congested and subways and flyovers are failing to be adequate. Vehicular traffic and electricity power generating stations are degrading the environment. Clean ground and dirty air! But then drainage and sewerage may pollute the watercourses. Public goods will then have to be defined so as to include the activities that try to do away with private bads.

Then, there develop what have been called urban agglomerations (though in definitional sense there are very small urban agglomerations in India) and what could perhaps be termed as multi-local habitations. The idea that everybody should know everybody else and that every citizen identifies himself with the city, has lost meaning in the present-day world. Plato's ideal city was to have 5040 persons, no more.

Further, urban localities were not unknown for poverty but slums are then the gift of development in urban locales and lack of similar development in rural counterparts. They are the product of push and push, rather than push and pull. More than 600 towns with population more than 50000 have more than 4 crore people in slums—around a quarter of their aggregate population. Mumbai's 50 per cent population lives in slums. Even Meghalaya is having more than 40 per cent urban population living in slums. Kerala is the only state, which has less than 2 per cent of urban population living in slums.

In addition, in many large States, the recent data shows that incidence of poverty, in urban areas is higher than that in rural areas. While in U.P. and M.P., the rural and urban incidence ratios are equal, in Kerala and Andhra Pradesh urban incidence ratios are more than twice of their rural counterparts. In Tamil Nadu, Maharashtra and Gujarat, urban incidence ratios are distinctly higher than their respective rural counterparts while in Karnataka urban incidence ratio is 1.5 times the rural counterpart. This leaves among the large states only Assam, Bihar, Orissa and West Bengal where urban scene is relatively better so far as poverty is concerned but they all have poverty ratio around or over 40 per cent except West Bengal where it is less than 30 per cent. They are the states having low urbanization rate as well.

It is true that for the country as a whole the tempo of urbanization had slowed down during the eighties and has further slowed down during the nineties, thanks to push-push factor. For urbanization levels of 1991, 1998 and 2001, see Appendix Table 1. The disaggregated picture is that in Uttar Pradesh and Tamil Nadu among the major states and Arunachal Pradesh among the smaller states the URGD is pretty high. In Tamil Nadu and Goa, the rural population has somewhat declined while it has risen in Lakshadweep and Daman and Diu. In the case of smaller states, it may be a matter of classification of habitations. Significant point though to note is that the URGD in the case of Kerala and Manipur is negative, which means the rate of growth of rural population is higher than that of urban population. We all know that rural habitations in Kerala are no worse, and perhaps better, than their urban counterparts. In fact, if there is filth in Kerala it is in bigger cities.

Thus, urban local bodies have great advantages of diverse economic activities, economies of scale and of scope in provisioning of services but have great disadvantage of shouldering many more responsibilities. There are around 3700 urban local bodies with 100 corporations, 1500 municipal councils and 2100 nagar panchayats, besides 56 cantonment boards – a kind of extra-constitutional body. For their state-wise distribution, see Table 1.

Let us further note a few legal facts. The Fifth Schedule Areas in many states and Sixth Schedule Areas in Assam, Meghalaya, Tipura and Mizoram have been specifically excluded from the operation of the 73rd and 74th Amendments under State legislation. The Parliament has to first extend the provisions through legislation. While the Parliament has passed legislation in respect of rural local bodies in 1996, it has yet to act to extend the provision for urban local bodies. As a result, in the states of Mizoram and union territories of Dadar and Nagar Haveli no municipal bodies exist. In Meghalaya, the Municipal Act is still under consideration. In Jammu and Kashmir and Sikkim, the Municipal Acts have been passed rather late. No place seems to have been declared urban in Arunachal Pradesh. In all these states there exists urban population. It simply means that many urban places are non-municipalized. In some States, under popular demand or as a populist measure, some nagar panchayats, as recently in Haryana, have been de-municipalized (Kulwant Singh, 2001). Elsewhere, which means in all large states, the Conformity Acts were passed before the deadline of June 1, 1996. Except Bihar and Pondicherry, municipal bodies have been constituted though there were cases of serious delays elsewhere for the first set of elections (Sivaramakrishnan, 2000).

Table 1: Distribution of State-wise Urban Local Bodies

	Municipal Corporations		*Municipal Councils*		*Nagar Panchayats*		*Urban Local Bodies*	
	April 1998	Sept. 2002	April 1998	Sept. 2002	April 1998	Sept. 2002	April 1998	Sept. 2002
Andhra Pradesh	7	7	94	109	15	1	116	117
Arunachal Pradesh	—	—	—	—	—	—	—	—
Assam	1	1	28	29	50	38	79	68
Bihar	6	5	70	32	94	80	170	117
Chhattisgarh	—	6	—	20	—	49	—	75
Goa	—	—	14	13	—	—	14	13
Gujarat	6	6	85	85	58	58	149	149
Haryana	1	1	81	21	—	46	82	68
Himachal Pradesh	1	1	19	20	28	31	48	52
Jharkhand	—	1	—	17	—	22	—	40
Jammu & Kashmir	—	—	2	3	67	67	69	70
Karnataka	6	6	121	124	88	87	215	217
Kerala	3	5	55	53	—	—	55	58
Madhya Pradesh	18	14	103	86	283	234	404	334
Maharashtra	15	19	229	224	—	2	244	245
Manipur	—	—	7	8	21	21	28	29
Meghalya	—	—	6	6	—	3	6	9
Mizoram	—	—	2	—	4	1	6	1
Nagaland	—	—	—	—	9	8	9	8
Orissa	2	2	30	33	70	68	102	103
Punjab	4	4	96	97	37	30	137	131
Rajasthan	3	3	11	11	169	169	183	183
Sikkim	—	—	—	—	—	8	—	8
Tamil Nadu	6	6	102	102	636	611	744	719
Tripura	—	—	1	1	12	12	13	13
Uttar Pradesh	11	11	226	193	447	417	684	621
Uttranchal	—	1	—	31	—	28	—	60
West Bengal	6	6	112	112	4	4	122	122
Andaman & Nicobar	—	—	1	1	—	—	—	1
Chandigarh	—	1	—	—	—	—	—	1
Delhi	—	1	—	1	—	—	—	2
Pondicherry	—	—	—	5	—	—	—	5
Dadra & N. Haveli	—	—	—	—	—	—	—	—
Lakshadweep	—	—	—	—	—	—	—	—
Daman & Diu	—	—	—	2	—	—	—	2
Total	*96*	*107*	*1494*	*1443*	*2092*	*2091*	*3682*	*3641*
July 2000	—	101	—	1430	—	2009	—	3540

1. Nagar Panchayats are known as notified area committees in Bihar and Jharkhand, notified area authorities in West Bengal, town area committees in Jammu and Kashmir, town committees in Nagaland, notified area councils in Orissa, and town panchayats in Tamil Nadu. 2. In Karnataka, municipal councils are of two categories: city councils and town councils, elsewhere they are municipal councils or municipalities. 3. In Mizoram, proposed to be set up.

Some Elements of Local Public Economics

Local public political bodies are expected to deal with local public affairs with the exercise of local public choice. In the economic domain, they are public goods, public utilities and public works of local nature or local character[9]. While public goods chiefly possess the characteristics of non-rivalry in joint consumption and non-excludability of any consumer in consumption of these goods like sweeping and street lighting. If all individual consumers consume the same amount of a good at the same time, then the consumption is said to be non-rival and therefore non-rival consumption is also referred to as joint consumption. (But you need not consume it jointly). Yet there are only a few pure public goods. For example, beaches on holidays, parks in fine weather and city streets during rush hours become goods of rival consumption. Non-excludability is often technical but it may be political or economic too. While technically it may be feasible to debar the consumers, who do not pay for the service, the cost of excluding them may be sometimes prohibitive. As their consumption cannot be priced to individuals all of whom are supposed to consume the same amount[10], they need to be financed from common pool of resources. Some scholars therefore prefer to call them common pool services. There are other public goods, which share the property of non-rivalry but not that of non-excludability for example the use of roads. Such public goods can be accessed on payment[11]. Important point to note is that local public goods are supposed to have local reach[12].

Public utilities are often natural monopolies and their services are provided through over-ground or underground networks. Some of these services like water supply or electricity can be priced with ease. As charges for some of the services are known as toll, some scholars prefer to call them toll services. Such business organizations are subject to special government regulations. Very often they are in the charge of municipal governments and sometimes in the charge of some parastatal organizations. Even if they are owned and run by private parties, they are subject to certain government regulations. Ownership and operation have often shifted between private and public hands as also between local and state/nation or para-municipals to parastatals. There could even be separation between ownership and operation.

Electricity supply is no longer a local affair unless electricity generation (through use of solar or wind) is restricted to non-conventional resources. Water supply is increasingly becoming a non-local affair. Unbundling of various levels of supply will permit distribution part to be handled through local authority.

Public works are constructed for public use or enjoyment especially when financed and owned by the government. Roads, culverts, bridges, flyovers and subways in the modern days and dug-wells, tanks and playgrounds in the olden days, are all examples of public works. They have quality of some degree of 'public-ness'. Many of the utilities such as waterworks could also be called so.

In theory the usual distinction made is between local and national. And we will not discuss here global ones. Except in Greece of City-States of olden days, there has always been made a distinction between local and non-local public goods/utility services. Further, it depends basically on the technology whether a particular service is a natural monopoly. Even a public good may change into a private good.

PART B:
URBAN LOCAL DOMAIN

Functional Domain of Municipalities

What should be dealt with by a particular local body would depend on the nature of the good as well as on the capacity/capability of that body as also on what other non-local bodies are doing in that local area. In our Constitution, matters of local public sphere are enumerated in the State List because the unit States were expected to constitute local bodies and assign them the tasks, functions and responsibilities and empower them with adequate resources so that the local bodies could look after the tasks assigned to them[13]. Since the unit States failed to do this job adequately, the State of India stepped in. The amendments evolved a uniform pattern of local bodies across the country with little scope in details, suggested some of the functions/responsibilities/tasks for devolution/delegation, if already not devolved/delegated, and exhorted the State Legislatures to endow the local bodies with such power, authority and resources as may be necessary for carrying out such functions. In respect of Schedule Fifth and Sixth Areas, the Parliament has yet to extend the provisions for urban local bodies.

Constitutional Position

Part XI of the Constitution deals with the relationship between the Union and the States and it has two chapters – Chapter I dealing with legislative relations and Chapter II dealing with administrative relations. Of the eleven articles dealing with legislative relations, Art. 246 delineate the legislative competence of the Parliament and the State Legislatures as regards the subject-matters. The clause (3) of the article stipulates exclusive power to the State Legislatures to make laws with respect to any of the matters enumerated in List II in the Seventh Schedule while the clause (2) stipulates co-extensive power to the State Legislature along with the Parliament with respect to any of the matters enumerated in List III in the Seventh Schedule. All subject matters related with local functions are listed in List II and List III and traditionally local powers of raising resources (taxes, user charges and loans) are also listed in the List II. As the local bodies are not legislative bodies (but only deliberative bodies), local bodies do not have any exclusive domain of their own. Their domain is co-extensive with and a subset of the state's functional domain.

Twelfth Schedule

Art. 243W suggests that the Legislature of a State may, by law, endow the municipalities with such powers and authority as may be necessary to enable them to function as institutions of self-government and further suggests that such law may contain provision for the devolution of power and responsibilities upon municipalities – subject to such conditions as may be specified – with respect to (*i*) the preparation of plans for economic development and social justice and (*ii*) the performance of functions and the implementation of schemes as may be entrusted to them including those in relation to the matter listed in the Twelfth Schedule. Art. 246 also suggests that the Legislature of a State may, by law, endow the Committees (the Wards Committees) with such powers and authority as may be necessary to enable them to carry out the responsibilities conferred upon them including those in relation to the matters listed in the Twelfth Schedule.

Certain things should be clear. First, this article is not a statutory binding for the State Legislatures. Second, provision for devolution of power and responsibilities, with conditions, is indicative. Third, the Twelfth Schedule is only illustrative; all matters listed therein neither need to be devolved, nor are they suggested to be exhaustive. Fourth, the schedule indicates only the subject-matters of functions, not the functions themselves that could be entrusted. Fifth, powers, responsibilities and authority may be devolved by the law in anticipation of functions and schemes that may be entrusted to them.

Some Exercises on Functional Domain

All major States had Municipal Laws as well as Municipal Bodies much before they came into existence in the present form. (They are thus the foster parents.) There might have been many Municipal Acts by which the municipal bodies were governed, partly because of reorganization of states in different phases. For example, there are four Municipal Acts in the State of Maharashtra (Pethe, et al, 2003) while Andhra Pradesh had two. Some States only amended their existing acts, others repealed the old ones and legislated new ones and still others have them for the first time. Usually there are two Acts – one dealing with municipal corporations and the other with other municipalities. The issue is what are the functions assigned to the urban local bodies – which are now of three levels: Municipal Corporations, Municipal Councils and Nagar Panchayats. Some small states do not have any urban local bodies; others do not have any municipal corporations. Among the major ones do not have any nagar panchayats. There are in existence cantonment boards as well, on which the Constitution is silent. As there has to be a division of local functions between different tiers of rural panchayats, the note has to be taken of the size of habitation in the legislations for different levels of urban local bodies. Large heterogeneity in urban local bodies even within a given category and wide spectrum of 'local public goods' and 'local public utilities' make the exercise rather difficult. Some State Acts have differentiated different levels within a given category like municipality.

However, scholars and researchers have been busy in collating the information related with the subject matters listed in the Twelfth Schedule and have tried to put the information in a tabular form.

While in many cases, earlier municipal Acts had elaborate details on functions that were devolved to urban local bodies, the amendment Acts did not specify them. In some other cases, they bodily lifted the subject-matters and listed them as functions in their respective Amendment Acts. In still other cases, an elaborate exercise was carried out and functions and sub-functions were listed. Further, as most of the major States had separate laws for municipal corporations and other municipalities, it could have been advisable that two/more different tables were prepared, also because what was needed for Patna would not be needed for Sewan. But then geographical peculiarities would require their consideration too. And if different State Legislatures think differently, we should rather welcome the approach rather than castigate them for non-uniformity in their conformity Acts.

We could see four such compilation tables: NIUA (2000), Sivaramkrishanan (2000), AIILSG (2001) and Singh (2001). While the NIUA (2000) has given separate summary tables for municipalities and municipal corporations with respect to 18 functions in the Twelfth Schedule as well as for 28 additional functions. While municipality table covers 12 States and the municipal corporation table covers three municipal corporations and three states. In detailed tables for each state, the NIUA (2000) cross-classifies the functions according as they have been made obligatory or discretionary and whether they fall in the category of (*i*) public health, (*ii*) medical relief, (*iii*) public works, (*iv*) education, (*v*) development and (*vi*) others. Sivaramakrishnan (2000) gives two tables for nagarpalikas—one for 18 functions (subject-matters) of the Twelfth Schedule and the other for 21 additional functions. But in the text he does point out there is little meaning in the distinction between obligatory and discretionary functions for discretionary activities do not come as a sequence after obligatory ones. Simply because a municipality is in arrears in payment of electricity dues for street lighting, which is a obligatory function, will not close down a primary school because education is listed as a discretionary item.

AIILSG (2001) did prepare the table for 13 states, including Delhi, showing which of the eighteen functions/subject-matters have been assigned to the nagarpalikas. Singh (2001) has concentrated only on three States of Kerala, Tamilnadu and West Bengal, showing which of the 18 functions devolved have been put in the category of obligatory or discretionary. Singh (2001) has also matched the entries in twelfth schedule with those in the State List and Concurrent List of the Seventh Schedule).

While these efforts are commendable, they are all partial and there are discrepancies between them as also in these tables and detailed Acts. However, this is inherent in the kind of exercise; after all it is matter of judgement whether to tick a particular subject-matter as yes if only an item or two out of that subject-matter is mentioned. There are not one or two but several Acts in some states! There is thus a lot of confusion as perhaps none of the scholars could have access to all Acts and amendments thereto.

Unfortunately some scholars have just counted the numbers as if a set of five core functions is equivalent another set of five functions of secondary importance.

Present Position of the Functional Domain

Based on the study of secondary sources, we come to following general pattern. All major states have assigned to their urban local bodies the responsibility of (*i*) 'public health, sanitation, conservancy, and solid waste management' (Item 6 of Schedule XII, Item 6 of State List of Schedule VII); (*ii*) 'provision of urban amenities and facilities such as parks, gardens and playgrounds' (Item 12 of Schedule XII, Item 18 of State List and Item 20 of Concurrent List in Schedule VII); (*iii*) 'burials and burial grounds, cremations and cremation grounds and electric crematoriums' (Item 14 of Schedule XII, Item 10 of State List in Schedule VII); (*iv*) 'vital statistics including registration of births and deaths' (Item 16 of Schedule XII, Item 30 of Concurrent List in Schedule VII); and (*v*) 'regulation of slaughter houses and tanneries' (Item 18 of Schedule XII, Item 15 of State List in Schedule VII). While the last two are regulatory in nature, the middle one is a serious problem only in metropolis. Somebody did comment that only the task that has really been left with the ULBs is that of 'jhadoo lagao'. I think scavenging in a town/city is a great duty.

Almost all the States have assigned to their urban local bodies the responsibility of (*vi*) urban forestry, protection of environment and promotion of ecological aspects (Item 8 of Schedule XII, Item 6 of State List in Schedule VII), major exception being Delhi; (*vii*) water supply for domestic, industrial and commercial purposes (Item 5 of Schedule XII and Item 17 of State List in Schedule VII), major exception being Delhi, Andhra Pradesh (in fact Hyderabad) and Madhya

Pradesh; (*viii*) roads and bridges (Item 4 of Schedule XII and Item 13 of State List in Schedule VII), major exception being Uttar Pradesh and Delhi; (*ix*) cattle pounds and prevention of cruelty to animals (Item 15 of Schedule XII and Item 15 of State List and Item 17 of Concurrent List in Schedule VII), major exception being Andhra Pradesh.; (*x*) public amenities including street lighting, bus stops and public conveniences (Item 17 of Schedule XII and Item 5 of State List and Item 20 of Concurrent List in Schedule VII), major exception being Andhra Pradesh.

With few exceptions, the states have assigned (*xi*) safeguarding the interests of the weaker sections of society, including the handicapped and the mentally retarded (Item 9 of Schedule XII and Item 9 of State List and Item 16 of Concurrent List in Schedule VII), and (*xii*) promotion of cultural, educational and aesthetic aspects (Item 13 of Schedule XII and Items 12/33 of State List and Item 25 of Concurrent List in Schedule VII).

What is important is that many States have reservation on the items listed in the beginning in the Schedule XII. While Andhra Pradesh, Gujarat, Maharashtra, and Delhi have reservation in assigning the responsibility of urban planning (including town planning) and urban poverty alleviation, Uttar Pradesh joins the abovementioned States when it comes to assigning the regulation of land use and construction of buildings and Madhya Pradesh will join them in not assigning the responsibility of slum improvement and upgradation. Karnataka and West Bengal would join them in not assigning the responsibility of planning for economic and social development.

It should be noted that matters that need to be locally dispensed with are all part of the State List. As there could hardly be a uniform division of functions and powers—both listed in the same list—they were advisedly enumerated in the State List so that a given State could take a contextual decision. A State of 15 crore with municipal bodies of 25 lakh could not be expected to devolve the same set of functions as a State of 15 lakh with municipal bodies no bigger than 25000. Yet, it is surprising that regulation of land use and construction of buildings in a city could not be trusted to the city government.

It is understandable that cities with slums having 50 per cent of their population cannot handle the problem on their own, or more precisely from their own resources. Could they do so there would not have sprawled the slums with such great proportions. Now, contribution of those living in slums is being recognized. Local bodies need to be supported in improving the living conditions in their slums. Yet, let it be under the auspices of respective city governments and through the wards committees.

Core and Non-core Functions

Urban local bodies are governments even if they are derivate of the their respective State governments. Therefore, they will carry out some regulatory function. But traditionally municipal Acts have classified municipal functions as obligatory and discretionary. Historically, it was the obligatory charge (rather than function) on the local bodies to defray the cost of local policing as, it was argued, the Imperial Government could not afford local policing throughout the country (Rao, 1965) and there were instances of thugee, burglary, waylaying and dacoity. In literature, many other dichotomous classifications prevail such as mandatory-optional, statutory-discretionary, statutory-delegated, traditional-additional and of common-pool funded and toll services. The additional functions have been called as transferred functions as the state governments earlier performed them and now they have been transferred. They cover activities, projects and institutions under both Plan and non-Plan categories (Kerala's First State Finance Commission' Final Report, 1996, p. 20). To all these can be added 'agency functions' where there is some role for local bodies in implementation of centrally sponsored schemes. While suggesting constitutional, legislative and administrative changes, the Eleventh Finance Commission recognized local functions to be of civic, regulatory and development character (Eleventh Finance Commission, 2000, p. 84). When it came to the identification of items in the Twelfth Schedule, it classified them as follows: item numbers 4, 5, 6, 14 and 17 as core functions, 9, 10, 11, 12, 13 and 15 as welfare functions, and 1, 2, 3, 7, 8, 16 and 18 as development functions (*ibid*, p. 312 and p. 313n).

Economists' choice has however been public goods and public utilities. Pethe *et al* (2003) prefer to discuss sets of municipal functions in terms local public good (LPG) and extended local public functions (LPG-E).

Practitioners have however preferred to classify local municipal functions as regulatory/administrative, service and development or regulatory, service, welfare and developmental. However, the Eleventh Finance Commission (2000) classified the subject-matters of the Twelfth Schedule in terms of core, welfare and development functions in one place and civic, regulatory and development at another. Six core municipal services, as identified by the National Institute of Rural Development (NIRD) and National Institute of Public Finance and Policy (NIPFP), are enumerated as: primary education; primary health; municipal roads; drinking water supply; sanitation; and street lighting (Eleventh Finance Commission Report, 2001 p. 75). While discussing the maintenance thereof the Commission adds three more civic services like cremation and burial grounds, public conveniences and other common property resources but deletes roads (*ibid*, p. 76). Other common property should hopefully include municipal roads (not specially mentioned) and parks, heritage buildings, etc. Sanitation is often detailed as scavenging, collection and disposal of refuse and drainage. Some scholars emphasise drainage and solid waste management.

Planning Commission had constituted a Working Group on Expenditure Norms under the chairmanship of Raja Chelliah, which concluded that the following functions be regarded as the core municipal functions: water supply, sanitation/sewerage, solid waste collection, primary education, primary health. The following will present a comparative picture of core functions suggested by some of the committees/commissions:

Zakaria Committee	Finance Commission	Planning Commission
Water Supply	Drinking Water Supply	Water Supply
Drainage/Sewerage	Sanitation	Sanitation/ Sewerage; Solid Waste Collection
Roads & Works	Municipal Roads	
Street Lighting & Electricity Distribution	Street Lighting	
	Primary Education	Primary Education
	Primary Health	Primary Health

It is important to note that primary education and primary health are not counted among the core functions by the Zakaria Committee while roads and street lighting are not counted as core services by the Planning Commission while Eleventh Finance Commission has counted them all along with drinking water supply and sanitation with some qualification. While Zakaria Committee had included electricity distribution (a public utility) in addition to street lighting (a public good), the Finance Commission restricted to street lighting. Further, roads and works of Zakaria Committee become just municipal roads in the Finance Commission. In fact, it may be a matter of style of writing, as many public works incidental to roads etc. cannot just be excluded. However, State Finance Commissions have taken more realistic view. For example, first Kerala Finance Commission suggested street taps rather than water supply (which, according to the Twelfth Schedule, means water supply for domestic, industrial and commercial purposes) because it is only in Thrissur among the municipal corporations, where the municipal corporation undertakes water supply. Andhra Pradesh mentioned cleaning of roads and drains, sanitation and drainage and street lighting.

According to Pethe *et al* (2003), the term 'core services' does not have a precise connotation in economics and they prefer the category of local public goods. They include street lighting, sanitation, and roads along with fire brigade in the LPG category and excludes water supply, which can be metered. Education and water can be added in the extended LPG category.

Multi-Body Functional Domain

In many States, the functions are delegated through executive orders rather than transferred through a piece of legislation so that, it is apprehended, they can be withdrawn easily. Even if they are not formally withdrawn, they can be effectively withdrawn or not delegated at all by instituting boards and authorities for municipal functions. Even, the Union Government over time has been introducing a good number of schemes in which local bodies are performing delivery or agency functions with no role in preparation or implementation. The District Rural Development Agency and the District Urban Development Agency are the cases in point, which are operating instruments of the Ministry of Rural Development and Ministry of Urban Development respectively. These are the ministries responsible for implementation of the new provisions. The Eleventh Finance Commission (2000, p. 83) has taken a different view on this issue and has suggested that they should discharge their duties in helping the local bodies emerge as institutions of self-government and should therefore take lead in integrating their agencies with the new set-up so that other ministries follow the suit.

The scene in many states is quite messy. Besides, urban local bodies there are Development Authorities—practically in all municipal corporations—and there are Special Purpose Authorities much at the wishes of the WB/WHO, first in water supply and later even in sanitation and drainage. While the representatives of city governments were not consulted in procurement of loans or in preparation and execution of the schemes by their respective state governments, the loan liability was passed on to the city governments under the presumption that it is a basically a municipal function. In some cases, even operation and maintenance was overtaken by parastatals. Of late, after the new dispensation, due to resentment of elected civic bodies, some of these functions have been restored to municipalities and functionaries are under the control of the municipal authorities. Then there are agencies, as noted above, for carrying out centrally sponsored schemes.

The present scene of management or mismanagement of local affairs is reminiscent of late nineteenth century's Britain where flourished a number of *ad hoc* local authorities like school boards, health boards, burial boards, highway boards with overlapping jurisdictions and a lack of coordination with omnibus local government. Golding (1955) has quoted a comment in terms of "a chaos of areas, a chaos of franchise, a chaos of authorities and a chaos of rates" Our present scene can be depicted by the following diagram (Fig. 1):

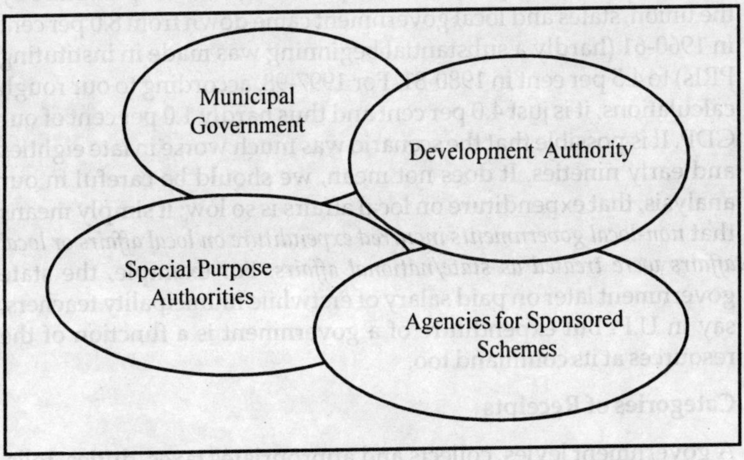

Fig. 1

The result is that there is a lot of confusion confounded with misallocation of resources and handicap in development of capabilities of local governments. There is a lot of frittering of energy of local people's representatives and officials in 'fitting their requirements with guidelines' and thereby making experts in manipulations. In Kerala, you should to build a house in Rs. 22000 and in Jaisalmer you should build a latrine close to your kitchen!

It has been noted by the Eleventh Finance Commission that there are many schemes dealing with these subjects in the State Plans and there are many centrally sponsored schemes and it suggests that such schemes should have been transferred to the local bodies long ago (p. 73). They should be transferred ere long along with funds and functionaries (p. 73 and p. 76). To that extent there would be no extra financial burden on the Union government or the respective state governments. The Commission has further suggested that the capital cost of the civic services would be met by the states while cost and operation and management would be borne by the local bodies from their resource pool including transfers from their respective states. Hopefully, operation and maintenance costs do not include all revenue costs such as interest charges on the capital borrowed by the State Government on behalf of the local bodies.

FINANCIAL DOMAIN OF URBAN LOCAL BODIES

It was pointed out by the Report of a Task Force chaired by Raja Chelliah that local expenditure as a percentage of all expenditure by the union, states and local government came down from 8.0 per cent in 1960-61 (hardly a substantial beginning was made in instituting PRIs) to 4.5 per cent in 1980-81. For 1997-98, according to our rough calculations, it is just 4.0 per cent and thus hardly 1.0 per cent of our GDP. It is possible that the scenario was much worse in late eighties and early nineties. It does not mean, we should be careful in our analysis, that expenditure on local affairs is so low: it simply means that *non-local governments incurred expenditure on local affairs or local affairs were treated as state/national affairs.* For example, the state government later on paid salary of erstwhile municipality teachers, say in U.P. But expenditure of a government is a function of the resources at its command too.

Categories of Receipts

A government levies, collects and appropriates taxes, duties, tolls, fees and cesses; it gets net proceeds of certain taxes/duties collected by government of another level; it can get a share in proceeds of certain other taxes/duties, again collected by government of another level; it usually receives general and specific grants from other governments and other bodies, besides donations/contributions by individuals; and it can receive property incomes and interest on loans made people, other governments or its own corporate enterprises. For utility services it can demand user charges. It can also raise loans. For the utility services such as water, it can demand user charges. It does receive some revenue for regulatory and administrative activities in terms of fees, fines and penalties but they are neither nor should be turned into revenue-raising propositions. The receipts in case of an urban local body may broadly be categorized as:

(*a*) Tax Revenue Receipts from (*i*) its own taxes, (*ii*) assigned taxes and (*iii*) shared taxes;

(*b*) Non-Tax Revenue Receipts: (*i*) property income in terms of rent, royalty, interest, and profits/dividends, (*ii*) user charges for public utility services such as water, electricity; and (*iii*) fees (like license fees), fines and penalties;

(*c*) Grants: (*i*) in lieu of withdrawn taxes, (*ii*) in aid of revenue to meet the shortfall in revenue (general grant) or in aid of certain desirable activities; and

(*d*) Loans for particular project or for any purpose.

A municipality may have its own enterprise like BEST/DTC/DMS and it can receive dividends. It may generate its own electricity like many cities did when local stations used to generate DC electricity or may purchase electricity and distribute to its residents as the NDMC does. While these are commercial enterprises they are neither supposed to make huge perennial profits nor incur perpetual losses. They may indulge in cross-subsidisation between different uses of the service or different sections of the society.

Constitutional Provision

A local government being a derivate of state government can do so under the provisions made by the state legislature or the state government. These provisions stipulate the bases and their rates, exemptions and rebates and concession and other conditions such as procedures and limits. So would be the case with assignment of tax proceeds and share in tax proceeds. Case would be no different in the matter of grants and loans. In fact, while there is no reference to loans and user charges, there are laid down broad guidelines in other matters in the 74th Constitutional Amendment Act. The Act repeats the existing laws and practices. The Art. 243X stipulates that, the Legislature of a State may, by law,

(*a*) authorize a Municipality to levy, collect and appropriate such taxes, duties, tolls and fees in accordance with such procedures and subject to such limits;

(*b*) assign to a Municipality such taxes, duties, tolls and fees levied and collected by the State Government for such purposes and subject to such conditions and limits;

(*c*) provide for making such grants-in-aid to the Municipalities from the Consolidate Fund of the State;

(*d*) provide for constitution of such Funds for crediting all moneys received, respectively, by or on behalf of the Municipalities and also for the withdrawal of such moneys therefrom, as may be specified in the law.

A redeemable feature of the 73rd and 74th Amendment Acts is the provision regarding constitution of State Finance Commission and its mandate and the direction to the Governor to cause every recommendation made by the Commission to be laid before the Legislature of the State. However, it is at the sole discretion of the Legislature to accept any of the recommendations. So far the experience is not very encouraging yet there is no point in getting dissuaded.

Present Financial Domain

A perusal of the taxation provisions in the state laws reveals that while power to collect certain taxes is vested with the municipalities, the rates and revision thereof, procedure of collection, ceilings and floors, method of assessment, exemptions and concessions etc. are reserved with government to be declared through notification.

Octroi and property/house taxes are two most significant municipal taxes from the viewpoint of revenue. Octroi, an indirect tax, was favoured in comparison to house tax, a direct tax, by the urban middle class composed of lawyers, traders and teachers, who came to power in municipal boards and councils, claimed Sivaramakrishnan (2000, p. 159).

Octroi[14] is an ancient tax on goods entering a city for sale, use or consumption. The East India Company15 collected it as a central tax between 1808 and 1835. It was condemned by Charles Trevelyan who was in 1828 asked by Bentick to enquire into hindrances caused by this impost (on more than 200 items). In fact, it was power of search, which could stop internal trade by the delay it would necessarily occasion, was used but for extortion. Its effect on national morals was far worse than on national wealth and it only exited the locals against foreign traders. East India Company, though reluctant, was compelled to abolish it. Provincial government did not impose it either.

Sivaramakrishnan (2000, p. 159) reports its reappearance in 1870 in Mirzapur. In 1864, principles of octroi as town duties were enunciated by same Charles Trevelyan, which were in essence (*i*) levy of impost on very few items of local consumption and not on items, which attracted customs with low rates (in the form of *chungee* which means handful) (Manager of Publications, 1951, pp. 145-58). Though it was an important source, practically all committees on tax reforms condemned it as it was always found to relapse into abuses every time and everywhere it was introduced.

Except for four states of Gujarat, Maharashtra, Orissa and Punjab where revenue position of municipalities is somewhat better, the compensation paid in lieu of this tax by the states such as Haryana and Madhya Pradesh has been quite low and payment is delayed. Eleventh Finance Commission (p. 76) recommends its replacement by a suitable tax. One may suggest its reintroduction in a way that traffic does not get obstructed and process is quickly completed. One can think of green and red channels in international terminals.

There is no state where property tax is not collected. It is rated as the single most important local tax. Property tax comprises of basic house/building tax plus service taxes such as water/drainage tax, lighting tax, and conservancy/scavenging tax. There is clear-cut division between local and non-local jurisdiction everywhere that immovable property (real estate) is taxed by the local government and movable property, by the non-local government. Usually, the rate is uniform but some cities did have progressive rates.

But its rates are archaic and administration is found to be lacking. There are instances when properties of same values are giving taxes from almost nothing to substantial. It has been reported by the Kerala Finance Commission (1996, p. 55) that a commercial property earning

Rs.10 lakh annually paid only Rs. 1291 as tax while a similar property paid close to Rs. 3.5 lakh. Reforms have recently been attempted in some municipal corporations. Switching over from annual retable/ ratable/ lettable value to unit-value based on zone of location, from inspection-based assessment to self-assessment by the owner/ occupier, from receiving demand note to filing returns, as with income tax—especially in certain corporations, have yielded substantial rise in tax collection. The yield could increase ten-fold in some cases. There is therefore need for accelerating such reforms elsewhere. States could be recommended for doing away with concessions and exemptions and amend their rent control acts. The Eleventh Finance Commission has suggested that the property tax should be made recoverable from the occupier (which is a practice in England) so that the tax is not avoided/ evaded for want of owner being elsewhere.

Some states permit advertisement tax while others permit entertainment/ theatre or show tax. Some permit terminal tax and others permit entry tax. Some states have permitted their urban local bodies to collect education cess and others have gone for development cess or drainage cess. Like water tax, lighting tax, animal/ vehicle (non-motorized) tax, and professional tax, there are innumerable taxes listed in the acts but they do not yield any sizable revenue. In some states, some of these taxes are adjunct to property tax so that cost of collection could be reduced as well as that people differently located in economic terms could be charged different rates for the same level of services such as street lighting and scavenging.

While municipal Acts have not specified the statutory assignment or division of net proceeds of taxes, this is a widely prevalent practice. Similarly, almost all states give general and specific grants-in-aid to their local bodies. They also pass on the moneys received for implementation of centrally sponsored schemes. Some of the states have transferred their schemes of local nature along with funds and functionaries. They have adopted a pragmatic approach of giving supervisory and controlling power to local bodies while retaining the power of appointment/ dismissal and promotion/ demotion with them. Kerala has shared its plan budget with its local bodies to the extent of 40 per cent.

PART C: ADEQUACY OF SERVICES AND RESOURCES

For a given level of expenditure, it is obvious that the less is the own revenue the more is needed the transfer to make the resources adequate. If an economy could be effected on expenditure without compromising the quantity, quality or intensity of services or more resources could be garnered from the local economy either as better tax efforts or more rational user charges (with due care for social justice dimension), there would be to that extent less need for transfer of resources.

With a view to keeping matter simple, we shall not be concerning ourselves in this paper with capital cost of providing infrastructure or the method of its financing though we understand its importance and criticality when there is so much need for undertaking such projects. Partly we are not sufficiently armed with the relevant data and partly because the emphasis of the Finance Commission is on revenue expenditure on maintenance and operation of services, also because there are only a few municipalities, which have any revenue surplus to spare for capital investment. Further, the data we are going to use are state aggregate, leaving no scope for seeing any revenue surplus, which could be invested in capital works. We understand if there are no works what are the urban local bodies going to maintain and if there are no utilities there is nothing for them to operate. Yet we shall be concerned only with operation and maintenance of municipal functions.

Our interest basically lies here in the fact whether own revenue of the ULBs in a particular state has been able to cover the expenditure on operation and maintenance of core civil services. We should however remember that such aggregative exercises are somewhat misleading as they hide the troubles of poor municipal bodies as if the prosperous ones have really transferred their surpluses to the poor ones, much in the same way as high per capita income may hide the fact of poverty. In other words, an aggregate surplus/deficit does not suggest that the ULBs in a particular state are severally in a state of surplus/deficit.

Subject to these limitations, adequate transfer—whether as assignment or sharing of certain taxes or pooled taxation proceeds or grants—would be equivalent to deficit in revenue resources.

However, if present expenditure itself is found inadequate in relation to some norms, and which may well be the case for inadequate availability of the resources, then inadequacy of resources has to be measured in terms of the difference with normative level of expenditure and the actual level of revenue. Of course, these norms have to be realistic by national parameters rather than by global parameters. Some scholars may suggest use of some potential level of revenue instead of present level of revenue as some studies have suggested, which could be realized but for inefficiency in administration. We have not done that.

Data Base and Consistency Exercise

However, before we embark upon to judge the level of inadequacy of resources, it would be proper to find the present scene of expenditure. For consistency requirement we have accepted the state-wise database for the year 1997-98 the latest year for which the Eleventh Finance Commission could gather detailed information on revenue and expenditure as there is no better dataset is available. While the expenditure is divided between that on *core services* (water supply, street lighting, sanitation, roads and burial and burial grounds) and *other services* (other than those listed above), the total revenue is divided between *own revenue* and *other revenue* – the former being divided between *tax revenue* and *non-tax revenue*.

We have considered those states, which have been covered in the Eleventh Finance Commission, ignoring Uttranchal, Chhattisgarh and Jharkhand as separate states. These states have been treated here as part of their parent states.

Data Problems

But the dataset available has innumerable problems; even if we ignore the fact in different states the texture of municipal services is different. If we accept the data mechanically, as does Govind Rao (2001, pp. 12-13), all ULBs would be found to incur in 1997-98 an expenditure of over Rs. 151308 crore while all PRIs spend about Rs. 20931 crore, suggesting that all local bodies spend roughly Rs. 172239 crore (which would be more than half the revenue expenditure of the Union Government of India). Based on this database, M.G. Rao (2001, pp. 12-13) wished us to believe that the total expenditure of all governments put together spent in a sum equivalent to 34.8 per cent of the GSDP (GDP?) while revenue collection and accrual stood at 18.3 per cent and 19.8 per cent respectively! He also tries to make us believe that the three levels of the government were spending almost equal amounts (*ibid*). Going into further details, one discovers from his exercises (*ibid*, p. 30-31) that (*i*) the ULBs in Maharashtra spend to the tune of 63 per cent of the NSDP of Maharashtra and all LBs put together to the tune of almost 66 per cent; (*ii*) the ULBs in Andhra Pradesh spend to the tune of 53 per cent of the NSDP of Andhra Pradesh and all LBs to the tune of 56 per cent; (*iii*) in West Bengal, percentage of own revenue to total revenue is more than 67 percent.

We did not believe it and checked up with other sources such as the RBI's analysis of state finances and Reports of the State Finance Commissions. We explored problems with some suspected cases and finally found that, in the case of three states, data had to be treated. We have ignored the states, which are too small for aggregate exercises like the ones attempted here.

Data Treatment

Checking each basic figure of expenditure and revenue for each level of municipality, seeing if there was a sudden jump, comparing core expenditure with own revenue/total revenue and total expenditure with own revenue/total revenue, computing ULB-state revenue expenditure ratio, and tallying total other revenue with transfers from the states to their PRIs/ULBs as given in the RBI analysis for dimensional purposes, we appropriately shifted the decimal point to the left in quite a few cases and used plausible proportions of core-total expenditure or own-total revenue so that various ratios and proportions are in line. In the case of Andhra Pradesh, expenditure figures, in the case of West Bengal, revenue figures and in the case of Maharashtra, both revenue and expenditure figures had to be adjusted. The details of the exercise are given in an appendix given in the end.

Table 2 presents the data for the aggregated picture of all ULBs. For Bihar only information that is available is about the 'other revenue'. The EFC has committed error of treating information not furnished as zero in many cases, including Bihar. ULBs do not exist in Anrunachal Pradesh, Mizoram and Sikkim. The EFC does report the information on the ULBs in union territories including NCT of

Delhi. We have changed the order of the States. Sixteen States, whose revenue expenditure was above Rs.30 crore, except Bihar, find place in alphabetic order. Then are placed smaller states and Bihar in the end.

Present State of Affairs

Mahrashtra and Rajasthan are the only two states where expenditure on core services is found to be higher than that on services other than the core. Which could mean that municipalities are in non-municipal business and perhaps non-municipal governments are in the municipal business. Which could also mean that funds for non-municipal schemes are flowing from governments of other levels and local governments as agents nominally or notionally handle the schemes. The figures are occurring on the both the sides of accounts. This is corroborated by the fact that in many major States such UP, MP, WB, Karnataka and Kerala, and also in states like Assam, Jammu & Kashmir, Goa, Meghalaya and Tripura, the ULBs spend much larger sum on services other than core ones.

Municipal Revenue Deficit (MRD) could be easily defined as the excess of municipal revenue expenditure (MRE) over municipal revenue receipts (MRR). That is, we have MRD=MRE-MRR. But when we define it respect of a state as MRD(S)=MRE-MR R, we commit a mistake because no local body does transfer its revenue surplus to any revenue deficit local body. It should not except in a case of an emergency; it should rather go for supplementing its capital receipts – received as loans or as capital grants – for raising its own infrastructure. But we can do no better than resort it. The Eleventh Finance Commission aggregated municipal revenues and municipal revenues for all three different levels of municipal bodies.

Of the 20 states whose revenue deficit/surplus can be calculated we find that in 1997-98, six states had revenue surplus whereas fourteen states had revenue deficit. Surplus states include Gujarat, Maharashtra, Andhra Pradesh, Rajasthan, U.P. and Manipur. In some cases like Manipur data may not be properly classified. Except in the case of Gujarat and Himachal Pradesh, the magnitude is so small as to account for the difference in the opening balance and closing balance. And there may be no wisdom in under-consumption if income is low! For example, in U.P., core expenditure is lower than that of Haryana, not to say anything of MP, Rajasthan, Gujrat and Tamil Nadu.

Table 2

Expenditure and Revenue of Ulbs For 1997-98 (Rs. Crore)

	Core Expenditure	*Other Expenditure*	*Total Expenditure*	*Own Revenue*	*Other Revenue*	*Total Revenue*
1. Andhra Pradesh	202.9	512.9	715.8	345.5	307.1	751.8
2. Assam	20.2	53.4	73.6	16.0	39.6	55.6
3. Gujarat	369.3	581.6	950.9	810.3	381.8	1192.1
4. Haryana	164.5	179.7	344.2	104.07	74.15	178.4
5. Himachal Pradesh	11.0	23.5	34.6	21.5	18.0	39.5
6. Jammu & Kashmir	12.0	63.1	75.1	3.2	33.8	37.0
7. Karnataka	151.8	294.0	445.8	162.4	254.4	416.8
8. Kerala	84.5	188.1	272.6	113.9	147.1	261.1
9. Madhya Pradesh	226.7	394.7	621.4	148.2	336.2	484.4
10. Maharashtra	2223.5	1754.9	4978.3	4503.9	674.4	5178.3
11. Orissa	39.7	98.2	137.9	85.2	32.1	117.3
12. Punjab	52.6	306.8	359.4	152.1	62.7	214.8
13. Rajasthan	349.7	139.3	489.0	380.2	129.8	510.0
14. Tamil Nadu	521.0	730.9	1251.9	658.8	566.3	1225.1
15. Uttar Pradesh	134.3	471.6	605.9	172.3	454.5	626.9
16. West Bengal	98.0	283.1	381.1	75.3	298.3	373.6
17. Goa	3.66	13.4	17.1	7.0	8.9	15.9
18. Manipur	0.2	2.7	2.8	2.6	1.3	3.9
19. Meghalaya	1.2	5.8	7.0	0.2	5.00	5.2
20. Nagaland	0	0.9	–	1.2	1.3	2.5
21. Tripura	2.5	8.1	10.6	1.2	6.0	7.2
22. Bihar	–	–	66.0	39.7	–	–

Is there a need to develop any other criterion to judge the scene better? One may think, on a long-term basis, a local government – nay any government – should generate enough revenue to meet its core activities/ duties. Then, Municipal Basic Deficit (MBD) can be defined as the excess of core expenditure (MCE) over its own revenue MOR). For all ULBs in a state, we can write MBD(S)=MCE-M O R Table 3 presents both municipal revenue deficit/ surplus (MRD) and municipal basic deficit/surplus (MBD). Surpluses are negative deficits.

Table 3
State-wise Municipal Revenue Deficit/Surplus and Basic Deficit/Surplus (Rs. Crore)

	Municipal Revenue		*Municipal Primary*	
	Surplus	*Deficit*	*Surplus*	*Deficit*
1. Andhra Pradesh	-36		-142.6	
2. Assam		18		4.2
3. Gujarat	-241.2		-441	
4. Haryana		165.8		60.43
5. Himachal Pradesh	-4.9		-10.5	
6. Jammu & Kashmir		38		8.7
7. Karnataka		29	-10.6	
8. Kerala		11.5	-29.4	
9. Madhya Pradesh		137		78.5
10. Maharashtra	-200		-2280.4	
11. Orissa		20.6	-45.5	
12. Punjab		144.6	-99.5	
13. Rajasthan	-21		-30.5	
14. Tamil Nadu		26.8	-137.8	
15. Uttar Pradesh	-21		-38	
16. West Bengal		7.5		22.7
17. Goa		1.2	-3.34	
18. Manipur	-1.1		-2.4	
19. Meghalaya		1.8		1
20. Nagaland		-1.2		
21. Tripura		3.4		1.3

Andhra Pradesh, Gujarat, Maharashtra, Uttar Pradesh and Rajasthan have both the surpluses. Their ULBs as an aggregate are able to meet their expenditure on core services from their own revenue and total expenditure from their total revenue. Apparently, they are facing no resource crunch. But as pointed out earlier, in some cases it may not be a case of satisfaction; for example, when expenditure on core/all services are poor by some normative minimum standards. Uttar Pradesh may be a case in point. There are states having primary surplus but revenue deficit, suggesting that they have undertaken many non-core activities while their core activities are perhaps being undertaken by other agencies. Small deficits may also be a reflection of low expenditure.

Let us repeat that there may be some ULBs not faring well in a State where ULBs as a fraternity are performing quite well and *vice versa*. Further, let it be pointed out in some cases it is possible that in view of the scarcity of resources, they may well be spending much less even on core services than desirable much in the same way as some poor do save. Similarly, in some cases, just the opposite is possible: an ULB is exerting to provide better services even if has to face deficit. Nobody knows which way lies prudence!

Adequacy of Services Provided at Present

This brings us to the question of checking the availability of resources against normative requirements. And we choose the national norms, ignoring geographical factors and, more than that, the issue of local choice and priority! A report on 'Augmentation of Financial Resources of Urban Local Bodies', better known as Zakaria Committee, had suggested two set of norms for operation and maintenance expenditure – one for core municipal services and the other for all municipal services – in per capita terms at 1960-61 prices according to the population size of the city. See Table 4. One may note as the size of a city increases, the proportion of expenditure on core services decreases.

Table 4: All-India Per Capita Norms for Core and All Municipal Services (Rs. in 1960-61 Prices)

City Size	*Over 20 lakh*	*Between 5 and 20 lakh*	*Between 1 and 5 lakh*	*Between 50000 and 1 lakh*	*Between 20000 and 50000*	*Less than 20000*
Water Supply	10.80	10.20	9.80	8.64	7.56	7.42
Drainage & Sewerage	12.20	11.90	10.80	9.30	8.70	8.20
Roads & Works	2.50	2.20	1,80	1.35	1.20	1.10
Street Lighting & Electricity Distribution	3.00	2.85	2.50	2.30	2.15	2.00
Core Services	**28.50**	**27.15**	**24.90**	**21.59**	**19.61**	**18.72**
Education	6.00	5.00	4.00	3.00	2.00	1.00
Medical and Health	3.00	2.00	1.00	0.75	0.50	0.25
Fire Fighting	0.50	0.40	0.30	0.20	0.10	0.05
Horticulture	0.50	0.38	0.20	0.08	0.06	0.05
General Administration	5.00	4.00	3.00	2.00	2.00	1.00
All Services	**43.50**	**39.03**	**33.40**	**27.62**	**24.27**	**21.07**
Core to All Ratio (%)	65.5	69.56	74.55	78.17	80.80	88.85
Population weights in 2001	0.196	0.163	0.244	0.010	0.182	0.114

Core services in these norms include water supply, sewerage/ sewage disposal, storm water drainage, construction of roads and paths and street lighting and electricity distribution – operation and management part, but not primary education and primary health. These norms are said to be very old as for example electricity distribution may not be a municipal function, let alone a core function, in many states. With per capita income having become more than double in around forty years, these norms in aggregative terms may be accepted as conservative ones and we therefore opt for them even if they are somewhat ambitious and even if the functions included here have no one-to-one correspondence with those included in the Eleventh Finance Commission list. Since suggested municipal domain is much larger, it should be possible for us to accept these norms for an aggregate exercise.

However, the detailed data that we have command over does not permit us to go for as detailed an exercise as this one. We therefore do not go for city-size norms but for nation-wide norms. We have also to update these norms. And if possible, we should take care of inter-state urban price differentials.

Nation-wide Norms

We choose to impose national composition of urban population in 2001 by size distribution of UAs/Towns[18]. The weighted averages turn out to be Rs. 30.13 for all services and Rs. 22.00 for core services by using population weights of urban habitations in different size-classes as suggested by Zakaria Committee, noted in the last of the table above.

Updating the norms

Using spliced all-India consumer price index for urban non-manual employees as deflator, Mathur (2001) has obtained the norms for 1997-98 at current prices. With the use of the same deflator, these weighted norms come out to be around Rs. 485 for all services and Rs. 355 for core services.

Converting National Norms into State-wise Norms

Using implicit national urban poverty line as numeraire, state urban poverty lines, are converted into price differential factors for different states, data being obtained from Saxena (2001),. Multiplication of these factors gives us the state-specific Zakaria norms at 1997-98 prices.

Projection of Urban Population

We then worked out urban population for each of the states for 1997-98 using rate of growth per annum during the decade between 1991 and 2001[19].

Desirable Expenditure

Multiplying the urban population with these norms, one can find out normative expenditure for each of the states for urban population. One may note that this population includes non-municipalised urban population. Subtracting the actual expenditures from the respective normative counterparts, the deficiency in provision of municipal services can be gauged with ease. See Table 5.

Deficiency in Service

In this exercise, we have used both the expenditures, core and total, and compared the actual ones with normative ones under the assumption that expenditure incurred reflects the level of service. We find that in none of the states, except Maharashtra, the ULBs as a whole are meeting the desired standards set in 1960s as far as core services are concerned. Part of the reason may lie in the fact that many of the core municipal services—like water supply and electricity distribution—are not provided by the municipal bodies and therefore norms may need to be moderated in certain cases. The scene is slightly better if we consider the overall gap. The ULBs in Gujarat, Haryana, Himachal Pradesh, Maharashtra and Punjab are incurring expenditure that would suffice expenditure on full Zakaria basket though they may be undertaking such other services, which may not be included in Zakaria basket. For details see Table 5.

A little calculation will show us that barring exceptions actual expenditure on core services by ULBs is abysmally low. Exceptions are Maharashtra exceeding its actual/norm ratio beyond 1, Haryana around 90 per cent, Rajasthan around 80 per cent, Gujarat and Himachal Pradesh around 60 per cent, and Tamil Nadu around 50 per cent. Actual core expenditure in Andhra Pradesh and Kerala is around 30 per cent of the norm. The ULBs in Assam, Karnataka, Madhya Pradesh, and Punjab spend below 25 per cent of the norms and UP, West Bengal and Goa end up with less than 15 per cent. But it is possible that the scene is not that bad for many of the core services are being handled by the para-statals and it is possible in some states the ULBs may be cost effective. The excess shown in the case of Maharashtra, cost may not be reflective of the level of services. These ratios dramatically improve when we consider all activities together as money may be forthcoming with ease for other (non-municipal) activities from other levels of the government for sponsored schemes. Maharashtra is a special case where partly for dominant position of Mumbai, partly for higher price level of services compared to urban Maharashtra, and for extra-municipal activities historically undertaken by municipal bodies in Greater Mumbai, they may be spending on many activities.

Table 5

Normative and Actual Expenditures In 1997-98

(Rs. Crore)

	Actual Expenditure		*According to Zakaria Norms*		*Zakaria Expenditure Deficiency*	
	Core	*Total*	*Core*	*Total*	*Core*	*Total*
1. Andhra Pradesh	202.9	715.8	703.7	961.4	500.8	245.6
2. Assam	20.2	73.6	83.1	113.5	62.9	39.9
3. Gujarat	369.3	950.9	644.7	880.8	275.4	-70.1
4. Haryana	164.5	344.2	177.6	242.6	13.1	-101.6
5. Himachal Pradesh	11.0	34.6	18.0	24.5	7.0	-10.1
6. Jammu & Kashmir	12.0	75.1	69.3	94.7	57.3	19.6
7. Karnataka	151.8	445.8	664.0	907.2	512.2	461.4
8. Kerala	84.5	272.6	301.6	412.0	217.1	139.4
9. Madhya Pradesh	226.7	621.4	757.6	994.1	530.9	372.7
10. Maharashtra	2223.5	4978.3	1584.1	2164.2	-639.4	-2814.1
11. Orissa	39.7	137.9	188.0	256.8	148.3	118.9
12. Punjab	52.6	359.4	227.4	310.6	174.8	-48.8
13. Rajasthan	349.7	489.0	443.4	605.7	93.7	116.7
14. Tamil Nadu	521.0	1251.9	1077.3	1471.8	556.3	219.9
15. Uttar Pradesh	134.3	605.9	1096.2	1497.6	961.9	891.7
16. West Bengal	98.0	381.1	680.7	930.0	582.7	548.9
17. Goa	3.66	17.1	25.5	34.9	21.8	17.8
18. Manipur	0.2	2.8	14.8	20.2	14.6	17.4
19. Meghalaya	1.2	7.0	11.1	15.1	9.9	8.1
20. Nagaland	0	–	8.1	11.1	8.1	11.1
21. Tripura	2.5	10.6	13.5	18.5	11.0	7.9
22. Bihar	–	66.0	403.2	560.9	–	–

We should also bear the fact in mind that there is no one-to-one correspondence between the activities enumerated in Zakaria Committee and those actually undertaken by or entrusted to the municipal bodies. The exercise serves the purpose of broadly gauging the dimension of the task to be addressed.

Desirable Expenditure and Actual Revenue

Finally, we need to see the gap between the expenditure that should have been incurred on operation and maintenance (with the assumption that utilities are in place!) by the urban local bodies and the revenues that were available to them because of their own efforts and that were made available – largely through transfers from other level of governments (primarily, the state governments). We have therefore gauged the gap between normative expenditure and actual revenue. See Table 6. We have not corrected the revenues for the potential, it should be noted, which better administration and better civic governance would have brought in and would bring in hereafter.

With the notion that at the least expenditure on core municipal services, which are said to be obligatory as well, should be met from municipalities' own resources, we have computed the two gaps – one between the normative expenditure on core municipal services and actual own revenue and the other between the normative expenditure on all municipal services and total revenue at its command. We may call them Normative Revenue Deficiencies (NRDs): Core-Own Deficiency (COD) and Total Revenue Deficiency (TRD).

We find that the ULBs as a whole in Gujarat, Maharashtra, and Himachal Pradesh can meet the expenditure on core services from their own resources. And these are also the states whose ULBs can meet full Zakaria basket with the resources at their command – their own and transferred provided that transfer is not withdrawn as some of the grants may be tied ones. Otherwise the gaps are large and therefore there is need for greater revenue realization as well as for larger transfers. If we just concentrate on core services and believe that they should be met with municipality's own resources, we find that ULBs in Rajasthan needs to raise its resources by 20 per cent while those in Punjab, Haryana and Tamil Nadu by 50-70 per cent and in Orissa and Andhra Pradesh by 100 per cent. The ULBs in

Kerala should raise their resources by 150 per cent and Karnataka by 300 per cent. What about UP, MP, Bihar, Assam and West Bengal? The scene is: Assam by 4 times, UP and MP by 5 times and Bihar and West Bengal by 8-9 times of the present level. Can they do so? In the short-run, they cannot. But in the long-run, they must. Since some of these services are public utilities, user charges commensurate with cost of supply would be a prudent practice—with some built-in cross-subsidization among users and uses.

Table 6
Actual Revenue And Normative Expenditure (Rs. Crore)

	Actual Revenue		*Normative Expenditure*		*Normative Revenue Deficiency*	
	Own	*Total*	*Core*	*Total*	*Core Gap*	*Total Gap*
1. Andhra Pradesh	345.5	751.8	703.7	961.4	358.2	209.6
2. Assam	16.0	55.6	83.1	113.5	67.1	57.9
3. Gujarat	810.3	1192.1	644.7	880.8	-165.6	-311.3
4. Haryana	104.07	178.4	177.6	242.6	73.53	64.2
5. Himachal Pradesh	21.5	39.5	18.0	24.5	-3.5	-15
6. Jammu & Kashmir	3.2	37.0	69.3	94.7	66.1	57.7
7. Karnataka	162.4	416.8	664.0	907.2	501.6	490.4
8. Kerala	113.9	261.1	301.6	412.0	187.7	150.9
9. Madhya Pradesh	148.2	484.4	757.6	994.1	609.4	509.7
10. Maharashtra	4503.9	5178.3	1584.1	2164.2	-2919.8	-3014.1
11. Orissa	85.2	117.3	188.0	256.8	102.8	139.5
12. Punjab	152.1	214.8	227.4	310.6	75.3	95.8
13. Rajasthan	380.2	510.0	443.4	605.7	63.2	95.7
14. Tamil Nadu	658.8	1225.1	1077.3	1471.8	418.5	246.7
15. Uttar Pradesh	172.3	626.9	1096.2	1497.6	923.9	870.7
16. West Bengal	75.3	373.6	680.7	930.0	605.4	556.4
17. Goa	7.0	15.9	25.5	34.9	18.5	19
18. Manipur	2.6	3.9	14.8	20.2	12.2	16.3
19. Meghalaya	0.2	5.2	11.1	15.1	10.9	9.9
20. Nagaland	1.2	2.5	8.1	11.1	6.9	8.6
21. Tripura	1.2	7.2	13.5	18.5	12.3	11.3
22. Bihar	39.7		403.2	560.9	363.5	

It is not clear to us as to whether transfers for centrally sponsored schemes are included in the other revenue and it is possible that different states have different practices. This is our considered view that these schemes along with funds and functionaries without external baggage be should be transferred to the local bodies. There could be instituted some training programmes for local body representatives and officials. But there should be no other encumbrances.

MAKING URBAN LOCAL BODIES SELF-RELIANT

Essentially, a government should be self-reliant in its primary duties. However, in a federal structure we consider it desirable that each citizen should consume a minimum of certain goods/services, irrespective of his/her domicile – with due respect to local choice. But different units would have perhaps different capacities to cater these services. Therefore, it would surely not be a case where each unit government would be totally self-sufficient to meet expenditure on activities in its sphere. We should therefore limit the sphere further. The principal canon employed in this paper had been that there is a core sphere expenditure on which should be met by local body's own resources. It is true that local resources may not be so neatly divided between public and private uses and those available for public uses into different tiers of governments – when they have concurrent jurisdictions. Transfers from one unit to another and one level to another may assume a myriad of forms. Yet, large transfers from other layers of government to a local government mean greater dependence. Therefore, our first attempt should be to make the local bodies earn their own revenue by transferring power to tax all local bases, which are tax-buoyant as well. Only then we should think of financial transfers. And as a matter of principle, financial transfers should be in the order of, in terms of magnitude and priority, (*i*) proceeds of assigned taxes, (*ii*) proceeds of shared taxes – preferably after pooling, (*iii*) untied grants and then (*iv*) specific grants (Chaubey, 1998; 2003).

It may be pertinent to see whether there exists any potential for greater taxation. Therefore, we conducted what may be called a feasibility exercise. We compare in this exercise core municipal requirement and total municipal requirement with per capita urban net state domestic product. As there exist no data for state net domestic product of urban area, we made a bold attempt.

Researchers working in the area of urban development tell us that less than 30 per cent urban population contributes close to 60 per cent to the GDP. It implies that urban productivity and therefore the per capita income is about twice the national average. Which means urban-rural differential, suggested by 30 population contributing 60 per cent, is 7:2 (=3.5). At lower level per capita income the urban-national productivity ratio may be higher but at higher level, this ratio should decline and tend towards 1 at very high level of urbanization. The logic is simple. When urbanization is 50 per cent they cannot contribute 100 per cent GDP!

In India till date urbanization in no state has exceeded the mark of 50 per cent and except Himachal Pradesh no state it is less than 10 per cent. We suggest, roughly speaking, 20 per cent urban population can contribute 50 per cent GDP, 30 per cent urban population can contribute 60 per cent GDP and 40 per cent urban population would contribute 70 per cent GDP and may be 40 per cent urban population contributes barely 75 per cent GDP. Keeping this in mind, in order to have an idea of urban per capita income we allotted the following sequence:

Urban Population Ratio (UPR)	10	20	30	40	50
Urban Total Differential (UTD)	30	48	60	68	75
Urban Total Per Capita Factor (UTPCF)	3.0	2.4	2.0	1.7	1.5

Further, for each state, allowing average marginal increase depending on the range, we find out the urban-total per capita factor and estimate per capita urban state net state domestic product—which we accept as per capita income in the absence of any other better measure. See Table 7.

Table 7: Urban Population and Income Ratios

State	*UPR*	*UTD*	*UTPCF*
1. Andhra Pradesh	27.0	56.4	2.1
2. Assam	12.7	34.8	2.7
3. Gujarat	37.4	65.9	1.8
4. Haryana	29.0	58.8	2.0
5. Himachal Pradesh	9.7	29.1	3.0
6. Jammu & Kashmir	24.9	53.9	2.2
7. Karnataka	34.0	63.2	1.8

Contd....

8. Kerala	26.0	55.2	2.1
9. Madhya Pradesh	25.0	54.0	2.2
10. Maharashtra	42.4	69.9	1.6
11. Orissa	15.0	39.0	2.6
12. Punjab	34.0	63.2	1.8
13. Rajasthan	23.4	52.1	2.2
14. Tamil Nadu	43.9	70.7	1.6
15. Uttar Pradesh	21.0	49.2	2.3
16. West Bengal	28.0	57.6	2.0
17. Goa	49.8	74.8	1.5
18. Manipur	24.0	52.8	2.2
19. Meghalaya	19.6	47.3	2.4
20. Nagaland	17.7	43.9	2.5
21. Tripura	17.0	42.6	2.5
22. Bihar	13.4	36.1	2.7

Note: The figures first two columns are in percentage whereas those in the third are in natural units.

In our exercise, we have considered the states that existed before late 2000 when three states were bifurcated. Uttranchal's NSDP figures are not available while Chhattigarh's and Jharkhand's are. We have therefore got the weighted average for composite Bihar and for composite Madhya Pradesh. In the case of Uttar Pradesh, Uttranchal being a small state will not materially affect the per capita income of Uttar Pradesh. While there is not much difference between per capita incomes of Madhya Pradesh and Chhattisgarh, there is substantial difference between those of Bihar and Jharkhand. Jharkhand's per capita income at Rs. 9551 is more than twice of Bihar's 4014 in 1997-98.

We have tried to find out the ratio of core expenditure to per capita income as well as that of total expenditure to per capita income. While per capita income is related to net state domestic product (urban), the expenditures are desirable ones. In poor states, price levels are lower and therefore expenditure norms in money terms are also somewhat lower. But the general pattern though not universal that emerges is: poorer is a state, the higher is proportion needed to flow to the ULBs in that state. See Table 8.

The ULBs in Goa and Nagaland join those in Punjab, Haryana and Himachal Pradesh (part of erstwhile Punjab) where core services as an aggregate need less than 1.0 per cent (0.8-0.9 per cent) of the

Table 8: Per Capita Expenditure Norms and Urban Per Capita Income (in Rs.) and Norm to Income Ratios (in Percentage)

	Normative Expenditure		*Per Capita Income*		*Expenditure Income Ratio*	
	Core	*Total*	*State*	*Urban*	*Core*	*Full*
1. Andhra Pradesh	357.55	488.50	11683	24404	1.465	2.002
2. Assam	269.01	367.42	7966	21866	1.230	1.680
3. Gujarat	371.31	507.29	16585	29232	1.270	1.735
4. Haryana	328.56	448.81	17530	35544	0.924	1.263
5. Himachal Pradesh	329.18	448.06	13488	40464	0.813	1.107
6. Jammu & Kashmir	303.48	414.71	9491	20537	1.477	2.019
7. Karnataka	399.81	546.25	12566	23358	1.711	2.339
8. Kerala	372.96	509.49	14231	30214	1.234	1.686
9. Madhya Pradesh	399.13	523.73	9393	20289	1.967	2.581
10. Maharashtra	421.91	576.41	18915	31192	1.353	1.848
11. Orissa	369.87	505.23	7973	20730	1.784	2.437
12. Punjab	303.48	414.53	18764	34879	0.870	1.188
13. Rajasthan	364.25	497.57	10997	24475	1.488	2.033
14. Tamil Nadu	440.06	601.21	15388	24793	1.775	2.425
15. Uttar Pradesh	325.43	444.60	7776	18218	1.786	2.440
16. West Bengal	319.89	437.05	11682	24032	1.331	1.819
17. Goa	421.21	576.47	32647	49075	0.858	1.175
18. Manipur	269.02	367.17	9039	19886	1.353	1.846
19. Meghalaya	269.61	366.77	10281	24800	1.087	1.479
20. Nagaland	268.93	368.53	13052	32342	0.831	1.139
21. Tripura	268.17	367.49	9658	24202	1.108	1.518
22. Bihar	296.87	412.99	5361	14451	2.054	2.858

urban net state domestic product while requirement of all services ranges between 1.1 per cent and 1.25 per cent. If they have adequate power to collect their own resources, they should be able to do so. Even Nagaland, as appears from its NSDP per capita figures, is not a poor state: its level is close to twice of Assam, Orissa and UP. Next comes Tripura where the ULBs need a claim of 1.1 per cent and 1.5 per cent for core services and all services. The ULBs in Assam, Gujarat and Kerala – all in different regions, at different levels of urbanizations, and with different per capita incomes – need 1.25 per cent of their respective urban NSDPs for core services and 1.70

per cent for all services. Assam may not afford it on its own but for Gujarat and Kerala, this should not be a problem. The same is the story is with Manipur, Maharashtra and West Bengal—again in different regions, at different levels of urbanizations and with different per capita incomes—where requirement of the ULBs for provision of core services is 1.35 per cent and for all services is 1.85 per cent. Manipur is much poorer than the other two and the ULBs therein may not be able to collect resources commensurate with its requirement. Jammu and Kashmir join Andhra Pradesh and Rajasthan where the ULBs need about 1.5 per cent of their respective NSDPs for core services and around 2.0 per cent for all services. Jammu and Kashmir is somewhat behind Rajasthan, which is somewhat behind Andhra Pradesh in terms of per capita NSDP but not necessarily in terms of urbanization. Even if Jammu and Kashmir is to be helped otherwise, its municipalities should try to stand on their own legs, as there are many states much poorer than it. The ULBs in Karnataka and Tamilnadu on the one hand and U.P. and Orissa are in that category, which requires around 1.75 per cent of their NSDP for core services and around 2.45 per cent for all services. While Andhra Pradesh is somewhat behind Tamil Nadu, Orissa and U.P. are far behind. They need transfer of resources at the moment. The ULBs in M.P. need a little less than 2.0 per cent of its urban NSDP and Bihar, a little more than 2.0 per cent for provision of core services. The requirement for all services is 2.6 per cent for the ULBs in MP and 2.9 per cent for Bihar. Though MP is somewhat richer than U.P., Bihar is far poor. There is need to flow resources to their ULBs from outside the state.

Undoubtedly such exercises are subject to many limitations yet they provide a clue to the solution. This exercise does show that the problem of resources for urban local bodies is not un-surmountable. The issue is to evolve a proper mechanism for transfer of resources from local people to local bodies and from higher level of governments to local bodies. And for very poor state, there may be no go but to go for transfer from the national government, where Finance Commission and planning Commission both have a role to play and the former is mandated by the constitution in this regard as well.

For greater revenue realization, it has been emphaised time and again that there exists a lot of potential but there is need for better functioning of local governments on the both the sides—providing better services and ensuring better compliance in the matter of general taxes. It seems that the things are improving after emergence of the new set up. State governments have to reform many archaic laws and lessen number of conditions. With rationalization of rates and method of collection it has been found that the yield of property tax has risen tremendously. Entertainment tax, which is somewhat buoyant and totally local in nature, should immediately be transferred to the local bodies by all states—at the moment Goa, Haryana, Kerala, Madhya Pradesh, Maharashtra and Utter Pradesh have done so. If octroi has to be abolished, some other equally buoyant tax should be transferred to the urban local bodies.

The cardinal principle of existence of any government, let alone an ULB, is that it should meet its expenditure (at least revenue one) on core services from its resources. Such an ULB can be said to be self-reliant. It is needless to say that they should not manage this balance by abdicating their responsibilities.

Transfer of taxes ensures taxation and representation both at the local bodies and that helps local people to assert in getting services and in checking misuse of resources. Followed by it would be sharing of pooled proceeds of state taxes with local bodies—both rural and urban. Then, grants should the last resort to transfer resources—resources should flow to the local governments as a matter of right, not as a concession or consideration. Only then the ULBs would be units of self-government.

We have not advised substitution of civic bodies by civil societies for the formers' primary duties. Civil societies are otherwise most welcome to supplement and complement. We have not advised absolving the municipal bodies of primary services by wholesale contracting out them to private bodies but they need not employ somebody needing service of two hours a day or once in a week. We have not dwelt on the good points of e-governance lest its use should be confused with good governance. The import of the Constitutional Amendments brought in the sphere of local governance of local public affairs lies in restoring the rule of democratically elected representatives. Selected young professionals, howsoever competent and smart, should not replace elected city fathers and village elders. The chief belief of democracy lies in its respect the wisdom of the electorate in electing right people, who have to be duly assisted for specialized jobs by selected professionals.

NOTES

1. For constitutional debate, see Singhvi (1989) and for Gandhi's reaction on learning that the Draft Constitution has no provision for village panchayats, which he thought should be the base of democracy, see Mathew (1996).
2. Rao (1966)
3. In Gandhian philosophy, Part III and Part IV of the Constitution, the word 'state' stands for the Government and Parliament of India and the Government and the Legislature of each of the States and all local or other authorities within the territory of India or under the control of the Government of India.
4. This was echoed time and again. The latest being assertion by Karnataka.
5. Tiebout, Charles (1956).
6. With development comes affluence (resources) to higher tier jurisdictions and effluents (duties) to lower ones. See Reagon (1972).
7. Chaubey (1998) has developed a framework wherein it has been shown that there are two kinds of activities in public sphere: intra-unit and inter-unit. Inter-unit activities will have the same standards but intra-unit activities of common nature may have of the same standard but for natural differences.
8. Plan assistance is given to a state in terms of grant and loan. A special category state receives it 90:10 grant-loan ratio while a non-special category state receives it in 30:70 ratio. All eight North-Eastern states, Jammu & Kashmir, Himachal Pradesh and now Uttranchal enjoy special category status.
9. These are extreme cases of market failure. Existence of externality in production and consumption of certain goods make the private marginal cost/benefit diverge from social marginal cost/benefit. Correction of externalities is devised through taxes of goods, fines for effluence, subsidies for effluence-abating devices and various controls.
10. The problem of non-revelation of preference is often referred to as the problem of free-riding and very often pointed out. But the problem of forced-riding is easily ignored. Street-light tax collected as adjunct to house tax will have to be paid by a blind citizen as well.
11. Ostrom couple has devised a four-fold classification based on presence/absence of possibility of joint consumption and excludability. They are known as individual (the same as private

good), collective goods (the same as public goods), common-pool goods (some people call them open-access goods) and toll goods. Toll goods are the ones, access to which could be denied—not necessarily through toll. See Ostrom and Ostrom (1977) and Chaubey (2004).

12. However, local goods, not necessarily public goods, may produce non-local bads.
13. Government of India Act (1919) had transferred the subject of local self-government to the provincial governments and therefore the Government of India stopped issuing any official instructions to them, which they were doing earlier. However, this Act had separate Schedules for local taxes.
14. It operated in India before Manu as also in Europe since Roman empire. It was levied on customs line. Later, the State sought a percentage from the proceeds where the privilege of levying was given to the city governments. Under the Regulation of 1805, octroi was levied on articles imported for consumption or use within the town.
15. East India Company, which was a trading company, has sought and got exemption from this duty from the Moghul rulers. G.
16. This was done in connection with construction of an index of decentralization for determining allocation to states for local bodies: In the case of panchayats, development functions have been divided between agricultural & allied and industries though the weights for both of them are the same. Eleventh Finance Commission (p. 310, 311n).
17. One may, on the parallel of primary deficit (consumption) and primary deficit (investment), development for services based on user services and others. But in fact, on deeper probing, one gets to know that all subsidizations are cross-subsidiazation.
18. Alternatively one could opt for state-wise composition of urban population by city-size.
19. Projecting total population and urban population means rural population has to be accepted as residual.

REFERENCES

Bird, R.M. (1998), *Designing Sate-Local Transfers for Uttar Pradesh* (Mimeograph).

Davey, Kenneth (1989), *Strengthening Municipal Government: A Discussion Paper*, Infrastructure and Urban Development Department, World Bank.

Dollery, Brian E. and Wallis, Joe L. (2001), *The Political Economy of Local Government*, Edward Elgar, Cheltenham.

Golding, L. (1955), *Local Government*, English University Press Ltd., London.

Government of India (2003), Economic Survey 2002-03.

Government of India (2000), *Report of the Eleventh Finance Commission for 200-2005.*

Government of India and UNCHS (2001), *Good Urban Governance Campaign: India Launch.*

All India Institute of Local Self-Government (2001) *Decentralisation and Municipalities.*

L.M. Sighvi Report on *Revitalisation of PRIs for Democracy and Development*, as excerpted in Kuruksheta (1989), Vol. 37, No. 5.

Mathews, George (1996), Panchayats: The Local Self-Government System in India, Included in *Decentralised Governance in Asian Countries*, edited by Abdul Aziz and David D. Arnold, Sage Publications, New Delhi.

Mathur, Mukesh P. (-), *Constitutional 74th Amendment Act and the Urban Local Bodies: A Brief Review*, National Institute of Urban Affairs (Mimeograph).

Mathur Om Prakash (2001), *Approach to State-Municipal Fiscal Relations*, National Institute of Public Finance and Policy, New Delhi.

National Institute of Urban Affairs (1998), *A Compendium of Municipal Legislations in Conformity With Constitution (Seventy Fourth) Amendment Act, 1992.*

Pethe, Abhay, Ajit Karnik and Dilip Karmakar (2003), Finances of Urban Local Bodies in Maharashtra: A Statistical Profile, Included in *India Infrastructure Report 2003*, 3i-Network.

Rao, M. Govind (2001) *Fiscal Decentralisation in Indian Federalism*, Working Paper 98, Institute for Social and Economic Change, Bangalore.

Rao, V. Venkata (1965), *A Hundred Years of Local self-Government in Assam*, Bani Prakas Mandir, Pathsala.

Reagon, Michael D. (1972) *The New Federalism*, New York University Press.

Reserve Bank of India (2000), *State Finances: A Study of Budgets of 1999-2000.*

Savas, E.S. (2000), *Privatization and Public-Private Partnerships*, Affiliated East-West Press Pvt. Ltd., New Delhi.

Singh, B.N. and Maitra, Shipra (2001), Formation of Wards Committee, Included in *Good Urban Governance Campaign: India Launch.*

Singh, Kulwant (2001), Urban Governance in India: Trends and Issues in Decentralisation, Included in *Good Urban Governance Campaign: India Launch.*

Sivaramakrishanan, K.C. (2000), *Power to People?: The Politics and Progress of Decentralisation*, Konark Publishers Pvt. Ltd., Delhi.

Srivastava, D.K. (2000), *Fiscal Federalism in India – Contemporary Challenges: Issues Before the Eleventh Finance Commission Report*, Har-Anand Publications Pvt. Ltd., New Delhi.

Final Report of First State Finance Commission of Kerala (1996)

Report of Second Himachal Pradesh State Finance Commission, 2002

Report of First Goa State Finance Commission,

Report of First Maharashtra State Finance Commission,

APPENDIX: TREATMENT OF FINANCIAL DATA OF ULBs IN CERTAIN STATES

Maharashtra

One could scarcely believe that in 1997-98 while revenue of all urban local bodies is Rs. 497762.26 lakh, its expenditure is Rs. 10365978.98 lakh, which is almost 21 times of the former. The problem was with whole data set. The Eleventh Finance Commission noticed large discrepancies in the figures for own revenue of municipal councils and municipal corporations furnished by the State Government, the Commission worked out the figures for own revenue for the years 1990-91 through 1997-98 on the basis of figures for the years for 1990-91 and 1994-95 as given in the SFC report and by applying thereto annual growth rates as indicated in the SFC report (EFC, p. 256n and p. 259n). But what is surprising is that the EFC simply accepted zero figures for other revenue while in the SFC report there are available figures to help one work out other revenue figures too. Actually, there are equally large and most disturbing discrepancies in the expenditure figures, which were uncritically accepted by the EFC! For example, total expenditure of all municipal councils is almost 25 times its revenue. Again, while in the case municipal councils other expenditure is 4 to 6 times the corresponding core expenditure, in that of municipal corporations, it is /6 to 1/18 times.

As there existed no nagar panchayats, we studies the data for municipalities and municipal corporations. In the Eleventh Finance Commission's Report, we found that other revenue was shown as nil in the case of municipalities, which we did not accept. From State

Finance Commission Report, we found by totalling the revenues of three categories of municipalities for the year of 1994-95 that other revenue forms Rs. 116.32 crore while own revenue is Rs. 408.61, which tallied with the figure reported in the EFC even by component. Accepting this ratio, we projected the figure for 1997-98, which comes out to be Rs. 20067.42 lakh as the correct figure for other revenue, which should largely include grants from the state. Along with own revenue of Rs. 70491.3 lakh, this will give total revenue of Rs. 90558.72 lakh. In the EFC Report, the expenditure of municipalities is Rs. 1720021.27 lakh, which is 19 times of improved revenue. Hardly believable! For 1994-95, we find per capita expenditure on various categories of services for each category of municipalities and also population size, our calculations showed that Rs. 248.6 crore were spent on core services and Rs.208.3 crore were spent on other services by 229 municipalities, total revenue expenditure being Rs. 456.9 crore, which is close to revenue expenditure given by the SFC (p. 101) as Rs. 467.48 crore. The core expenditure as given in the EFC is 6.6 times of that given in the SFC, while other expenditure as given in the EFC is 21.3 times of that given in the SFC. Scaling down the core expenditure for 1997-98 by SFC/EFC ratio for 1994-95, which is now found to be around Rs. 39572 lakh, and accepting other/core expenditure ratio for 1994-95, we estimate the other expenditure for 1997-98 to be around Rs. 33157.07 lakh. The total expenditure of municipalities comes out to be Rs. 72729.07 lakh.

In the case of municipal corporations, the revenue figures reported in the State Finance Commission for 1990-01 through 1994-95 broadly tally with their counterparts in the Eleventh Finance Commission Report. Except for one correction for printing error, we accept the figures for 1997-98: own revenue Rs. 379895.96 lakh, other revenue Rs. 47376 lakh and total revenue Rs. 427270.96 lakh. But in the case of expenditure, we find position to be very uncomfortable. The core expenditure declines from Rs. 602795.58 in 1990-91 to Rs. 110509.54 in 1991-92, which is less than one-fifth of the former. Then, it gradually rises to become Rs. 291826.85 lakh in 1994-95, still less than one-half of what it was in 1990-91. Then, it becomes Rs. 567972.84 lakh in 1995-96, still less than what it was in 1990-91. Then it becomes four times next year (Rs. 2244312.33 lakh) and again four times still next year (Rs. 8195804.75 lakh), which is more than 19 times the total revenue. However, in the SFC Report, the core expenditure is Rs. 60358 lakh in 1990-91, suggesting that there is error in placing of decimal point to the right—raising it only 10 times. From detailed exercise on figures available in the SFC, we find that in 1994-95 while the core expenditure is Rs. 120154 lakh, other expenditure is Rs. 93556 lakh and therefore total expenditure ratio is Rs. 213710 lakh. The core-total ratio is 0.5622. For 1997-98 the Department of Urban Development had projected total expenditure of Rs. 325099 lakh, which can be divided in terms of the above ratio as Rs. 182780 lakh as core expenditure and Rs. 142329 lakh as other expenditure. Our figures, which are given below, are based on this exercise.

	Expenditure (Rs. Lakh)			*Revenue (Rs. Lakh)*		
	Core	*Other*	*Total*	*Own*	*Other*	*Total*
Municipal Councils	39572	33157	72729	70491	20067	90558
Municipal Corporations	182780	142329	325099	379896	47376	427272
Urban Local Bodies	222352	175486	497828	450387	67443	517830

COMMENTS

ABHIJIT DATTA: Functions come first and finance comes second. Functionary is an Indian innovation in the sense that it is a convenient method of suggesting that whatever people are employed at the state level will be at their disposal at the local level. The fiscal decentralization does not assume that. Fiscal decentralization assumes that once the funds are given, it is for the local authorities to have the type of functionaries that they want to employ. It should not be thrust on them. In our situation, it is being imposed mainly because of the peculiar problems of the personnel structure and personnel management at the state level.

Many people think that because all the governments are in a financial mess, decentralization can be slowed down. I do not believe that decentralization costs anything. There is enough money in the kitty. Decentralization only menas transfer of subjects to local bodies. The real problem is not finance, but personnel. Because decentralization assumes contraction of the size of the government from the point where decentralization starts and expansion of the kitty and size of the government at the point of the recipient. If decentralization is really to be meaningful, then the Central Government and the State Governments must simultaneously contract. If they refuse to contract, then the problem arises. We should be very careful in giving an impression, a false impression, that decentralization is very costly, very difficult. The difficulty lies with the people who are decentralizing.

T.N. DHAR: The Planning Commission in the 1980s went for an exercise called high estimation and no estimation and afterwards certain norms were given, on the per capita expenditure that is incurred. Then, a certain minimum level could be reached. We upgraded those costs in terms of inflation, put them and then worked it out. If the states are poor, we give weightage on the volume of money required. Thus we came to a figure known as X. Then, if the devolution from the state is at this level, which is recommended, and they are able to raise their own revenues, then what is the gap? We found that can be again on the estimation of low, medium and high. Then the only alternative that we had at that time was to see in how many years' time this gap is filled. Is it two years. five years or ten years? The only alternative available to us is that we stretch it by two or three times so that at that level of recommendation hopefully they would be able to fill that gap.

But the main point flowing from this is, while we may have suggested how many times this gap, the disease is known, we know that the local governments, as they are constituted at present, whaterve they mean, it is beyond their capacity to meet these needs, unless they got one time push at some point.

More power of taxation should be given. It is a fundamental principle that lower the taxation the more difficult either to impose or to govern. It is a universal phenomenon. Only the benefit tax can be recovered. It is possible to do that. But those taxes, where the benefits are spent on the community as a whole, it becomes very difficult.

Therefore, the approach of the Twelfth Finance Commission seemed to be reasonable, to take up two or three services such as drinking water, solid waste disposal and sanitation and fill the gap.

6

Municipal Financial Resource Mobilisation:
Status, Concerns and Issues

–Gangadhar Jha

Two inter-related developments marked the closing years of the 20th century. First is globalisation that came to the fore after the demise of the bi-polarised global politics. Globalisation brought-in a vigorous worldwide revolution in communication and information due to unprecedented technological revolution and, above all, an unprecedented growth in international financial flows that is uninhibited by national boundaries. Nations across the globe were compelled to go for structural adjustments to enhance national competitive abilities, global trade and foreign direct investments (Rabinovitch 1999). Role of cities became all the more important in this process, as they are important centres of economic activities and "engines of economic growth". By virtue of this powerful economic role, cities contribute about 60 per cent to the GDP. It is, therefore, now believed that what will happen to the national economies in future is now largely contingent on what happens to the cities in terms of their institutional and fiscal capacities in providing urban infrastructure support to production activities and improving the quality of life of its growing inhabitants.

Second equally important development was initiation of virtually a wave of decentralisation across the globe. There was increasing realisation in the eighties of the last century that centralised planning and development initiative in the past failed to enhance national development. As a result, developing countries in particular adopted decentralisation in a big way. Decentralisation constituted an important agenda in the scheme of World Bank funding in a large number of countries (Davey 1989). More than 60 countries in Europe including the erstwhile command economies, now the 'countries in transition', Latin America. Asia and Africa have adopted decentralisation initiative and are in the process of strengthening it (Rabinovitch 1999).

These two phenomena emerging towards the closing years of the last century have implications for cities in two ways. First, globalisation and the accompanied accentuated shift towards market economy have prospects for accelerating the process of urbanisation (level of urbanisation) and urban growth (concentrated demographic growth in the metropolitan and class-I towns). Second, cities are called upon to increase their revenue enhancement efforts for financing augmentation of municipal services and urban infrastructure for (*i*) improving the quality of life of urban population, and (*ii*) attracting investment for generation of employment and income. Institutions of urban local self-government have, therefore, occupied the center-stage; they are called upon to manage change brought about by increasing demographic growth within their jurisdiction. An effective, efficient and responsive discharge of the devolved functions and management of change requires institutional and fiscal capacities in ample measure. On the contrary, the units of urban local governments (ULGs) especially in the developing and transitional economies have been experiencing serious fiscal stress (Bahl and Linn 1992; Bahl 2000; Bird 1994; Jha 1998).

The paper, therefore, analyses fiscal capacity on the basis of available municipal financial data on revenue structure and trends in own revenue. Subsequently, it discusses policy issues for revenue enhancement from tax and non-tax sources including user charges, by accessing the capita market and through effective and innovative urban management systems. This is done by looking into innovative ways of local financial resource generation by the institutions of urban local self-government in India and abroad.

Institutional Capacity

Decentralisation has impacted local government units in several ways. One of the impacts is addition to their functional domain. It has led to rising expectation on part of the local population from the local government. Local governments, however, lack institutional capacity for performing functions entrusted to them. The literature on municipal capacity building suggests that capacity building is driven, among other things, by three factors viz. (*i*) human resource development; (*ii*) organisational development and (*iii*) institutional and legal framework (Pellenburg *et al* 1996). These three important parameters together contribute to strengthening of financial resource mobilisation, financial management system and hence the fiscal capacity.

Fiscal capabilities and financial wherewithal are critically important for addressing all the three dimensions mentioned above. Putting in place a sustainable financing system calls for strengthening decentralisation through fiscal decentralisation, that has several useful spin-offs. It improves over-all revenue mobilisation by broadening the tax-net, enables sub-national governments to capture tax base, which is below the thresholds of taxes of higher levels of government, and it enhances efficiency in terms of improved level of services, accountability, willingness to pay and overall development of jurisdictions (Bahl 1999; Musgrave 1983). There is now an increasing realisation in several countries that have gone for decentralisation that it needs to be reinforced by fiscal decentralisation (Bird 1994). It creates conditions for ULGs to take expenditure decisions and steps to finance these decisions by using their tax authority. Such decisions are taken in public gauge for which they are accountable.

Decentralisation enhances quality and effectiveness of governance as well. From a financial perspective, the main factor related to governance is that it provides accountability and transparency. This means that elected officials take responsibility for affairs of municipal governments including the appointment of senior staff. Financial accountability is achieved through adherence to regulations of higher levels of government (e.g. avoided deficit budgeting, followed prescribed accounting standards, and ensure effective tax collection procedures), budget approval by elected officials, periodic reporting, and independent audits. Transparency involves making decisions in public and full disclosure of information used in making decisions. Good governance provides investors with a positive level of comfort.

Existing State of Municipal Finance

Analysis of structure and trends in municipal finance is constrained by non-availability of organised data on municipal finance on a regular basis. Eleventh Finance Commission (EFC) is the only source that contains a time series data on municipal finance. Hence the analysis is based on the EFC data. These have been supplemented by data from some of the second round of State Finance Commissions (SFCs) that have submitted their reports and wherever these reports contain data on municipal finance.[1]

Revenue Structure

Municipal Corporations: Revenue from own sources constitutes the most important indicator of financial wherewithal of any level of government. Analysis of revenue structure of all the municipal Corporations in all the states taken together indicates that the revenue from own sources improved between 1990-91 and 1997-98 with substantial setback in the year 1994-95 (Table-1). Revenue from own sources increased from 75.72 per cent to 79.62 per cent during this period. Such a rosy picture at the national level notwithstanding, dependence on state transfers has increased in a number of states. In the states of Gujarat, Haryana, Himachal Pradesh, Karnataka, Kerala, Madhya Pradesh, Maharashtra and Uttar Pradesh, revenue from own sources declined during the period. In the states of Haryana, Madhya Pradesh, Uttar Pradesh and Karnataka and Keral, the decline has been quite steep. The second SFC data for Karnataka indicates an improvement in the growth rate of own source revenue. It increased at a CAGR of 19.91 per cent between 1996-97 and 2000-2001 (Karnataka 2002). The second SFC data for Andhra Pradesh indicate that the revenue from own sources of Municipal Corporations in the state has declined from 28 per cent during 1990/91-1997/98 to 18.22 per cent during 1996/97 – 2000/01 (Andhra Pradesh 2002).

Municipal Councils: Revenue structure of Municipal Councils (MCs) at the national level seems to have remained steady during 1990/91 – 1997/98. Revenue from own sources of all the MCs in all the states taken together remained around 59 per cent (Table-2). But the situation in individual states worsened during this period. In as many as a dozen states, revenue from own sources declined. Such states include Andhra Pradesh, Assam, Gujarat, Haryana, Himachal

Pradesh, Karnataka, Keral, Madhya Pradesh, Rajasthan, Tamil Nadu, and Uttar Pradesh. In some of them, it declined rather steeply. Examples are Assam, Keral, Himachal Pradesh, Madhya Pradesh, and Uttar Pradesh (Table-2). Data from the second SFC for the states of Andhra Pradesh and Karnataka indicate that the dependence of MCs on state transfers has increased in recent years as the revenue from own sources has declined from 37 per cent in 1996-97 to 31.06 per cent in 1999-2000 in Andhra Pradesh and from 49.94 per cent to 36.90 per cent in 2000-01 in Karnataka.

Nagar Panchayats: Nagar Panchayats (NPs) present much more grim a situation with respect to revenue from own sources. At the national level, it declined from about 53 per cent in 1994-95 to 39.76 per cent in 1997-98. Of the 13 states that have NPs, revenue from own sources declined in as many as eight states (Table-3). It needs to be emphasised that NPs constitute the entry point for urban settlements from where they graduate to the higher size categories. NPs, therefore, need to be serviced and regulated well so that their graduation to municipalities and corporations is smooth.

Trends in Municipal Finance

Municipal Corporations: Analysis of data on revenue from own sources of Municipal Corporations in all the states taken together suggests a nominal decline in the CAGR between 1990-91 and 1997-98 (Table-4). However, individually, in some of the states (Andhra Pradesh, Tamil Nadu West Bengal, Gujarat and Rajasthan) the growth rate (CAGR) was fairly high. In other states, the own source revenue did not grow at an impressive rate. In four states including Karnataka, it increased at lower than 10 per cent. Taking the rate of inflation into account, the growth in own revenue thus appears to be at most nominal in real terms in these states. In Andhra Pradesh as well the second SFC data reveal that the CAGR has declined from 28 per cent during 1990-91 and 1996-97 to 18.38 per cent between 1996-97 and 1999-2000 (Andhra Pradesh 2002). In Karnataka, growth rate has increased lately as the data culled from the Second SFC suggest that revenue from own sources increased from Rs. 67.26 crores in 1996-97 to Rs. 552.61 crores in 2000-01 representing a CAGR of 19.91 per cent (Karnataka 2002) Data on growth in per capita own revenue at constant price would have thrown light on trends in real terms. Constraints on the availability of data, however, do not permit such an analysis.

Disaggregated data on revenue from own sources for different types of urban local bodies are not available in most of the second SFC reports that are available now. This for all the urban local bodies in Punjab grew at a CAGR of 20.21 per cent that seems to be impressive even after taking the rate of inflation into account. In Rajasthan, however, this declined from Rs. 219.69 crores in 1996 to Rs. 119.38 crores in 1999-2000. CAGR, therefore, not only declined but became negative (-11.48%) during this period (Rajasthan 2001). This is largely explained by a decline in revenue from Tolls and Octroi.

Municipal Councils: EFC data for Municipal Councils for all the states taken together suggest that revenue from own sources increased at a CAGR of 16 per cent in nominal terms that seems to be quite impressive. However, situation in the individual states was not so rosy. In as many as six states, it increased at a CAGR of less than 11 per cent in nominal terms. This indicates a nominal increase in revenue from own sources in real terms. The second SFC reports for Karnataka and Andhra Pradesh indicate an improved situation. Revenue from own sources increased at a CAGR of about 32 per cent in the former and at 15.42 per cent in the latter in nominal terms.

Dominant External Revenue and the Growth in Own Revenue

Conceptually, a dominant share of transfers in the total local revenue need not be looked at as an aberration in local finance. Urban settlements' contribution to the total GDP is substantial. Yet they do not have a legitimate share in the total national resources. Transfers from central and state governments could be taken as a proxy for the share of local governments in the national resources. Hence a high share of external sources in the total local revenue need not to be looked as an evil. However, this should not make them too complacent to ignore the potential of resource generation from own sources. The test lies in at least a 5 per cent per annum increase in real terms in revenue from own sources along with an increased share of revenue of external sources. Table-4 reveals that in some of the states with dominant external revenue (Haryana, Keral, Uttar Pradesh, Karnataka, and Madhya Pradesh), growth in own source revenue of Municipal Corporations was below ten per cent in nominal terms. This indicates a dependency syndrome.

Amongst the Municipal Councils, dependency syndrome is visible in as many as five states. In another five states, it increased just around ten per cent in nominal terms. The situation amongst NPs is not better either.

The analysis of revenue structure, growth in revenue from own sources and the dependency syndrome suggests that in a fairly large number of states municipal finance is not in a happy situation. In such a situation an analysis of per capita revenue and expenditure at constant price would further bring the fiscal stress of municipal governments in sharp focus. Non-availability of recent data on municipal finance constrained such an analysis.

Strategy for Resource Mobilisation

It should be obvious form the above that fiscal decentralisation has to be at the top of the agenda for municipal financial resource mobilisation. Other equally important aspects of the strategy and the issues involved relate to the very revenue sources of the urban local self-government. These are (*i*) tax sources; (*ii*) non-tax sources; (*iii*) fiscal transfers; and (*iv*) borrowings. Whereas fiscal transfer depends on discretion of higher levels of governments, other elements in revenue structure are within the competence of the ULGs that can be used by them effectively for generation of additional financial resources. Other residual spheres of intervention for revenue enhancement relate to (*i*) municipal asset management and (*ii*) political risk management.

Fiscal Decentralisation

Tax Sources

Analysis of revenue structure of municipal governments as well as trends in revenue from own sources in the preceding section of this paper does not reveal a rosy situation of municipal finance in major states of this country. A common feature of urban local finance across the developing countries is inadequate own sources of revenue. The devolved sources of revenue do not match a wide range of functions required to be performed by them. This has led to increasing dependence of ULGs on higher levels of government. Bahl and Linn found that in the cities studied by them, median share of local revenues in financing local expenditures was as low as 30 per cent in the Caribbean countries (Bahl and Linn 1992). This, including shared taxes, was around 63 per cent in the transitional countries (Bird and Wallich 1993).

This is explained by what Bird (Bird 1994) calls "vertical imbalance" (dependence on the revenue of higher levels of government) and "horizontal imbalance" (uneven access to local public resources). Local finance is thus characterised by a mismatch between functions devolved to ULGs and the devolution of tax authority (Jha 1998). This mismatch is exacerbated by lack of (*i*) buoyancy and elasticity in local fiscal instruments, (*ii*) taxes without a wide base, (*iii*) abolition of buoyant and elastic source of revenue- (Octroi), and (*iv*) dependence on only one or two taxes that are not easy to implement (Dillinger 1991). Octroi-a buoyant and elastic source of revenue- has been abolished in Napal, largely in India and Pakistan. Tax on annual rental value of land and buildings (Property Tax) has lost its buoyancy and elasticity due to a host of administrative, legal and behavioral reasons (discretionary considerations and corrupt practices). Taxes like Betting Tax, Tax on Animals, Tax on Vehicles without tires do not enjoy a wide base. Addressing the mismatch between functions and revenue would entail (*i*) a review of local functional domain and shift of functions that are in nature of state functions (curative health, medical colleges) from the domain of local governments to the domain of states, (*ii*) putting in place concept of core municipal function, agency function and transferred function and financing of only the core municipal functions (water supply, sanitation, solid waste management, drainage, street lighting and cremation grounds) out of own revenue and (*iii*) relating the core function with the size categories of towns.

An important aspect of municipal finance in India is that whatever local fiscal instruments have been devolved to local governments, by and large, these instruments do not have a nexus with urban economies that are growing over time. This is an anathema and needs to be addressed through devolution of tax instruments that have a direct nexus with the urban economies. One of the contradictions characterising urban local finance in less developed countries is that even though urban economies keep on growing over time, city governments are becoming impoverished. Taxes to be devolved to the ULGs, therefore, have to be related to the growth in economic base of cities and towns. Buoyancy of local tax instruments depends on their nexus with city economies.

Local Taxes as well must conform to certain basic tenets of local taxation. Local taxes need to be visible, non-sensitive to business cycle, sustainable, should not lead to exporting of tax burden outside the local jurisdiction and should have low administration cost (Bahl

1999). The theory of fiscal federalism as well suggests that the local tax base should be immobile (Oats). Local taxes should yield stable revenue and it should be easy to administer (Bird 1994). Taxes, which largely qualify these tests, include Sales Taxes, Income and Payroll Taxes, Property Taxes, Motor Vehicles Tax and Business Tax. Local Income Tax in the form of piggybacking on central income tax especially seems to be persuasive (Bird 1994).

Local Fiscal Instruments

Sales Tax on retail transaction has been a major source of revenue in U.S.A. Russia has targeted retail sales tax on luxury items. In the Philippines and South Africa, difficulties in getting at the retail sector, has led to taxation of gross sales by business type. Apparently, retail Sales Tax becomes difficult to administer especially in the developing countries due to non-keeping of books of accounts by retailers. Income and payroll taxes are levied in Russia and USA. In India, in some of the states, a similar tax is imposed on professionals, employees and trade. It is known as Tax on Professions, Trade and Calling. However, the Indian Constitution has capped this tax at Rs. 2500 per annum. Moreover, in several states, this tax has been taken over by the state governments. Property Taxes are universally a local tax but are imposed on different bases in different countries. These are discussed subsequently.

Promising Areas of Local Tax Reform

Promising areas of local tax reforms are (*i*) piggybacking on the prices of petroleum products, and electricity charge, (*ii*) devolving of (*a*) Entertainment Tax, (*b*) Stamp Duty, and (*c*) Motor Vehicles Tax. (*iii*) Another equally important aspect of municipal financial resource mobilisation relates to devolution of fiscal autonomy to the municipal governments so that they could set their own rates. In India, municipal laws provide for minimum and maximum limits of tax rates within which ULGs have the autonomy to decide the rate. In case the ceiling exceeds, an approval of the state government is mandatory. In the state of Madhya Pradesh, law provides for state approval only if tax rates need to be reduced. This is an innovative provision to prevent populist measure, if any. The concept of self-governance, however, suggests giving autonomy to ULGs in every sphere of local finance. That could be possible only by reviving the list of local taxes that was introduced in the Government of India Act of 1919 but abolished subsequently in the Government of India Act of 1935. The local list not only needs to be revived but refurbished as well by adding some new local fiscal instruments discussed above. The National Commission to Review the Working of the Constitution, however, has not agreed to its restoration as it thought that the time is not yet ripe for this (National Commission 2002). Also Professions Tax needs to be devolved back to the ULGs and the existing constitutional cap at Rs. 2,500 needs to be enhanced. Already there is a thinking to increase the cap.

An increasing demand on local services, abolition of Octroi, loss of buoyancy and elasticity of annual rental value (ARV) based Property Tax and the consequent fiscal stress of ULGs in India have become compelling reasons to innovate new sources of revenue. These compulsions have already led some of the municipal governments to introduce new sources of local revenue. In the national capital, the Municipal Corporation of Delhi (MCD) imposes a Toll Tax on commercial vehicles that enter the MCD jurisdiction. Different types of vehicles have to pay different rates, which range, from Rs. 25 per entry to Rs. 500 per entry (BOX 1). MCD also levies a Tax on consumption of electricity at a low rate of 2 paise per unit and yet the revenue yield is impressive.

In the state of Madhya Pradesh, which has been thinking lately to bring back Octroi, a few municipal governments introduced a Paryavaran Kar (Tax on Environment) on the goods vehicles, which unloaded consignments in the city (Raipur). Also a Niryat Kar (Tax on Export from local area) was imposed to generate additional revenue. These were, however, withdrawn at the instance of the state government on grounds of resistance from traders. The Pune Municipal Corporation in Maharashtra levies a Street Tax at the rate of 5 per cent of ARV as a piggybacking on Property Tax for part financing an elaborate scheme of improving traffic and transportation (Jha 1998). In the state of Haryana in India, the state government introduced an elaborate scheme of taxation to mobilise revenue for ULGs after the abolition of Octroi (Boxes-I and II below). This as well could not get off the ground due to lack of political will and the political risk management involved in it. The scheme of local taxation as conceived in Haryana was, nevertheless, quite commendable for mitigating fiscal stress of municipal governments. The state governments need to give serious thought to it.

Enhancing Revenue from Existing Taxes

There exists substantial scope for revenue enhancement from existing local taxes. Tax administration is constrained by (*i*) not-so-effective tax administration, and (*ii*) difficulties encountered in administration of the major tax - the Property Tax

Box I : New Fiscal Tools Innovated by Cities

Pune:

- Street Tax @ 5 per cent of ARV
- Use of Land as resource
- Transfer of Development rights
- Marketing of FSI

Raipur:

- Niryat Kar (Export Tax)
- Paryavaran Kar (Environment Tax)

Municipal Corporation of Delhi

Toll Tax on Commercial Vehicles including government Vehicles

(a) Tempos and Taxies: Rs. 25 per entry (monthly coupon, Rs. 500)
(b) Buses and mini trucks: Rs 50 per entry (monthly coupon, Rs. 1000)
(c) Six wheeler trucks: Rs. 50 per entry
(d) (monthly coupon Rs. 1500)
(e) Ten wheeler trucks and trawlers: Rs. 200 per entry (Monthly coupon Rs. 3000)

Sixteen wheeler trawlers: Rs. 500 per entry (Monthly coupon Rs. 5.000)

Effective Tax Administration

Maladies in tax administration relate to (*i*) lack of effective and objective valuation of tax base, (*ii*) assessment of demand, billing and collection. Widening of tax-net, addressing the question of under assessment, review of exemptions of lands and buildings from Property Tax are required to be objectively addressed. Some of the

Box-II: New Fiscal Tools Innovated in Haryana

- Local Area development Tax @ 4 per cent of the value of goods moving from one area to another within the state
- Tax on Profession, Trade and Callings
- Fire Tax @ one per cent of ARV
- Rs. 100 tax on Driving License
- Five paise per unit on power consumption
- Rs 2,500 per year on hotels, restaurants, banquet halls, petrol pumps, nursing homees, gas agencies, private schools and colleges, furniture show rooms, milk dairies, indusrial units.
- Rs. 1,500 per year on private laboratories, commerical colleges, computer centers and show rooms of big companies.
- Rs. 1,000 per year on workshops, service stations, ice factories, flour mills
- Tent houses, cable operators, printing; presss, medical and general stores.
- Levies on registration of new vehicles

cities have now gone for tax mapping for widening the tax-net. Physical surveys of lands and buildings by using GIS base maps tried in the cities of Ludhiana, Indore, Mirzapur, Ghaziabad, Agra, Lucknow, Kanpur and other cities have yielded encouraging results for widening of local tax-net. It has also helped in imparting objectivity and transparency in valuation and assessment of Property Tax.

Poor tax collection is another area of concern for local tax administration. In the state of Gujarat in India, which is amongst some of the progressive states with respect of urban administration, average collection ratio was only about 40 to 46 per cent (NIUA 1993). A study for the Eleventh Finance Commission revealed that 47 per cent of the sample municipal bodies were collecting only up to 50 per cent of PT demand. Statistics for other municipal bodies as well depict poor tax collection (Jha 1998).

Non-realisation of potential of revenue from tax sources due to poor tax-administration is a major reason for low revenue mobilisation. To give an example, the first State Finance Commission (SFC) in Rajasthan believed that there was a potential for additional revenue generation of about Rs. 1544 million against the actual generation of Rs. 2129 million (Rajasthan 1995).

Tax collection and generation of additional revenue could be ensured through (*i*) a scheme of incentives and penalties for municipal staff and the taxpayers and (*ii*) by profitably adopting the ABC Analysis, which is usually applied in management of inventory in an organisation or a project. An innovative scheme of incentives and penalties tried in Delhi in the recent past led to three times increase in PT revenue in five years (Sharma 1991). Some city governments have put in place friendly payment gateways like collection through banks and web-based tax collection. Indore Municipal Corporation has introduces a system of group health insurance of senior citizens. This enables the senior citizens to avail of free hospitalization up to Rs. 20,000 provided they have paid Property Tax. A few cities have put in place a tax collection system by involving banks and on-line payment of PT.

Refurbishing Major Taxes

Octroi and PT have traditionally constituted the mainstay of municipal finance in India. In India, it is abolished in all states except in the states of Punjab, Orissa and the municipal corporations in Maharashtra and Gujarat. In the State of Punjab, it was abolished though; the same was restored in 2002 following an order of the Punjab High Court. ARV system of PT, which was imported from Britain during the colonial rule, is suffering from a host of infirmities (Jha 1991). Analysis of data on revenue from PT reveals that share of PT in the total tax revenue is declining. In the state of Rajasthan, the share of PT in total revenue is only about 2 per cent!

Decline in fiscal role of PT in India is due to a host of administrative and legal reasons. Revenue generation from PT depends on an updating of the base according to the prevailing rental values. This is hardly done despite a legal provision for this in municipal laws. Other administrative reasons pertain to lack of transparency in determination of the base and rationalisation of rate structure. The greatest harm to PT is inflicted by the Rent Control Laws (RCLs). The provision for determination of fair rent in the RCLs has been extended by the courts for determination of even ARV for PT. This has depressed the base and hence loss of revenue productivity (Jha 1993). Other arguments against the existing system of PT relate to broader issues of rising land values that it is unable to capture and its inability to achieve urban development objectives.

Insurmountable problems in ARV system have led to abandoning of ARV as the base of this tax in some states and to switch over to a new system of PT based on unit values. Though there are variations of this model of PT, broadly it envisages a zonal rate for different homogenous zones in to which the city jurisdiction is divided. Zonal rate constitutes the basic tax to be paid by all lands and buildings without any exemption. Elements of progression are brought into the system on the basis of location, quality of construction, age of buildings and land use. These are graded and different values are imputed to different grades. The unit values are then determined in the form of a ready reckoner. These values are applied in determining the base by multiplying the carpet area with the unit values per sq. feet. The simplest variation of this system that is also known as the Area Detail System (ADS) exists in Patna in Bihar. It has only three locations, three column qualities of construction, three uses so that it works on the basis of a 27 matrix in Patna (Vaidya 1996).

The system seems to be objective, simple to administer and easier for the taxpayers to comprehend. This imparts transparency to the determination of the base. When introduced in Patna, despite a reduction in the rate from 69 per cent to 9 per cent, the revenue increased substantially. These positive attributes of the system have led to its snowballing effect in other states. The system first introduced in Andhra Pradesh, has now traveled to Ahmedabad in Gujarat, Rajasthan, Uttar Pradesh, Madhya Pradesh, Tamil Nadu and now MCD in Delhi has decided to replace the ARV system by a Unit Value system of PT. Besides adopting a Unit Value system of Property Tax, the State Government of Uttar Pradesh has also amended municipal laws for de-linking the standard rent concept of the Rent Control Law from valuation of Property Tax base.

Transparency, objectivity and simplicity of the unit value system not withstanding, the system is unlikely to enjoy buoyancy and elasticity as the unit values are frozen. In order to address this problem the unit values would need to be reviewed periodically and indexed with inflation. This involves hard political risk management. Karnataka, a state in India, has therefore opted for a capital value system. Capital values announced by the government periodically for the administration of Stamp Duty are taken as the base of PT. Though this is an artificial capital value created through fiat, it would still be a better value than the market value for which there hardly exists any market evidence in the developing countries due to several and severe distortions in the real estate market.

In any scheme of refurbishment of PT, what is important is that it has to be conceived within the existing legal framework in each country so that it could be sustainable in law. Also intervention is required on all the four important organs of PT viz. (*i*) nature of base, (*ii*) valuation and assessment practices, (*iii*) rate structure, and (*iv*) collection efficiency. Isolated intervention on any one of these organs is unlikely to enhance revenue productivity of this tax. All these organs would need to be addressed at the same time.

Any tax is said to be as good as it is implemented[2]. Revenue enhancement from PT calls for innovative tax administration backed by a computerised PT Information System and taxpayer-friendly payment gateways. Widening of tax net requires comprehensive property contact surveys using GIS base maps (Tax Mapping). A pilot project in Rajnagar locality of Ghaziabad covering an area of only 2.17 sq. mts, for tax mapping using the GIS base maps has resulted in increase in an annual rental value of Rs. 3.26 crores. PT demand increased from Rs. 40 lakhs to Rs. 78.2 lakhs including Water Tax and Sewerage Tax. (IPE 2003a). A similar ongoing-exercise in Agra that is presently continuing suggests that the total number of properties to be brought on the tax records will increase from the existing about 1.41 lakhs to an estimated 2,80 lakhs. Revenue increase will, therefore, be substantial (IPE 2003b)

Using Land as Resource

Land is emerging as a resource for revenue enhancement. ULGs have started using it in innovative ways. Amongst several innovative use of land as a resource in India, two innovative practices deserve special mention. The City and Industrial Development Corporation (CIDCO) in New Mumbai generated massive funds to finance development of New Mumbai by providing all the needed urban infrastructure including its connectivity by rail and road over the creek with the island city of Mumbai. Funds generated by using land were used even for providing shelter to the economically weaker sections of the society. CIDCO was created by the state government under the Companies Act, in which the state government holds equity. It did not have to spend huge funds for development of New Mumbai. A second example pertains to Delhi. During implementation of the Master Plan for Delhi (1961-1981), which was the first ever-urban planning exercise in India, land was used as a resource to generate substantial amount of funds. A seed capital of Rs. 120 million was initially created by the central government for acquisition and development of about 61 thousand acres of land for various land uses. The seed capital thus created was revolved to more than Rs. 223 billion by 1981 which was used to provide basic infrastructure (Jha 1986). Cost of acquisition and development of land was met from the funds thus generated and the entire sale proceeds of the developed land were credited to the fund.

In addition to using land as a resource, there are interesting land based non-property taxes which are used to generate financial resources and also to regulate the use of land in a number of countries. These include Vacant Land Tax, Tax on Land Value Increment and Betterment Levy.

Land based Non-Property Taxes

In India, Chennai Municipal Corporation levies a Tax on Vacant Land (VLT) at the rate of Rs. 104 per ground (290 sq. ft.). The Municipal Corporations of Delhi, Kolkata and Mumbai as well levy this tax on the capital value (CV) of land. MCD levies it at the rate of 5 per cent of CV. Mumbai Municipal Corporation levies the same at the rate of 12 per cent of CV. More than generating the resources, VLT is used to regulate the use and development of vacant land, which will add to the housing stock.

A number of countries in Latin America, Australia, Syria, Turkey and other Afro-Asian countries have taken recourse to VLT. Peru taxes vacant land on an increasing scale. The rate of tax is doubled every year till the vacant land is developed. In case one owns additional plot of land, it attracts additional tax burden (Smith 1979). In Ecuador, it is levied at the rate of 10 per cent. In Chile, it is levied at the rate of 3 per cent, which graduates to 6 per cent of land value over a period of three years, and frozen at this. In Buenos Aires (Argentina), Vacant Land Tax is levied at 5 to 10 per cent. In Syria, it is levied at a graduated rate on the basis of land values. In Australia, a surcharge of up to 5 per cent is levied on unimproved urban land. Vacant land is taxed in Taiwan, Turkey, Senegal, and Korea and even in Pakistan.

Tax on Land Value Increment

Land values appreciate largely due to improvements brought about by the city governments through city development initiatives. Land Value Increment Tax (LVIT) is used with the basic objective of mopping up some of the land value increment for the use and benefit of the community at large.

There are two varieties of LVIT. It is imposed in some countries on the realised increased in land value. In others, it is levied on unrealised value increments. Israel and Malaysia impose this tax on the realised value. Italy, Taiwan levy it on unrealised value. In Sydney (Australia), land value increment is recovered partly through tax at the time of change in zoning from rural to urban at the rate of 30 per cent.

LVIT, however, is a tax imposed by the central governmental and is not very productive largely due to problems confronted in assessment of land value increments. There are ways, however, to get over the assessment problems and share the proceeds of this tax with the municipal authorities.

A popular tax for sharing in the land value increment is Stamp Duty used extensively in India. Though imposed and administered by the state governments, the proceeds are shared with municipal bodies. As the land value increments are brought about by local development initiatives of municipal governments, there exists a rationale and justification for its devolving to ULGs.

Betterment Levy

This as well is levied to recover increase in urban land values resulting from implementation of specific urban development project. The proceeds from this levy are used to meet capital cost of the project. It is levied on the project beneficiaries and continues till the full capital cost of the project is recovered. It has, however, been constrained by two problems. First is the element of arbitrariness in assessing the extent of land value increments in quantitative terms. The second is the physical distance of properties from the implemented project up to which the properties are supposed to have benefited. Additionally, how does one distinguish which part of the land value increment is due to natural increase (scarcity value) and which is due to the impact of the project in question?

Non-Tax Sources

Generation of additional financial resources calls for innovative approaches. Traditionally known sources of revenue have a limit up to which they could be stretched. Non-tax sources have, therefore, constitute promising areas of resource mobilisation. Non-tax sources include fees, charges, price, remunerative municipal projects and enterprises and land based mechanisms of revenue generation.

Special Assessment District

Special Assessment District (SAD) is a popular device used extensively in USA. SAD is used to recover the cost of upgrading a service in a given area within a city. The cost of upgrading the level of service is recovered from beneficiaries by imposing a charge on the assessed value of beneficiary properties and is collected along with PT (Johnson 1993). Cost is recovered in the form of contribution that is used to service the debt incurred for service up-gradation. SAD has been used in California, Maryland and Taxes in U.S.A (Kirwan 1989). Levy of SAD in the developing countries could be formalised by providing for this in the Town Planning Legislation. The authority to administer it, however, would need to be vested in municipal governments. Alternatively, it could be put in the municipal law itself.

Valorisation Charges

Practiced in Columbia, it is similar to SAD. Valorisation charges have been used to finance street improvements, sewer extension and similar projects through a system of charging. The cost of public works is allocated to properties that benefit from projects directly. Cost is allocated in direct proportion to benefits conferred (Doebele, Grimes and Linn; Bird 1994). As a cost recovery mechanism, Valorisation Charges are allocated on the basis of assignment of prescribed benefits to properties in the demarcated series of equally wide parallel zones along the project. Adjustments are made to take account of variation in the lot size and frontage.

Development Impact Exactions (DIE)

DIE, practiced widely in USA, is yet another innovative mechanism to recover the cost of service resulting from the construction of new housing stock by builders. As it is charged on the builder for additional services that are required to be augmented by the civic authority, it mitigates the adverse impact on the community (Johnson 1993). DIE takes into account (*i*) competent local comprehensive planning system, (*ii*) a well thought out capital improvement programme, and (*iii*) development of an impact monitoring system.

In India, the Municipal Corporation of Hyderabad, has recently introduced it as an Impact Fee. The Ahmedabad Municipal Corporation as well has introduced it.

Development Charge (DC)

Whereas DIE is used to recover the added cost of a housing project, DC is used to recover the cost of providing services and infrastructure in already existing housing areas, which do not have such services, or the services are deficient. It is used also in situations of altogether new development. Provision of services in un-serviced residential and non-residential areas is examples of the levy of development charges. MCD in Delhi has been taking recourse to DC in unauthorised colonies on the basis of unit area. In new development areas, DC is included in the price of land and capitalised.

User Charge and Cost Recovery

Amongst the non-tax sources, User Changes constitute the most important mechanism for cost recovery.

Water supply is most suited for imposition of user charges. Yet almost all the municipal governments and the parastatals have been incurring deficits in provision of this service. To give a few samples, the second SFC report of Tamil Nadu reveals that during the years 1995/96 to 2000/01, deficits incurred in the areas under Municipal Councils and Town Panchayats was about Rs. 229 crores. However, there was a surplus of Rs. 430.28 crores in the Municipal Corporation areas. In Himachal Pradesh, accumulated deficit between 1997-98 and 2001-02 was Rs. 1552.33 crores (Teotia 2003). In Kolkata, collection through water charges was Rs. 8.29 per KL against an estimated cost of Rs. 63.10 KL in 2002. On sewerage, revenue collected was Rs. 25 per capita per annum against an expenditure of Rs. 112 per capita per annum (IPE 2003c). In the hill town of Manali, the accumulated losses on account of water between 1998/99 and 2002/03 were about Rs. 43. crores (Gupta and Teotia 2003).

Services provided by a public organisation are grouped as (*i*) public-goods and (*ii*) non-public or exclusionary goods. In case of the latter, users are identifiable and they could be excluded if they do not pay for the use of services. Water supply, sewerage, urban transport, solid waste collection, maintenance of parks and gardens qualify for imposition of user charges. Economic rationale of cost recovery entails that user charges have to be based on the unit cost of providing a service.

There exist a wide range pf practices for recovery of capital cost and operations and maintenance cost. Capital cost, in case of water supply, is recovered through one-time connection charge, development charge and betterment levy. But these instruments recover only a fraction of the total capital cost. A substantial one-time connection charge in water supply and sewerage projects now forms part of the HUDCO funded projects. In some of the cities, cost recovery has been successfully tried by using land as resource (CIDCo in New Mumbai and DDA in Delhi during the First Master Plan through a Revolving Fund). In development of new area, capital cost is capitalised as part of land price.

Practice of recovery of operations and maintenance cost is not different. Municipal governments and parastatals are not recovering even the maintenance cost. In India, maintenance cost recovery through user charges is hardly one-third of the total operations and maintenance cost (NIUA 1993, TRF 1997).

Many municipal bodies are, however, levying user charges in quite inefficient manner. Most of them adhere to piggybacking of user charges on PT or the ferule size as a proxy for water consumed. Charging on the basis of metered water use is not yet prevalent in a large number of cities and towns on the pretext that meters do not work especially if the water quality is not good. In this age of technological advancement, this argument does not seem to hold ground. Charging for water as piggybacking on PT is a bad system of charging especially when PT is suffering from depressed base and a number of infirmities characterise its administration. This makes the service delivery inefficient and inadequate. Efficiency requires to charge "wherever possible" (Bird 1994). Besides being an important tool of cost recovery, User Charges have commendable attributes. User charges enhance efficiency. Like price in a market economy, it provides a signal to municipal bodies for the demand of services. It ensures economical use of the service by preventing misuse and abuse of the services provided. It disciplines both the users and the abusers and fits into the very economic rationale of local government to improve efficiency, "to ensure that local citizens get in local services what they want, and are willing to pay for" (Bird 1994).

There is now evidence, though not on a very large scale, that compulsions of paucity of funds with the state governments and disciplining of borrowings by the Reserve Bank of India, the era of financial profligacy is waning out. State Governments are not in a position to meet fiscal gap of the cities and parastatals on a continuous basis. Almost all water supply systems are experiencing huge deficits. The Irrigation and Public Health Department in Himachal Pradesh revised water tariffs in March, 2001after a gap of nine years relating the charging on the basis of metering and fixing penalties for not installing of meters within a stipulated time. As a result, revenue doubled in a year (Teotia 2003). However, the order for charging was withdrawn in July, 2001 by introducing a flat rate regime again and freezing the same at Rs. 40 per month. Karnataka State Government has issued directives for a minimum charging and revision of tariffs on a periodical basis. In Chandigarh, the Chandigarh Administration has substantially revised tariffs for water (Gupta and Teotia 2003). The State Government of Punjab increased tariffs in July 2003 not only for the current year but has issued directives for further upward annual revision up to 2007-08 according to rates suggested by it (Punjab 2003).

All the directly chargeable services have, therefore, to be charged on the basis of costs. In any scheme of User Charge, the needs of lower income groups can be taken care of by working out an innovative cross-subsidy structure based on subsidy (*i*) from one income group to another, (*ii*) from one land use to another, and (*iii*) from one account to another. The Mumbai Municipal Corporation's Bombay Electric Supply and Transport (BEST), which provides electricity and transport, electricity account gives subsidy to the transport account, which incurs deficit.

Institutional Finance

Requirement of funds for augmentation of urban services and urban infrastructure is astronomical largely due to rapid pace of urbanisation and growth as also deficiencies in the existing level of services. There exist two options to finance capital investments. First is on "as-you-go" basis, which entails investment in one go. The other is to use surplus on revenue account, which is generally hard to come by due to fiscal stress afflicting most of ULGs. Softer option for financing urban infrastructure, however, in most of the developing countries is through budgetary support by the central/ state governments and directed credit. These have done a lot of harm to infrastructure financing per se as they hardly motivate the municipal governments to rationalise pricing and cost recovery in provision of urban infrastructure and services.

Municipal bodies need an access of funds by raising the same from financial institutions and from the capital market. Every country has, by now, financial institutions in one form or the other. In India, the leading financial institution to fund urban development projects is HUDCO at the national level. It has an urban infrastructure window that funds infratstructure development projects. Most of the states in India have constituted their own urban infrastructure finance institutions (Kerala, Karnataka, Tamil Nadu). Tamil Nadu has created an Urban Development Fund, which is managed as an asset management company in collaboration with leading non-banking financial institutions like HDFC, I&LFS and ICICI. The experience of this has been rewarding and it is now being replicated in other states. Tamil Nadu Urban Development Fund now borrows from the capital market to augment its funds.

An important role of institutional finance should be to promote efficient use of funds advanced. Hence financial institutions need to provide technical assistance for improving the municipal management system. They also need to use their funding for leveraging reforms in municipal management and cost recovery. Financial institutions also need to gradually come out of the system of guaranteed regime of lending. As discussed subsequently, it amounts to a perverse incentive to borrowers and adversely affects motivation for a rational system of cost recovery. HUDCO is now increasingly striving to come out of such a system of funding. It has provided a non-recourse line of credit of Rs. 10 billion to the Bangalore Mahanagar Palika without any state guarantee (Urban Finance 2003).

Directed Credit

Directed credit approach relied upon in a big way in East Asian countries retarded the development of market-based capital financing mechanism in Asia. It also increased vulnerability of East Asian economies to volatile flows of international capital (Stein 1998). In India, LIC and the pension funds have mandated investment in socially prioritised sectors that has semblance of directed credit.

Accessing the Capital Market

As mentioned earlier, urban infrastructure (UI) in developing countries is generally financed through plan or budgetary allocations from the higher levels of government or through lending by financial institutions (FIs). Both these methods are not conducive to promote an efficient use of scarce resources. Plan or budgetary allocations, by their very nature, are treated as soft money. Pricing and cost recovery, therefore, does not constitute a serious agenda in such a system of funding. Municipal governments or the UI agencies, therefore, are not found pro-active due to such an assured flow of soft funds. Similar is the case with guaranteed regime of lending by the FIs. As guarantee is given by the higher levels of government, borrowing organisations never care for pricing and cost recovery for repayment of loan. These two traditional systems of funding, by and large, make cost recovery initiative rather subdued. It has led to a mindset that UI is a social welfare service. Motivation for cost recovery in such a system becomes a casualty. Accessing capital market through appropriate debt instrument is, therefore, desirable.

This is, however, predicated on a number of imperatives. First, there must exist a long-term debt market. UI, by its very nature, involves lumpy investments and cost recovery is not feasible in the sort run. Hence there has to be a long- term debt market. Second, UI projects have to be commercially viable or else no investor will like to put one's money in such projects.. Third, accessing the capital market requires investment grade credit rating. This again brings back up-gradation of skills and innovative management practices as an imperative. Fourth, financial reporting and accounting system needs to be such that it provides information on (*i*) innate financial strength, and (*ii*) financial performance of municipal governments for raising funds from the capital market. Fifth is the availability of funds for project development as the mortality rate in development of commercially viable or bankable projects is fairly high at least in the beginning.

The aforesaid imperatives for accessing the capital market appear to be daunting. These have been addressed in the Indian cities in a number of ways, which are replicable.

India has been dealing with imperatives mentioned above since 1994 under an Indo-USAID collaborative program for commercialisation of UI, developing a market based UI finance system and a long-term debt market. It envisages improving internal municipal management system and financial management through municipal institutional capacity building initiatives. Known as Financial Institutions Reform and Expansion – Debt Market

Development (FIRE-D) launched in 1994, it initially made available a House Guarantee (HG) fund of US$125 million to be raised form the US capital market. The FIRE-D programme requires to structure commercially viable projects for water supply, sanitation and solid waste. These are the sectors that are eligible for funding out of the HG fund. Commercially viable UI projects (CVUIP) are funded out of the HG fund. But only up to 50 per cent of project cost. The balance needs to be raised from the Indian debt market. As HG money is available for a period of 30 years, CVUIPs become instruments to help develop a long-term debt market in India. The programme through policy advocacy in various states, technical assistance to the cities as also putting in place a series of mechanisms and processes including the credit rating of city governments has enabled some of the cities to access the capital market by issuing municipal bonds.

The problem of credit rating has been addressed by supporting CRISIL and ICRA - the two reputed credit rating organisations- to develop a methodology for municipal credit rating. Improving skills and management capabilities is addressed through technical assistance to the city governments. Accounting and financial reporting system has been dealt with by involving the Institute of Chartered Accountants, India which has developed generic guidelines for preparing accounting manuals. As a result, the state of Tamil Nadu has become the first state to switch over to double entry accrual based accounting system for municipal governments across the state. Maharashtra is presently engaged in groundwork to switch over to an accrual based accounting system. It has triggered municipal accounting reform in a number of cities. A Task Force created by the CAG of India looked into this issue and its report has further flagged the need for accounting reform at the local level.

As regards project development fund, at the national level, HUDCO has created a fund for financing project development and structuring. Some of the state governments have as well taken the initiative to create similar funds for financing project development initiatives. Andhra Pradesh Urban Infrastructure Finance Development Corporation in the state of Andhra Pradesh, Gujarat Urban Development Corporation and also the Gujarat Municipal Finance Board in Gujarat, Kerala Urban Development Finance Corporation in Keral, Urban Development Fund in the state of Madhya Pradesh created as a debt service reserve fund by intercepting the transfers to the municipal governments for debt, Urban Development Fund in Punjab are some the initiatives so far taken by some of the state governments. Urban project development could be supported through these financial institutional mechanisms.

In some European and South American countries, local government credit markets have been developed in stages beginning with a central government financed loan fund that applies commercial standards and practices. The next stage is loans provided by commercial banks; the third is bond issuance in the domestic capital market. Central governments can encourage this transition by channeling funds to commercial banks and promoting credit enhancement measures through pooled funds, grant intercept mechanisms, guaranteeing loans, and passing legislation that permits local government assets and revenues to be used as loan collateral. They can also assist municipalities with project structuring and strengthen financial management through a combination of regulations and technical assistance.

In Canada, municipal credit market is focused on issuing bonds in the domestic capital market. A few of the larger cities also issue bonds in international markets. Six of ten Canadian provinces have established municipal finance authorities, which pool borrowing requirements of the municipalities within their jurisdictions and issue debentures. These authorities have access to the municipal tax base in the case of default and five of the six receive additional credit enhancement through a provincial guarantee of their debentures. Other provinces either directly assist municipalities in accessing capital markets, create large municipalities with strong economic bases, or provide direct loans to municipalities. All provinces set limits on municipal borrowing levels and debt service costs, prescribe and monitor accounting and financial management standards, and provide technical assistance to local governments.

Due to a number of policy-support by the central and state governments, the process of accessing the capital market is snowballing in India and, by now, the following cities including a pooled financing institution, have accessed the capital market for raising of funds. Nevertheless, two conditions need to be addressed through policy intervention. First is that local governments must demonstrate they are financially and operationally stable and have the ability to repay loans. Second is the availability of lenders who are satisfied with the local government's ability to service loans and the legal recourse available to them in case of loan default.

Municipal Bonds Issued by the City Governments

City	*Year*	*Size of Issue (Rs. million)*	*Govt. Guarantee*	*Credit Rating*
1. Bangalore	1997	1250	Yes	A-(SO)
2. Ahmedabad	1998	1000	No	AA(SO)
3. Ludhiana	1999	100	No	LAA-(SO)
4. Nasik	1999	1000	No	AA-(S0)
5. Nagpur	2000	500	No	LAA-(SO)
6. Madurai	2001	300	No	LA+(SO)
7. Indore	2001	500	Yes	A(SO)
8. Kolkata	2001	500	No	AA(SO)
9. Ahmedabad (Tax Free)	2002	1000	No	AA(SO)
10. Hyderabad (Tax Free)	2002	825	No	LAA+(SO)
11. Tamil Nadu (Pooled Finance)	2002	304	–	LA(SO) AA(SO)

Barring Tamil Nadu pooled finance organisation, nine cities have so far accessed the capital market. Ahmedabad has done it twice. These cities have raised Rs 6,975 millions from the capital market. Also barring Bangalore and Indore, other cities have accessed the capita market without a government guarantee. Municipal Corporations of Ahmedabad and Hyderabad and the Tamil Nadu Water and Sanitation Pooled Fund have issued tax-free municipal Bonds. Requests of the Visakhapatanam Water Supply and Sewerage Board and the Hyderabad Water Supply and Sewerage Board are presently under the consideration of the central government for tax-free municipal bonds.

Keeping the total number of municipal Corporations in the country, this does not appear impressive. Nevertheless, what is important is the beginning that has been made. It has motivated cities to be pro-active. It has led to a change in the mindset. Urban infrastructure and services are no longer treated as social welfare services. There is a better appreciation now at all levels that these involve cost of production that needs to be recovered through rational pricing and cost recovery. It has led to motivation on part of city managers to adopt innovative management system. In order to give fillip to the development of municipal bond market, the central government amended the Income Tax Act for issuance of tax-free municipal bonds and permitted Rs. 2,000 million in 2001-02 and Rs, 5,000 million in 2001-03 to be raised through tax-free municipal bond. It also introduced municipal accounting reforms as mentioned earlier. The central government introduced two incentive funds to motivate the state governments to introduce reforms for attracting investments in urban settlements.

In the budget of 2002-03, the Finance Minister introduced (*i*) Urban Reform Incentive Fund, and (*ii*) City Challenge Fund. Urban Reform Incentive Fund (URIF) with an initial outlay of Rs. 500 crore has been set up to provide reform linked assistance to the states. Detailed Guidelines have been formulated to give financial assistance to states for introducing reforms that have been identified in the Guidelines. City Challenge Fund is an incentive based grant facility that will support cities to fund transition costs of moving towards sustainable and creditworthy institutional systems of municipal management and delivery, and sector level reforms (e.g. in the urban water and sanitation sector). This fund will meet expenses to be incurred by cities to finance the cost of developing a reform program and its implementation. Credit worthiness and hence sustainability of reforms is to be used as benchmarks for assessing the proposals. Importantly, the fund will support those reform programs that are developed and owned by municipal governments.

Amongst several factors inhibiting development of municipal bond market (*i*) lack of credit worthiness of large number of city governments and municipalities, (*ii*) problem of credit enhancement, (*iii*) need for technical assistance, (*iv*) lack of robustness in revenue generation from own source of revenue, and (*v*) lack of professional skills for structuring and development of commercially viable or bankable projects, (*vi*) lack of confidence amongst the lenders about the ability of local governments to service the debt are important factors. A recent Municipal Bond assessment study in three states has reiterated some of these concerns (NIUA 2002). Quite many of these concerns will be, hopefully, addressed by policy initiatives discussed above. These factors apart, there are other issues relating to widening and deepening of capital market, adherence to SEBI regulation and the extent of financial disclosures and related issues (Bagchi and Kundu 2003).

Pooled Financing

The nascent market based urban infrastructure finance system by accessing the capital market through floating of Municipal Bonds, is generally amenable, by and large, to very large Municipal Corporations in sprawling metropolitan cities that have strong economic base. Small and medium towns whose number is substantial (5161 according to the 2001 Census) are not in a position to access the capital market on stand-alone basis largely due to their lack of credit worthiness individually. Moreover, it will not be cost effective as well. Pooled financing structures exist in the U.S.A., Canada (Bond Banks), and even in Southeast Asia viz. the Philippines (Local Government Unit Credit Guarantee Corporation) and Malaysia (Local Government Credit Guaranty Corporation) to support borrowings by smaller municipalities. These are state sponsored intermediaries that borrow on its own financial strength for a number of smaller municipalities that are individually not in a position to access the capital market on their own. Pooled finance mechanism thus serves as debt fund for small and medium size municipal entities. A spin-off of this structure is that it can be used to leverage urban reforms in small and medium towns.

A beginning has been made in the state of Tamil Nadu by creating Water and Sanitation Pooled Fund (WSPF) in August 2002. Managed by a multi-sector Tamil Nadu Urban Infrastructure Financial Services Ltd. (TNUIFSL), it finances and refinances water supply and sanitation projects of municipalities in small and medium size towns (FIRE-D 2003). It raised Rs. 30.4 crores from the capital market through Bond issue to finance small water and sanitation projects in 14 municipal areas at 9.20 per cent rate of interest with 15-year maturity. Of this, Rs. 16 crores was granted the status of tax-free Municipal Bonds. Bond issue was structured with a multi-layered credit enhancement mechanism that secured a credit rating of AA(SO) by FITCH and LAA(SO) by ICRA. A catalytic element in structuring of this Bond issue was the Direct Credit Authority (DCA) Guarantee that the USAID now offers for supporting development of commercially viable infrastructure projects, augmentation of infrastructure, private sector participation, decentralisation and ensuring access of urban poor to the basic urban services.

Pooled finance structures like the one in Tamil Nadu needs to be encouraged in other states as well. With this end in view, the

Government of India has formulated Guidelines that will help create pooled finance structures in states (India 2003). The Guidelines identify small and medium towns with a population of up to a million. It envisages (*i*) facilitating development of bankable urban infrastructure projects, (*ii*) reducing the cost of borrowing with appropriate credit enhancement measures, (*iii*) raising funds from the market for bankable projects through Bonds, (*iv*) support municipal bodies in project development for urban infrastructure, and (*v*) restructuring of existing costly debts. Triggering pricing and financial management reforms in small and medium towns as well as facilitating development of Municipal Bond markets are other objectives that the Guidelines envisage for the State Pooled Finance Entity (SPFE).

The Guidelines envisage creation of SPFE and operated by state governments. They will issue debt securities on behalf of the municipal bodies without state guarantee. Escrowing of resources for servicing of debt, setting up Debt Service Reserve Fund and getting them managed by trustees of the Bond issue are other mandates for SPFEs. The central government is to support SPFEs through Pooled Finance Development Fund (PFDF). For this, Rs. 50 lakh has been proposed for the year 2003-04 as a token amount. An allocation of Rs. 400 crores has been made in the Tenth Plan for this initiative.

Central assistance from PFDF is to be given for (*i*) reform packages for the municipal and urban local bodies concerned, and (*ii*) contribution to the Debt Service Reserve Fund (DSRF). Contribution to the DSRF would be to the extent of 50 per cent of the DSRF requirement as determined by a credit rating agency or 10 per cent of the amount to be raised from the market whichever is less. This will be admissible for a minimum of AA rating. The balance amount is to be contributed by the State/Union Territories Government.

Public- Private Partnership (P-3)

P-3 has come handy in recent years in the municipal sector due to its several spin-offs. It facilitates financing of urban services, augments the level of services, enhances efficiency of service delivery system, and brings in new technology. P-3 is pushed through either by way of privatisation or by contracting out of services to private operators and providers. Interesting forms of privatisation have immerged like BOT, BOOT, BOO, BOLT and others. However, in order to enhance efficiency and effectiveness of the delivery system, municipal government and urban infrastructure agencies are going for management contract. Privatisation has not yet materialised on a scale as required in less developed economies. There are only sporadic examples of privatisation. Water supply is privatised in Manila. Interestingly, two private providers were granted concession for eastern and western parts of the city to promote competition. After privatisation, the efficiency of the delivery system increased and the tariffs decreased (Dumol 2000)[3] . Other examples are Buenos Aires, and Macao. France has had a long history a privatisation of water supply, which is also practiced in U.K.

In India, privatisation in water sector has been limited to management contracts rather than concession contracts. Presently two very large water supply projects with private sector participation are being implemented in Tiruppur (Rs. 1,023 crores project in Tamil Nadu) and in Visakhapatanam (Rs. 4.100 crores industrial water supply project). Concession contract and management contracts, besides enhancing efficiency of the system, contributes to cost saving and hence make available additional financial resources. Some of the water supply undertakings (in Indore, Faridabad, for example) have profitably gone for energy audit that has helped them in additional cost savings.

Privatisation and contracting out have been tried in a number of services like solid waste collection, street light maintenance, maintenance of parks and gardens, collection of Octroi with substantial cost savings and efficiency enhancement in a number of cities. Cost savings in the wake of privatisation/contracting out, implies additional resource generation.

Asset Management

Municipal governments generally own assets like land, plants and equipments. Many of them do not, however, have an inventory of assets owned by them. They are, therefore, not in a position to have efficient and optimum use of their assets. They are also not able to leverage their assets for raising funds from the market. It has come to light that Municipal Corporations do not have knowledge of lands owned by them. Initiatives taken in asset management in recent years in Ludhiana, Indore, Lucknow and Agra have brought to light substantial amount of new found land belonging to them but not on their office records. These now could be leveraged for generation of additional resources. Asset management also helps in using passive assets for remunerative uses.

Political Risk Management

Paying taxes and user charges is perhaps the most unpleasant thing. Hence no body likes to pay these. It requires provision of quality services that induces the users to pay for. A hike in taxes and user charges, though quite legitimate for financing of augmented supply of services, leads to agitation and political unrest. Here comes the skill of political risk management. It lies in the political domain of local governance. Mayors and Chairpersons along with elected Councillors have a pivotal role in managing political risk of tax and tariff increases. They need to appreciate that good economics is not a bad politics if they need to be re-elected. But this would call for a strong Mayor system or the cabinet form of local government so that Mayors and Chairpersons could have a popular and dominant position for political risk management.

We have discussed in the preceding pages leading contemporary issues and practices in financial resource mobilisation. There are many more interesting community based financing practices (Orangi Pilot Project, in Pakistan; Allandur Sewerage system in Tamil Nadu; solid waste collection in Ludhiana in Punjab and elsewhere). Constraints on the size of this paper do not permit to discuss those innovative financing practices. Nevertheless, these have provided much needed insights into how a communitarian government, which a municipal entity is supposed to be, can conceptualise innovative ways of doing things and adopt innovative practices. Such practices and experiences are emerging day by day. What is, therefore, needed is to be innovative in finding out solutions to the complex civic problems.

We end up this rather long discussion by a simple, persuasive and useful rule of financing urban services:

If the beneficiaries of a service can not be identified and excluded from consuming it, finance it by taxes; if the beneficiaries can be identified and excluded, finance it through user changes; if the service provision requires long term investment of huge funds (as in UI projects), finance it by borrowing; and if the local communities could be organised, try to devise community based financing and implementation process.

Table 1: Revenue from Own Sources of Municipal Corporations in Major States (Per centage)

Sl. No.	*States*	*1990-91*	*1994-95*	*1997-98*	*2000-01*
1.	Andhra Pradesh	40.15	51.45	59.49	46.91*
2.	Assam	28.95	63.51	88.68	N.A.
3.	Gujarat	74.55	77.76	73.54	N.A.
4.	Haryana	82.08	52.72	45.45	N.A.
5.	Himachal Pradesh	86.02	78.19	65.49	N.A.
6.	Jammu & Kashmir	Mun.Corpn. does not exist			
7.	Karnataka	45.75	34.23	32.37	60.8
8.	Kerala	79.61	79.1	48.92	N.A.
9.	Madhya Pradesh	52.88	50.17	35.92	N.A.
10.	Maharashtra	89.41	89.09	65.51	N.A.
11.	Orissa	67.24	86.15	84.56	N.A.
12.	Punjab	83.17	92.39	85.54	N.A.
13.	Rajasthan	79.29	78.28	88.23	N.A.
14.	Tamil Nadu	56.22	62.98	67.44	N.A.
15.	Uttar Pradesh	35.71	24.47	27.7	N.A.
16.	West Bengal	19.22	94.99	94.08	N.A.
	All States	*75.72*	*20.52*	*79.62*	*N.A.*

Source: Report of the Eleventh Finance Commission for 2000-2005 and Second SFC Reports of Karnataka and Andhra Pradesh

* Pertains to the year 1999-2000

Table 2: Revenue of Municipalities from Own Sources in Major States (Per centage)

Sl. No.	*States*	*1990-91*	*1994-95*	*1997-98*	*2000-01*
1.	Andhra Pradesh	N.A.	43.47	46.71	31.06*
2.	Assam	97.25	63.51	88.68	N.A.
3.	Gujarat	56.11	54.55	54.07	N.A.
4.	Haryana	67.97	81.81	65.9	N.A.
5.	Himachal Pradesh	60.95	49.26	38.1	N.A.
6.	Jammu & Kashmir	3.42	3.2	2.41	N.A.
7.	Karnataka	54.93	64.13	49.93	36.9
8.	Kerala	64.69	63.93	41.1	N.A.
9.	Madhya Pradesh	38.07	40.29	28.72	N.A.
10.	Maharashtra	N.A.	N.A.	N.A.	N.A.
11.	Orissa	56.17	64.49	68.87	N.A.
12.	Punjab	77.39	75.3	85.39	N.A.

Contd.

13. Rajasthan	82.35	84.85	72.34	N.A.
14. Tamil Nadu	62.57	63.61	54.59	N.A.
15. Uttar Pradesh	39.19	27.43	25.36	N.A.
16. West Bengal	21.17	24.33	21.06	N.A.
All States	*59.51*	*60.92*	*58.85*	*N.A.*

* Pertains to the year 1999-2000

Source: Report of the Eleventh Finance Commission for 2000-2005 and Second SFC Reports of Karnataka and Andhra Pradesh

Table 3: Revenue of Nagar Panchayats from Own Sources in Major States (Per centage)

Sl. No.	*States*	*1990-91*	*1994-95*	*1997-98*
1.	Andhra Pradesh	N.A.	38.91	40.08
2.	Assam	89.07	94.72	40.01
3.	Gujarat	72.36	79.72	67.62
4.	Haryana	N.P. does not exist		
5.	Himachal Pradesh	72.35	70.54	67.62
6.	Jammu & Kashmir	14.7	15.5	16.02
7.	Karnataka	57.74	64.34	47.57
8.	Kerala	Nagar Panchayat does not exist		
9.	Madhya Pradesh	31.91	48.12	13.88
10.	Maharashtra	Nagar Panchayat does not exist		
11.	Orissa	68.16	63.18	63.69
12.	Punjab	64.23	67.13	77.99
13.	Rajasthan	67.46	68.87	66.06
14.	Tamil Nadu	37.67	38.13	24.63
15.	Uttar Pradesh	33.31	46.35	35.31
16.	West Bengal	3.72	6.45	5.26
All States		*49.84*	*53.11*	*39.76*

Source: Report of the Eleventh Finance Commission for 2000-2005

Table 4: Growth in Own Revenue of Municipal Corporations in Major States (Per cent)

Sl.No.	*States*	*Revenue from Own Sources*	*Revenue from External Sources*	*CAGR* Own Source Revenue*
1.	Andhra Pradesh	59.49	40.51	28
2.	Assam	88.68	11.32	14.1

Contd.

3.	Gujarat	73.54	26.46	18.4
4.	Haryana	45.45	54.55	14.4
5.	Himachal Pradesh	65.49	34.51	17.26
6.	Jammu & Kashmir	Mun.Corpn does not exist		
7.	Karnataka	32.37	67.63	10.3
8.	Kerala	48.92	51.18	7.5
9.	Madhya Pradesh	35.92	64.18	3.6
10.	Maharashtra	65.51	34.49	12
11.	Orissa	84.56	15.44	16.4
12.	Punjab	88.54	11.46	13.5
13.	Rajasthan	88.23	11.77	18.9
14.	Tamil Nadu	67.44	32.56	25.5
15.	Uttar Pradesh	27.7	72.3	5.8
16.	West Bengal	94.07	6.93	107.04
	All States	*66.11*	*33.89*	*-1.3*

* CAGR relates to the period 1990-91 to 1997-98

Table 5: Revenue Structure and Growth in Own Revenue of Municipalities in Major States, 1997-98 (Per cent)

Sl.No.	*States*	*Revenue from Own Sources*	*Revenue from External Source*	*CAGR* Own Source Revenue*
1.	Andhra Pradesh	46.71	53.29	9
2.	Assam	34.63	65.37	3.7
3.	Gujarat	54.07	45.93	14.1
4.	Haryana	65.91	34.09	11.6
5.	Himachal Pradesh	38.1	61.9	13.2
6.	Jammu & Kashmir	2.41	97.59	10.82
7.	Karnataka	49.94	50.06	13.8
8.	Kerala	41.11	58.89	11.2
9.	Madhya Pradesh	28.72	71.28	9
10.	Maharashtra	N.A.	N.A.	19.6**
11.	Orissa	68.87	31.13	12.3
12.	Punjab	85.39	14.61	-11.4
13.	Rajasthan	72.34	27.66	17.5
14.	Tamil Nadu	57.59	42.51	10.9
15.	Uttar Pradesh	25.36	74.64	2.7

Contd.

16	West Bengal	21.06	78.94	13.9
All States		*58.85*	*41.15*	*16*

* CAGR relates to the period 1990-91 to 1997-98

* * Relates to total revenue

Source: Report of the Eleventh Finance Commission for 2000-2005

Table 6: Revenue Structure and Growth in Own Revenue of Nagar Panchayats in Major States (Per cent)

Sl.No.	*States*	*Revenue from Own Sources*	*Revenue from External Source*	*CAGR* Own Source Revenue*
1.	Andhra Pradesh	40.08	59.92	4.4
2.	Assam	40.02	59.98	4.8
3.	Gujarat	Information included in Municipalities		
4.	Haryana	Nagar Panchayats do not exist		
5.	Himachal Pradesh	67.62	32.38	21.23
6.	Jammu & Kashmir	16.03	83.97	25.16
7.	Karnataka	47.57	52.43	33.
8.	Kerala	Nagar Panchayats do not exist		
9.	Madhya Pradesh	86.12	13.88	1.6
10.	Maharashtra	Nagar Panchayats do not exist		
11.	Orissa	63.69	36.31	9.1
12.	Punjab	77.99	22.01	12.3
13.	Rajasthan	66.06	33.94	15.7
14.	Tamil Nadu	18.55	81.45	20.8
15.	Uttar Pradesh	35.31	64.69	13
16.	West Bengal	5.2694.74	81.7	
All States		*39.78*	*60.22*	*15.8*

* CAGR relates to the period 1990-91 to 1997-98

Source: Report of the Eleventh Finance Commission for 2000-2005

REFERENCES

Andhra Pradesh (2002). Second State Finance Commission Report, State Government of Andhra Pradesh, Hyderabad.

Bahl, Roy W and Johannes Linn (1992). Urban Public Finance in Development Countries, New York : Oxford University Press.

Bagchi, Soumen and Kundu, Anirban (2003). "Development of Municipal

Bond Market in India : Issues Concerning Financing of Urban Infrastructure", Economic and Political Weekly, Vol.XXXVIII, No. 8, February, 2003.

Bahl, Roy (2000). "Sustainable Local Government Financing Strategies in Developing Countries and Transition Countries", City Development Strategies, No. 3, Second Quarter.

Bird, Richard M. and Christine Wallich (1993). "Fiscal Decentralisation and Inter governmental Relations in Transitional Economics" Working Paper No. WPS 1122, Washington D.C. : The World Bank.

Bird Richard M. (1994). "Financing Local Services : Patterns, Problems, and Possibilities" paper presented for Global Report on Human Settlements, April.

Davey, Kenneth (1989). Strengthening Municipal Government, Discussion Paper, Washington D.C.: The World Bank.

Dillinger, William (1991). "Property Tax Reform ,Washington D.C.: The World Bank.

Doebele, W.A. et al (1989). "Participation of Beneficiary in Financing Urban Services, Land Economics 55: 1

Dumol, Mark (2000). The Manila Water Concession, A Key to Government Officials' Diary of the World's Largest Water Privatisation, Washington D.C.: The World Bank.

FIRE-D (2003). Project Notes, Note No. 31, Indo-US Financial Institutions Reform and Expansion Project-Debt Market Component, May, 2003.

Gupta, J.P. and Teotia, Manoj K.(2003). Study on Urban Management in a Hill Town : A Case Study of Manali in Himachal Pradesh, Interim Report,sponsored by USAID under the FIRE-D project, CRRID, Chandigarh.

India (2003). Draft Guidelines for Pooled Finance Developmemnt Scheme, Ministry of Urban Development & Poverty Alleviation, circulated in the Seminar on Municipal Accounting jointly organized by the Ministry of Urban Development and Poverty Alleviation and FIRE-D Project in New Delhi, 2003.

IPE (2003a). Mapping of Properties and Developing GIS for Property Tax Enhancing, Infrastructure Professionals Enterprise, Ghaziabad.

IPE (2003b). Agra Municipal Reform Project, Supported by Japan Bank of International Cooperation, Infrastructure Professionals Enterprise, Pvt. Ltd., Agra.

IPE (2003c). Kolkata Environmental Improvement Programme: Capacity Building Programme, Inception Phase Consultancy Final

Report, Annex-B: Resource Mobilisation and Improved Financial Management , supported by DFID, Inftrastructure Professionals Enterprise, Pvt. Ltd., New Delhi.

Jha, Gangadhar (1986). "Revolving Fund as a Technique of Financing Land Development: A Critique" in K.S.R.N. Serma (ed.) Financing Urban Development in India, New Delhi: Indian Institute of Public Administration.

Jha (1991). Property Tax in India: Existing Practices and Issues for Reform, paper presented as part of a World Bank study on Financing Urban Services in India, Washington, D.C.: the World Bank, Country Operations Department.

Jha, Gangadhar (1998 a). "Enhancing Municipal Fiscal Capability: Issues in Local Resource Mobilisation" in Konrad Adenauer Foundation (ed.) Local Government Finances in India, New Delhi: Manohar.

Jha, Gangadhar (1998 b). Project Development Experience in Urban Environmental Infrastructure (Mimeo) Vol. I. Proceedings of an International Seminar, New Delhi, and NIUA.

Jha, Gangadhar (1993). "Reforming Property Tax: The Legal Issues", Nagarlok, Vol. XXV, No. 4, October-December.

Johnson, Thomas (1993). "An Alternative Method of Financing Urban Development in Less Developing Countries", Journal of Construction, May, 7:4.

Karnataka (2002. Report of the Second State Finance Commission, State Government of Karnataka, Bangalore.

Kirwan, R.M. (1989). "Finance for Urban Infrastructure", Urban Studies, Vol. 6.

Mathur, O.P. (1999) "Governing Cities: Facing upto the Challenges of Poverty and Globalisation" in O.P. Mathur (ed.) India, the Challenges of Urban Governance, New Delhi: National Institute of Public Finance and Policy.

Musgrave, Richard A. (1983). "Who should Tax, Where and What?" in Charles Mclure (ed.) Tax Assignment in Federal Countries, Canberra: Centre for Research on Federal Financial Relations, Australian National University.

National Commission (2002). Review of the Working of the Constitution, Report of the National Commission to Review the Working of the Constitution, Vol.l, New Delhi.

NIUA (1989). Upgrading Municipal Services: Norms and Financial Implications (Mimeo) Vol. I, New Delhi, National Institute of Urban Affairs (NIUA).

NIUA (1993). Urban Development Strategy for the State of Gujarat (Mimeo) Vol. I, National Institute of Urban Affairs, New Delhi.

NIUA (2002). Development of Municipal Bond Market in India: Municipal Bond Assessment Studies, National Institute of Urban Affairs, New Delhi.

Pettenburg et al (1996). "Building Capacities for Better Cities" Discussion paper for Habitat II, Rotterdam, IHS.

Punjab (2003). Notification No. 2/2/2003-3LGIV/6510, dated 2nd May, 2003, State Government of Punjab (Department of Local Government), Chandigarh.

Rabinovitch, Jonas (1999). "From Urban Management to Urban Governance: Towards a Strategy for the New Millenium" City Development Strategies, No. 1 October.

Rajasthan (1995). Report of the First State Finance Commission, State Government of Rajasthan, Jaipur.

Rajasthan (2001). Report of the Second State Finance Commission Rajasthan for 2000-2005, State Government of Rajasthan, Jaipur.

Sharma, M.P. (1991). "Property Tax Collection: A Case Study of Municipal Corporation of Delhi", Urban India, 11: 1.

Smith, Roger S. (1979). "The Effects of Land Prices" in Roy Bahl (ed.) The Taxation of Urban Property in Less Developed Countries, Madison : The University of Wisconsin Press.

Stein, James (1998). "USAID's Strategy for Promoting Bond Market Development in Southeast Asia", in Gangadhar Jha (ed.) Project Development Experience in Urban Environmental Infrastructure, vol.I (mimeo), papers and presentation at an International Seminar, New Delhi: National Institute of Urban Affairs.

Teotia, Manoj K. (2003). Draft Himachal Pradesh Development Report, submitted to the Planning Commission, CRRID, Candigarh.

TRF (1997). Municipalities in India: The Devolution Paradox (Mimeo) Vol. I & II, Calcutta: Times Research Foundation.

Urban Finance Newsletter, Vol. 6, No. 3, September, NIUA, New Delhi.

Vaidya, Chetan (1996). "Property Tax Innovations in India", paper presented at the Policy Seminar on Property Tax Innovations in India, organised by NIUA, NIPFP and CCI, New Delhi, August 29-30, 1996.

COMMENTS

K.K. PANDEY: Why is municipal financing needed? Because the core services are the main determinants of the quality of life and living standards. Ultimately, the equity part is more important, particularly in our welfare state, both types of equity, horizontal and vertical; horizontal across the cities and vertical within the cities and among different areas. That is why even the UN Millennium Declaration includes services and gives emphasis on inclusive cities, so that the poor, women and children, are not deprived access to the basic services.

Another important area is environment. This is related to core municipal services, but include new dimensions, which reflect congestion air pollution, water pollution and noise pollution, which are closely linked to core municipal services.

The last one is demand side productivity, which is most important in the current context of macro economic development, and the focus is to make India a developed nation by the year 2020.

Two-thirds of the GDP comes from the urban areas. The economic rate of return on core municipal services is 2 to 3 times higher than the investment. These services provide an enabling environment for the productivity of households and firms. This is the driving side or the demand side of services.

There are successive studies on the supply side. There is wide gap between what the municipalities have and what they require. This mismatch ultimately leads to low equilibrium thread of low recovery, low operation and maintenance, low investment and ultimately low level of services. In this scenario, our municipal governments have problems of solvency. They do not generate enough cash to operate and maintain services. The problem is service level solvency, budgetary solvency, medium tern and long-term solvency.

Coming to the fiscal transfer, we have fiscal transfer from the state, which are used basically as a tool of crisis management. A vast majority of the fiscal transfers, which are given to the local bodies, are used for debt repayment and are straightaway deducted from the local government, or are not used, or are not directly given to the local bodies and hence are not reflected in the books of accounts. Similarly, whatever comes to the municipal bodies is used towards payment of salary. This affects the overall functioning. Whatever the municipalities get is being used towards payment of salaries and whatever is left is used for maintenance of services. Here the worst affected part is the core operation and maintenance, replacement and repair of services.

In this scenario, the gap is enormous. Whatever is coming from the Central Commission is only Rs. 14 per capita and the gap is more than Rs. 400 to Rs. 500 per capita. If we work out on the basis of the Planning Commission norms, the requirement is about Rs. 900 per capita. If we take replacement value of urban infrastructure, we take 8 per cent as operation and maintenance and 10 per cent towards replacement and repair. Whatever is coming is a very small amount for that purpose.

We should recognize and we should realize that we cannot really match this gap of Rs. 400 per capita through resources from the Central Finance Commission, or the State Government or any other public sector agency. So, the gap can be bridged only by involving all the stakeholders through participatory funding in a participatory manner.

The other point is productivity enhancement, which is the focus of the current phase of the 21st century. We have golden quadrilateral of east-west and south corridors. A lot of towns are within some range of this corridor. So, we should consider the internal towns and specify allocation to them. The third is environment.

Another aspect is seed capital. This money should be used as seed capital to enable the towns to mobilize more resources.

Another important area is the Local Area Development Fund of MPs and MLAs. Equally important are resources from business, industry and trade like parivartan in Ahmedabad. In Delhi, Maruti is operating a children's park. The third is community resource on the pattern of Andhra Pradesh Janmabhoomi or Namak Namey in Tamil Nadu, or some project in Indore in Madhya Pradesh. We have resources from business, industry and trade and also the constituency fund. The Finance Commission devolution should be linked with the ability of the local bodies to tap local elasticity.

The third is the institutional structure. In Tamil Nadu, they have the Tamil Nadu Urban Development Fund. They have a number of other agencies, which are supporting local bodies in terms of planning, financing and monitoring. They are enabling them to have access to the capital market, and they have come up with a number of documents, like guidelines, check lists and manual. The Central Finance Commission should focus on these three areas of activities.

K.C. SIVARAMAKRISHNAN: It is necessary that we need effective dissemination of some of these practices. In the past 10 years, I have noticed that we are in a position to talk a little more cogently about decentralization than before.

One of the reasons is that in spite of all these measures, distortions are permitted to exist and there are all sorts of kickbacks. There is continued preference for this type of arrangement. Whether it is the local leadership or the city or municipal leadership. The search for the patrons continues to be the organizing principle for funding.

The second point is that we have rich cities and poor city governments. It is a policy issue to be really addressed. Unfortunately, we also have a couple of mindset problems. It has been mentioned in Prof. Chaubey's paper that all that is urban is not municipal. Yes, I have been maintaining that this is true across the world. But now we have another problem. All that is municipal is not urban.

Just now the Tamil Nadu Government has issued a draft notification saying that 536 of the 611 town panchayats may be degraded; converted again into panchayats, mainly because these are town panchayats, towns just by name, and as panchayats probably they will be able to access the Central Government funds.

The fact that the Ministry of Rural Development in the Government of India has a huge Rs. 10, 000 crore budget, being given directly to the panchayats makes a mockery of decentralization. Because it is not decentralization; it is a question of saying panchayats are holy, panchayat are manipulable, panchayats are manageable, they can be bought or their tails twisted by money. You cannot just talk about decentralization on the one hand and, at the same time, have huge Central Government grant, which it is almost impossible to administer on any kind of rational basis. A part of the problem is the rather cavalier approach.

India is one of the few countries in the world, which has got a credible census. We have had this census definition of what is urban for a long time. A few years ago, when the Tamil Nadu Government decided that they will make all these town panchayats into nagar palikas, though Tamil Nadu is one of the few states which has some kind of revenue criteria before municipalization, that criteria was not applied. As a result of the decision to make them into urban, the Tamil Nadu urbanization level shot up to the top of India. Next week, it will go down to the 4th or 5th position because of their recent decision.

The advisory jurisdiction of the Central Finance Commission is much more important than its statutory jurisdiction, whatever it is. Somebody at some point of time has to say that this is not the way to run the state. The Tenth Finance Commission, headed by Shri K.C. Pant, made a very straightforward statement that the impact of the local governments is much more than the impact of the Central and State Governments. That is a serious statement, particularly in a situation of shrinking of sovereign space and globalization. We have to recognize that the national government appears to be capable of doing less and less on the economic scene, compared to before, and the state government even less. I do believe across the world, certainly with regard to developing countries, for that matter even others, the local government may very well be the government of the first and last resort, because there is no escape from it.

It is necessary that the Finance Commission also says, "before you ask us to augment the funds of the state, so that the local bodies" needs can be dealt with, try and be consistent as to what your rural local bodies and your urban bodies are. At least the Election Commission say, when we conduct the election, please do not change your boundaries, please do not create new districts, please do not meddle around with them. I think that kind of umpiring is also necessary.

A series of basic facts that Prof. Chaubey refers to relate to the functional domain, that it is illustrative, it is indicative, it is not exhaustive. It is necessary that we address this question. A few people have raised it. The Twelfth Finance Commission whould also address this.

The purpose of the Seventy-Third and Seventy-Fourth Amendments was not cosmetic. It was certainly a political purpose. But is was also intended, article 243(g) and 243(h) very clearly says, that these are supposed to be institutions of self-governance. These are not institutions of dogcatchers, these are institutions of self-government. The schedule has to be read along with the main provisions of the Constitution. We need not have gone through the process of amending the Constitution and then ratifying it by the required number of states, if we merely wanted to add a few more pages to the Constitution. The Constitutional Amendment Act is not a masterpiece of legislative drafting.

In the month of July 2003, the parliament spent two whole days discussing the Seventy-Third and Seventy-Fourth Amendments. Surprisingly, on both days the quorum was available in both Lok Sabha and Rajya Sabha. No newspaper picked it up, because nobody walked into the well of the House and nobody shouted. The Parliament Standing Committee on Urban and Rural Development its Thirty-Seventh Report have very categorically stated that the items listed in the Eleventh Schedule should be regarded as mandatory and the legislative discretion given to the State is only rulemaking. It is not a question of just taking away the substance of these functions.

Therefore, I think it is very important for us to realize all these things and to take these two Constitutional Amendments as a whole. It is not possible for any Constitution to be exhaustive and list all the items. The substance is already there. I do not think that we will be serving the purpose of decentralization by all the time saying it is illustrative. Because, after all is said and done, many of the instrumentalities of the state are illustrative. After all the theory of governance, at least as far as the institutionalities of government are concerned, a certain amount of vagueness or opaqueness is always useful for governmental power. So, when they say it is only illustrative they can do various kinds of other things. Therfore, I Think it is very important that we recognize that the Constitution as a whole looks upon this as an institution of self-government and any attempt to dilute this by constantly referring to the illustrative or indicative nature would be counter-productive.

With regard to the amendment whereby the Finance Commission was brought in, the Finance Ministry itself was not in favour of this amendment, when it was being discussed in the Joint Parliamentary Committee. By and large, the theory is that decentralization at any given time may be an additional point of stress on the efficiency and fiscal prowess of the national government. It has been the general theory. Across the world, international experience shows that decentralization, if it is accomplished at all, it is accopmplished by a combination of political forces, market related problems and also the inability of the upper level governments to deal with a whole variety of services. Therfore, the Central and Provinial Governments realized at some point of time that in order to hold on, let us give up some; otherwise, we will have to lose everything.

On the role of the Finance Commission, we are one of the few countries of the world, which have this mechanism of the Finance Commission, and it has worked well, as far as the Centre-State transfers are concerned. But one of the reasons why it has worked is that the Constitution itself clearly recognizes the divisible pool.

Therfore, the Constitution has already created a certain platform upon which the Finance Commission from time to time enters with confidence. It becomes a rational and cogent exercise.

In the case of local government, augmenting the funds of the state government so that the local bodies can be helped, becomes an exercise in proper channel. It is a needless constraint on the Finance Commission. As far as states are concerned, by and large, they have used expediency in this business. They say, please augment my resources, and then I can decide what I will do with the local government.

The whole question is whether the Finance Commission can consider the concept of a divisible pool, as far as local governments are concerned. Now it is not that such a divisible pool is ruled out. In article 243(h) we did mention assigment of taxes, which may be collected by the state. So, I think the element of that concept is there.

The Finance Commission can certainly float this idea. Here again, the advisory jurisdiction is much more valuable. You can say, let the State Finance Commission also go into this. In the case of the First State Finance Commission of Maharashtra, a certain per centage of the entertainment tax, vehicles tax and professional tax will go to the local bodies. The Pubjab Finance Commission said that five taxes would get into the divisible pool, lke stamp duty, motor vehicles tax, electricity duty and entertainment tax. In terms of the concept, the Finance Commission can definitely say, please have an independent tax domain; consider this. You can put it in such a way that it would be very difficult for the State finance Commission to ignore that advice.

The terms of reference of the Central Finance Commission are something that have been honed over a period of time. Every term of reference that is issued by the President every five years has a certain consistency and continuity about it. But this is not the case with regard to SFCs. Een before the first generation came, one of the very first things that Raja Chelliah did was to get together a group of people and said, how can we help the SFCs by creating an independent tax domain for the local bodies, what all items can possibly go in and, secondly planning the concept of divisible pool and how it can work. The details will have to be worked out. I am sure, there is enough data to decide on that.

There is a great deal of ambivalence about what is urban. We do not understand the extent and the spatial aspect of urbanization in the country. Public policy response to urbanization has been largely one of irritation and responding to what was considered to be your day-to-day problems. One of the things, which we do not understand adequately, is the kind of spatial character of urbanization that confronting this country.

In terms of percentage, 27 per cent urban of the total population is not a very high figure. Probably, after the decision by Tamil Nadu, it will drop down by one percentage point or so. It does not matter. These percentages do not make much sense for a large country like India. But for a few states they definitely do, like Maharashtra, Gujarat, Tamil Nadu, several southern states, western India, western Uttar Pradesh, North East and so on.

There are many many urban habitations of the northeast, which have not really been brought in within the municipal rubric. But, more importantly, it is very clear that the future of urbanization is going to be mainly one of the large multi-municipal, multi-jurisdictional agglomerations.

A few years ago, we brought out a book called Future of Urbanization. This is the result of detailed research on the subject. About 90 per cent of the urban population in Maharashtra, Gujarat, Karnataka, Andhra Pradesh and Tamil Nadu will be in corridor shaped urbanization complexes. These complexes and these agglomerations will have neither a core nor a periphery. They will be multi-municipal and they will be a combination of both rural and urban local bodies. In the best of times, it is not very easy to deal with this. This is where the bulk of the urban population is going to be and there is a financial angle to this.

In the so-called metropolitan areas, here again the Constitution provides a particular platform, and this is the metropolitan planning committee. Only one state, West Bengal, has set up the Metropolitan Planning Committee. Even there the West Bengal Government dragged its feet unitl there was a change in the political configuration of the Calcutta Municipality, when they found that having the metro concept is perhaps a useful way of dealing with parties.

There have been discussions about equalization funds and discrepancies in contiguous jurisdictions. On the basis of the cenus configuration, experts can identify a few areas, which are multi-municipal which also comprise rural local bodies and urban local bodies. As far as those areas are concerned, is it possible to create some kind of financing entity so that there is equalization and metropolitan view of financial resources? How can you mobilize resources at the metropolitan level? Whether it is the Hyderabad Metropolitan Area, or the Bangalore Metropolitan Area, or certainly the National Capital Region, Where you have tremendous disparities, these are very important points.

In Delhi for instance, buildings in the MCD area are under the 74th amendment but if you go across the street, you are not under the Seventy-Fourth Amendment, because the New Delhi Municipal Committee does not come under the Seventy-Fourth Amendement. It is a rich urban local body. There are therefore tremendous disparities. If we really look ahead, even 5 or 10 years, the position may become still worse.

The National Capital is one of the richest places in Asia. Still, do we have an intelligent mechanism whereby resources of the National Capital are pooled and allocated carefully? It still proceeds on the basis of the Central Government expenditure. Prof. Datta has very rightly pointed out what is it that the States should do, what is it that the municipalities can do. So, I think there is another opportunity, where the Finance Commission can look into this. If merely 48 to 50 per cent of the urban population is going to be concentrated in about 20 agglomerations in the country, what is the appropriate financing mechanism? Raising these issues and giving some possible ways in which the State Finance Commission can go into, would perhaps be useful.

As far as synchronization is concerned, the Eleventh Finance Commission have already made a number of recommendations. I would suggest, two or three conceptual issues. There is still time for the Central Finance Commission to go into them. As far as the sharing of resources between the State Government and the local governments are concerned, even in the best of times, as far as the existing situation is concerned, you will only be devising a sharing formula for sharing bankruptcy, and not resources.

Therefore, you have to address the issue of independent taxation domain; secondly, the divisible pool and, thirdly, what you will do, as far as the bulk of the urban people and concentrations are concerned. These are areas where you have the eminence and the ability to flag the issue. But you are not obligated to take a very narrow view of what your position is. As far as money is concerned, it is essentially between the state and the local bodies.

As far as the local governments are concerned, there is such a great degree of ambivalence between the states. The states today are waking up to the dangers of decentralization, as far as their own political authority is concerned. Almost every month some new forms of dilution are taking place.

The local government is rarely assaulted frontally. Now the Constitution says you cannot supersede. So, the local governments will not be assaulted frontally, whether they are rural or urban; they would only be undermined.

RAVI KANT JOSHI: The speakers have mentioned no doubt that more resources should be given, more functions should be given to local bodies, there should be equity between the transfer domain and financing and all that. Yes, there is no disagreement on those points. Along with that, two things are happening after the Seventy-Fourth Constitutional Amendment, one of which is globalization. I would like to draw attention to that.

What we have observed, particularly in the last decade, is that a lot of civic action movements are going on and we are seeing suo motu efforts by the local bodies. To me this is a heartening feature.

Essentially, what has come out is that while the Seventy-Fourth Constitutional Amendment has created the feasibility for a new fiscal arrangement, it has not taken place. Decentralization has not made any dent and the kind of devolution that has taken place has made no impact, because Rs. 400 crores makes no difference. In fact, the individual budget for water requirement of the Bombay Municipal Corporation is Rs. 400 crores a year, or perhaps more than that.

However, what we see is heightened civic action, because some people have now started asking for action. When you say that the cities are competing, at the same time, people have started feeling that is is the quality of the urban infrastructure and the quality of the urban life that is determinant for his productivity, human productivity. So, the urban citizen is now sensing that his productivity, his earning capacity, is dependent on the quality of the urban infrastructure and urban life. Simultaneously, we see umpteen numbers of cases where in the local bodies are taking suo motu improvement effort. Nothing is happening, no more further devolution of resources, no more enabling orders and still the local bodies are coming out and making some effort.

At CRISIL, we carried out a study of 33 municipal bodies in

Karnataka and it has come out that cities have significant revenue potential. The argument is that the cities do not have resources.

The states will have to play a major role in future. The Twelfth Finance Commission needs to create a macro framework. They have not only a fiscal role, but also a non-fiscal role. They will have to come out with the umpiring role, saying that this is the thing, this is the order. The Eleventh Finance Commission mentioned that the local bodies should go for double entry accounting system and CAG should look into it. For 55 years no ICA or CAG bothered about the accounting system or budgetary format statement of the municipal bodies. Today fortunately, we have the CAG report, the task force report, on what should be the municipal accounting format and budgetary format or what way they can go ahead. Such a catalytic role facilitates the states, SFCs and the local bodies to realize their potential.

Municipal finances are of average quality. It is not that their finances are very bad. No doubt they are bad. But compared to the last 50 years, they are not very bad. We have done a case study of Karnataka. The State transfers are above the average compared to the other states.

We studied the state level data and the micro data of the 33 municipal bodies. In order to carry out internal improvement, the total amount required will be Rs. 7,200 crores. No doubt they have great revenue potential, which is not being utilized today. If they come out with 100 per cent own revenue improvement, they can come out with Rs. 4,200 crores. Even if the municipal bodies go ahead with 100 per cent of their own potential, the picture is that there will be a shortage of Rs. 3,025 crores.

The state will therefore have to contribute. Today it is in a distorted way, to improve the own revenue increment.. The municipal bodies do have the potential, which has to be explored. Now given the macro context of the urban improvement required, or the basic minimum improvements required at the city level, this is insufficient. Both will have to club their efforts in order to meet the situation.

There is high dependence of the local bodies on the state. We have such a public finance structure, wherein this is being looked upon as ex gratia or grant in aid. It is not treated as a legitimate share of the local bodies. You do not want it to be like in South Africa, where have three separate spheres. The Government of India Act 1919, had three separate spheres. But that sharing should not be considered as dependency ratio, but a legitimate right. One will have to work out what is their real legitimate share and how much more they should get, which they are not getting because of their inability to perform or other extraneous factors.

The transfer as per centage of total revenue is 53 per cent and the own revenue is insufficient to cover the resultant gap in state funding. The municipal bodies have to step up their efforts to meet the current deficit. Over and above that, there is a reduction in the state share.

If there is a reduction in the share of the states to the local bodies, then the state should transfer its own share, or its responsibility, to the municipal bodies. I am asking them to cover the deficit out of the state share.

The lending programme has such a great potential to recover 85 per cent. ADB loan has been given to these towns. What is the problem? Why this deficit? It is not attributable to the large loan size, or to the revenue limitation of the municipal bodies or the state. It has become an uneven grant or loan ratio, which the State Government wishes to change.

If we look at the micro reform, it shows that administrative re-organization is required, modernization of the financial system, accounting reforms, control system, rationalization of the accounts, bank reconciliation and so on.

At the macro level, there are 5 players in non-fiscal framework for revenue sharing, TFC can come out with a catalyst role the SFCs addressing the state and local relations for horizontal equalization.

Urban services have a national priority. The national government will have to treat water supply, sanitation and solid waste management as 3 or 4 basic core services of national importance.

Local public goods are becoming very important today . Urban local goods are becoming more important. Somewhere, like defence or something like that, national priority will have to be given for this minimum service. Who funds that and who actually spends it will be immaterial, whether it is the Centre or the State. But somewhere that kind of improvement will have to come.

These are alignments of the funds with the common approach. There are so many international donor agencies, funding of lending agencies. I have a feeling that sometimes with all their bona fide interests, they are causing harm to our local bodies. The way the funds are to be administered, there has to be convergence.

T.N. DHAR: Another thing to be discussed seriously is urban corridors. That is how the development has been taking place. The mechanism of the district planning committee was meant to integrate these corridors. But they have not been operationalized, at least not in my state. We passed the Act. The state has to nominate. That has not taken place. So, the horse is not drinking the water. We have a separate planning head. The urban development in-charge does not know what the rural development in-charge is doing Apart from the multiplicity of agencies operating, there are the parastatal forms that obtain in the state. I do not know how it is operating in other states. There may be parastatals of different forms. This is applicable to the States and the Centre, because the Centre also has parastatals. The district urban authority and the state development authority are parastatal.

The district planning committee and metropolitan planning committee is something on a larger scale, this must be operationalized and made effective. This is one way of solving this urban rural divide, because one is the area of divide and the other is continuity that occurs. This must happen.

ABHIJIT DATTA: There are two or three areas that the TFC should avoid.

One is making a very positive recommendation regarding the municipal tax or property tax in particular. Secondly, they should not make any detailed recommendation on infrastructure financing of municipal bodies. These matters are not included in the Terms of Reference of the State Finance Commission, as provided in the Constitution, nor are these provided for in the constitutional Terms of Reference and the Presidential Terms of Reference for the Twelfth Finance Commission. Because, if the municipal taxes, the property tax in particular, if these are dealt with by the Finance Commission, then it transforms itself into a Tax Commission, for which it has no jurisdiction and it has no expertise.

So far as infrastructure financing is concerned, including to some extent DPC and MPC, if they deal with this question, then it will be transgressing the role of the Planning Commission, which is outside the domain of the Finance Commission.

These are two issues that have been raised in the seminar very forcefully. But I would express my word of caution in this, because both the existing property tax valuation in the country, as well as the existing method of valuation of stamp duty are not market driven. Any sensible Tax Commission must approach the tax reform from the point of view of linking the tax base with market indicators. This is something that no State level Commission or the Central Commission has done so far.

So far as property tax is concerned, it is misnomer to say that this valuation is linked to the ARV. It may be there in law. In practice, it has nothing to do with that. Twenty years back, after the Jairam Toleram case was decided, after that the states have gone in for discretionary rent, which in fiscal terms is called presumptive valuation. This presumptive valuation is not restricted to conventional valuation. The difference between conventional valuation method and the presumptive valuation like ASP is that in conventional valuation, the executive cannot tamper with the valuation method. If there is annual valuation method or capital valuation method, the executive can tamper with this method. The presumptive valuation, on the other hand, does away with the valuation process altogether and fixes the rate at zero valuation. So, it falls short of a true tax in an economic sense.

It is true that we hear of some improvements of tax revenue, property tax revenue, arising out of some of the reforms that have gone in during the past few years. But if one looks at it, one sees that the initial tempo of revenue generation has flattened down. Unless this type of artificial valuation is repeated over and over again, this tempo cannot be sustained. I think that is also due to measures like newer property discovery and newer methods of collecting property tax and so on, and not due to per se its valuation.

The Bangalore system is basically partly based on unit value system and partly based on artificial rental data, monthly rental data. It is combination both. It is not wholly artificial, but it is substantially artificial. That is given up now. As it was explained yesterday, the Government has come out with a new notification saying that capital valuation should be introduced. But, at the moment, there is no preparation for making it capital value based. Even Bangalore would need to have some time to adjust itself from the ARV related value to capital value system. This adjustment, in my view, might take about 10 years or so.

Judging from the experience of East European countries, which have moved from artificial valuation to capital valuation, there are steps for doing that. The obvious step is, how do you know what is the actual value? You do not do it through your conventional assessment system. You do it by involving property dealers, by involving builders and so on, who are very much embedded in generating and creating black money, to declare what is the true value. Then, on that basis, you build it up. Simultaneously, what you do is to free land market from all the restrictions, particularly at the state level, so that the generation of black money gets reduced and property value becomes more and more market oriented. Then only you get property valuation, not before that.

To call any valuation system, which looks like a market value, or declare it is the capital value, is not easy because you are not getting the date. It is all manipulated data from the market. So, I think, this market orientation is essential. Unless you are able to do that, we will not be able to collect the valuation yields of property taxation in a proper sense of the term, whic includes stamp duty also.

All over the world, except South Asia, stamp duty has more or less been abandoned. Even in Britain it is almost abandoned. There is a nominal rate. In our country, for well over 100 years, the stamp duty rate was 3 per cent, until Maharashtra brought in the idea of raising it. They raised it to 13 per cent and all the State Governments followed it up. Now there is pressure to reduce it.

Stamp duty is a fee for evidentiary effect. It is a benefit tax. If the Concept of benefit taxation is accepted, the users of this benefit should get the upper limit of tax. You cannot misuse it for revenue generation purposes. Unless one understands the underlying difficulties of property valuation, one should not be too hasty in making a judgment about the right type of taxes.

I am suggesting capital value again and again because the rental value is on the way out. All over the world, there is a movement away from the rental value. But there is not a single instance of any country, which has opted out of the capital value. It is more rational, at what levels the government can tax, a single base tax for income tax, stamp duty, property tax and so on.

The last point is about valorization, valuation of property tax, property increment and so on. These are primarily American experience, and these experiences also emanate from the same kind of difficulties that we face, but in an acute form and so on. If there is buoyant property tax, then there is no need for valorization and other parallel property taxes.

OM PRAKASH MATHUR: In Karanataka, the entire state has shifted to capital valuation, except in Bangalore. Bangalore has not yet shifted to capital valuation for one simple reason. The capital valuation has two components. One is the land component and the second component is the building structure component. The proportion between the two, what should be the tax rate on land and what should be the tax rate on the structure, that is under dispute. The Bangalore Municipal Corporation wrote to the Government that if you want to maintain the garden city character of the Bangalore city, then you have to lower the tax rate for the land component and increase the building component. Currently, it happens to be the other way round. This is precisely what is holding out the extension of the capital value system to the Bangalore City Corporation area. The self-assessment system is slightly different.

The purpose of the stamp duty is nothing else but to have the evidentiary value of the transaction in a court of law that the transaction has taken place. The stamp paper is the only document that is taken as evidentiary value of the transaction. The stamp duty is continuing in our country simply because the revenue from stamp duty is close to Rs. 18,000 crores. That is what is preventing the doing away of stamp duty, as many other countries have done .

But it not quite right to say that all the states have done away with it. What they have done is, excepting the conveyance component; they have done away with all other transactions. We are still continuing with 68 instruments, which are subjected to stamp duty in part. The conveyance part is still being maintained in most countries. The rate is nominal. Much as we have tried to say that the higher rates are not revenue friendly, the State Governments do not accept this plea. If you look at the fate of URIF, it is simply stuck on one component, namely stamp duty, out of 7 components. All the State Governments are agreeing on all the other 6 components, excepting one, which is on lowering of the stamp duty to 5 per cent, within the duration of the Tenth Five Year Plan.

V. SATYANARAYANA: I think the time is ripe for the urban sector to explore further revenues. I do not think we can find a better time than this in the next 5 or 10 years. All said and done, a lot of work is going on and there are isolated islands of innovation. We do really need to create a condition for that growth to really take off in the urban sector.

We also need to remove the disincentive that exists in our urban sector, be it financial or institutional. If you take the current financial structure of HUDCO, it is actually a disincentive for the urban sector reform as a whole. It is not a problem of HUDCO, it is a problem of the Government of India, which created the HUDCO, more in terms of guaranteeing back the financial structure rather than the market. Base.

Secondly, there is the issue of the institutional structure in the urban sector, of multiplicity and multi-municipal. Could we have one economic entity, one economic unit? Be it the corridor or be it the urban agglomeration, whatever the formation, could we have one single entity? We do confess there is lack of capacity with multiplicity of institutions. Could we actually take a position of moving into one institutional structure for service delivery and economic management?

Thirdly, while the jury system is still out, we could create umpires for service delivery, for example, regulated framework. Somebody has to actually drive the reform process or the instruments of reform process, which could be the regulatory framework. Independent declaration of the work framework for water and sanitation would perhaps be the role model for the future.

Lastly, I think the Sarkaria Commission and Planning Commission numbers seem to be way below what is happening in the country right now. I would strongly urge you not to use those numbers, because those numbers are very very low, compared to the present on-going works. The numbers are for water alone. It looks like a per capita expenditure of Rs. 3,000 per head. Similarly, for sewerage it is probably in the same range of Rs. 3,000. If one goes by the existing capital costs, the existing norm of Rs. 9 for all services may seem very low. It is better to get information from the on-going projects before you choose the normative approach."

D.K. SRIVASTAVA: The Finance Commission has been asked to consider the issue of augmenting the Consolidated fund of the State in order to supplement the resources of the local bodies. There is also reference to the restructuring of public finances in the country as a whole. This is actually a repetition of the reference that was also given to the Eleventh Finance Commission. It only indicates that the structure of public finance as understood, between the States and the Centre, the States and the local governments, in the macro framework and in terms of their inter-dependence, there is something clearly not right with the way the finances have been devolving over time. It has not been set right even subsequent to the recommendations of the Eleventh Finance Commission. It is a continuing problem.

It might be appropriate if we take the issue of financing the work of the local bodies in the context of the overall restructuring, and that is way in which it might be useful to look at some of the issues that you actually said should be excluded from the purview of the Finance Commission in terms of the narrow class, or could be considered in terms of the broader class. But we do not intend to get into this without proper expert advice. So, even if we look at the system of property taxation, or other tax issues that relate to urban local bodies, we will do so only after consulting the experties available in the country.

On the issue of financing of urban local goods it is true that in terms of the lesson that we received at the under –graduate course is that the nature of the gravity of the economy shifts to urban areas as industrialization takes place and as the service sector grows. In fact, the economic activities and population gravitate upwards to urban areas. As a matter of fact, in our case, urbanization is very slow. Urbanization is determained, not by the process of urbanization, but by the notifications of the State Governments. Therefore, the true content of urbanization is not contemplated. I think it is very clear from international experience that population will gravitate subsequently to urban areas. Therefore, the problems that we face today would become even more aggravated over time, as we go along.

It also brings out the fact that though the economic activities have already gravitated towards urban areas, there is certainly on dearth of the resource base that is there. It is really a question of getting the alignment right.

In this context, I would make the following propositions:

Firstly, in the context of the provision of local public goods, a re-assessment of the revenue resources is almost always a more efficient alternative than transfers from higher tiers. The more distant the source of transfer, the less efficient is the dispensation.

Secondly, in the absence of any significant borrowing by urban local bodies, the actual expenditure is bound to be equal to the actual revenue receipts. Therefore, the market for local goods is always secured at the existing tax prices. Of course, the market is cleared at a very low level of quality and adequacy of the local public goods.

Thirdly, imposing a uniform exogenous norm, such as the update of the Sarkaria Commission estimates for locally provided goods, is a method used by unitary governments. It is not consistent with the weightage for efficiency through democratic decentralization. In the decentralized provision of urban local public goods, differential preferences and differential costs are the key to search for efficiency.

Fourthly, the pre-condition to preference revolution at the local level and optimal goods decision is adequacy of institutions entrusted with local goods. Elected representatives, autonomous State Finance Commissions and other local agencies are the key to decentralized governance. At present, these institutions are peripheral and endogenous to the State Governments, lacking in technical activities and of true autonomy. Now the prevailing model is the habit persistence and not strong institutions, which are required by a model of democratic decentralization.

Fifthly, the Central Finance Commission can play a vital role by facilitating the creation of, and augmenting, the strength of institutions required for democratic local governance, by focusing on information, incentives and institutions, rather than filling in any gaps, however normatively determined.

These are some of the pre-conditions according to which, if we look at the financing of urban local bodies, we would probably make headway.

7

Municipal Data: Tables, Charts and Diagrams

–Om Prakash Mathur

Definitions

1. "Municipalities" refer to urban local bodies comprising municipal corporations, municipalities and nagar panchayats.
2. Revenue receipts of municipalities consist of own revenue receipts and state transfers to municipalities. Own revenue receipts of municipalities comprise tax receipts and non-tax receipts of municipalities. Tax receipts of municipalities comprise taxes that are levied and collected by municipalities, whereas non-tax receipts comprise fees, interest, fines, duties, charges, and rents etc.
3. State transfers to municipalities include all transfers made on revenue account head of State Budget.
4. Revenue expenditure of municipalities consist of expenditure on establishment and salaries, operation and maintenance and expenditure on debt servicing.

Data Adjustments

A. Urban Population

1. Urban population of states, for purposes of this study, include the population of statutory towns.

2. Adjusted urban populations of states are used to calculate er capita municipal receipts and expenditures.

B. Municipal Receipts and Expenditure

1. For the year 2001/02, data pertaining to municipal receipts and expenditure was not available for Karnataka and Punjab. Annual change of 1999/2000 to 2000/01 is applied to arrive at the estimated per capita municipal receipts and expenditure for the year 2001/02. Further, the estimated per capita amounts of 1999/2000 and 2000/01 are multiplied by the adjusted urban population of the state to arrive at the estimated amounts of municipal receipts and expenditure.
2. For the year 2000/01 and 2001/02, data pertaining to municipal revenue receipts and revenue expenditure was not available for Orissa. Annual change of 1997/98 to 1998/99 is applied to arrive at the estimated municipal receipts and expenditure for the year 2000/01 and 2001/02. The proportion of expenditure on establishment and salaries of the year 1999/2000 is applied to the estimated revenue expenditure of the years 2000/01 and 2001/02 to arrive at the estimated expenditure on establishment and salaries. Further this estimated expenditure on establishment and salaries is deducted from the estimated revenue expenditure of the year 2000/01 and 2001/02 to arrive at the estimated expenditure on operation and maintenance for the respective years.

3. For the period of 1997/98 to 2001/02, and for the years 1997/98 to 1999/2000, per capita receipts and expenditure for municipalities in Bihar and Uttar Pradesh are applied to arrive at the estimates for municipalities in Jharkhand and Uttaranchal. These are then added to arrive at the estimated municipal receipts and expenditure of Bihar for the period of 1997/98 to 1999/2000, and for Uttaranchal for the period of 1997/98 to 1999/2000.

In Karnataka, to arrive at the estimated expenditure on establishment and salaries for the year 2000/01, the proportion of expenditure on establishment and salaries to revenue expenditure for the year 1999-2000 was used to arrive at the estimate for the year 2000/01. Further, the annual change of per capita amount of expenditure on establishment and salaries and as well as the operation and maintenance from 1999/2000 to 2000/01 was applied to arrive at the estimated per capita expenditure on establishment and as well as operation and maintenance for the year 2001/02. Further, estimated per capita amount was multiplied by the adjusted urban population of the state for the year 2001, to arrive at the estimated amount of establishment and salaries and operation and maintenance.

5. In Karnataka, the annual change from 1999/2000 to 2000/01 was applied to arrive at the estimated per capita own revenue receipts and state transfers for the years 2001/02. Further, the estimated per capita amount was multiplied by the adjusted urban population of the state to arrive at the estimated amount of own revenue receipts and state transfers.
6. In Uttaranchal in absence of information on state transfers to municipalities for the year 2001/02, figures of the year 2000/01 are used for the year 2001/02.

Table 1
Relative Share (%) of Revenue Income of the Central Government, Tax and Non-Tax Receipts of State Governments and Own Revenue Receipts of Municipalities in the Combined Revenues of the three Tiers of Government

Tiers of Government	*Years*			
	1997/98	*1998/99*	*1999/00*	*2000/01*
Central Government	63.78	62.72	62.81	61.91
State Government	33.39	34.31	34.39	35.11
Municipalities@	2.84	2.97	2.80	2.98
Total	*100.00*	*100.00*	*100.00*	*100.00*

Note: @ Based on estimates provided by the state governments.

Source: 1. Receipts Budget, 2003-04, Government of India
2. Revenue Receipts, State Finances, Reserve Bank of India.
3. Information related to the finances of municipalities is provided by the Urban Departments and Directorates of Municipal Administration of states.

Table 2: Municipal Own Revenue Receipts as a % of State Own Revenue Receipts

States	1997/98	1998/99	1999/00	2000/01
Andhra Pradesh	4.52	4.92	4.47	4.73
Assam	2.10	2.26	1.85	1.83
Bihar	1.36	1.04	0.77	0.82
Chattisgarh	–	–	–	10.87
Goa	1.62	1.71	–	2.02
Gujarat	13.43	12.13	12.59	11.97
Haryana	3.17	2.48	2.03	1.62
Himachal Pradesh	1.61	2.01	1.08	2.20
Jammu and Kashmir	0.79	0.93	1.02	1.20
Jharkhand	–	–	–	–
Karnataka	2.69	2.77	5.14	4.87
Kerala	2.89	3.07	3.08	3.16
Madhya Pradesh	5.27	6.22	5.71	4.94
Maharashtra	21.04	24.33	21.06	21.94
Manipur	0.05	0.06	0.05	0.04
Orissa	4.46	5.57	3.97	3.45
Punjab	6.23	8.58	9.94	10.69
Rajasthan	6.39	3.02	0.83	0.95
Tamil Nadu	6.32	5.70	6.37	6.17
Tripura	0.02	0.02	0.03	0.02
Uttar Pradesh	2.05	2.08	1.88	1.89
Uttaranchal	–	–	–	5.89
West Bengal	6.16	6.30	6.34	5.33
All States Average	*8.04*	*8.27*	*7.81*	*8.09*

Note: denotes data related to state own revenue receipts is not available.

Source: 1. Revenue Receipts, State Finances, Reserve Bank of India.

2. Information related to the finances of municipalities is provided by the Urban Departments and Directorates of Municipal Administration of the states.

Table 3: Municipal Own Revenue Receipts as a % of GSDP

States	*1997/98*	*1998/99*	*1999/00*	*2000/01*	*2001/02*
Andhra Pradesh	0.42	0.42	0.41	0.45	0.48
Assam	0.12	0.13	0.11	0.12	0.12
Bihar	0.07	0.07	0.07	0.07	0.07
Chattisgarh	–	–	–	0.43	0.41
Goa	0.20	0.20	-	0.27	0.26
Gujarat	1.30	1.20	1.30	1.34	1.16
Haryana	0.27	0.25	0.19	0.16	0.20
Himachal Pradesh	0.13	0.14	0.15	0.15	–
Jammu and Kashmir	0.05	0.05	0.07	0.08	–
Jharkhand	–	–	–	0.05	–
Karnataka	0.29	0.26	0.50	0.50	0.51
Kerala	0.29	0.28	0.28	0.29	0.29
Madhya Pradesh	0.44	0.48	0.49	0.50	0.36
Maharashtra	1.88	2.02	1.83	2.32	2.16
Manipur	0.12	0.11	0.09	0.08	0.06
Orissa	0.27	0.32	0.25	0.26	0.24
Punjab	0.69	0.73	0.94	1.00	1.07
Rajasthan	0.49	0.22	0.06	0.08	0.12
Tamil Nadu	0.60	0.52	0.61	0.61	0.62
Tripura	0.03	0.03	0.03	0.03	0.04
Uttar Pradesh	0.12	0.13	0.13	–	–
Uttaranchal	–	–	–	–	–
West Bengal	0.31	0.28	0.28	0.27	0.27
All States Average	*0.65*	*0.64*	*0.64*	*0.71*	–

Notes: GSDP figures are of position as on 21-10-2003

- denotes information is not available for GSDP.

Source: 1. Same as source 2 of Table 2

2. Directorate of Economics and Statistics of State Governments.

Table 4
Municipal Own Revenue Receipts, Per Capita and Annual Average Growth Rate

Rank	*States*	*Per Capita 2001/02*	*Annual Average Growth Rate (%) 1997/98 to 2001/02*
1.	Maharashtra	1493.33	9.11
2.	Punjab	932.38	16.50
3.	Gujarat	809.45	2.24
4.	Goa	510.64	14.57
5.	Andhra Pradesh	386.83	14.09
6.	Kerala	371.11	12.59
7.	Tamil Nadu	355.50	5.45
8.	Himachal Pradesh	335.55	11.87
9.	Karnataka	321.96	22.46
10.	Chattisgarh	321.55	-
11.	West Bengal	215.77	6.60
12.	Haryana	207.81	-0.89
13.	Orissa	194.50	1.05
14.	Madhya Pradesh	188.67	-3.47
15.	Assam	153.25	6.13
16.	Uttaranchal	113.67	-
17.	Rajasthan	80.68	-30.38
18.	Uttar Pradesh	79.54	9.79
19.	Tripura	58.93	19.23
20.	Jammu & Kashmir	48.18	18.01
21.	Manipur	41.55	-5.16
22.	Jharkhand	39.46	-
23.	Bihar	39.46	3.56
	All States Average	*482.14*	*7.68*

Notes: - denotes not applicable.
Source: Same as source 2 of Table 2.

Diagram 1

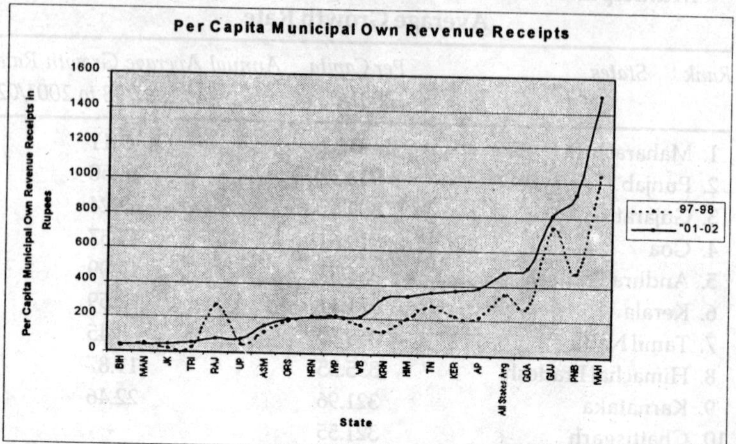

Table 5

State Transfers as a % of Municipal Revenue Receipts, 2001/02

Rank	*States*	*Transfers (%)*
1.	Jammu & Kashmir	83.71
2.	Tripura	83.48
3.	Rajasthan	83.33
4.	Uttar Pradesh	74.48
5.	Uttaranchal	63.71
6.	Jharkhand	61.99
7.	Bihar	61.99
8.	Himachal Pradesh	58.48
9.	Madhya Pradesh	54.75
10.	West Bengal	54.33
11.	Karnataka	51.92
12.	Chattisgarh	50.14
13.	Manipur	46.50
14.	Kerala	44.45
15.	Orissa	44.16
16.	Haryana	39.46
17.	Tamil Nadu	33.70
18.	Goa	33.61
19.	Andhra Pradesh	30.70
20.	Assam	29.65
21.	Gujarat	17.81
22.	Maharashtra	13.82
23.	Punjab	10.12
	All States Average	*31.72*

Source: Same as source 2 of Table 2.

Table 6

Municipal Revenue Expenditure, Per capita and Annual Average Growth Rate

Rank	States	Per Capita 2001/02	Annual Average Growth Rate (%) 1997/98 to 2001/02
1.	Maharashtra	1253.71	6.51
2.	Punjab	1008.12	17.22
3.	Himachal Pradesh	955.45	13.02
4.	Gujarat	865.12	7.11
5.	Goa	604.18	13.24
6.	Andhra Pradesh	508.88	14.47
7.	Kerala	493.17	10.65
8.	West Bengal	487.49	10.33
9.	Tamil Nadu	481.79	0.96
10.	Madhya Pradesh	427.66	-2.59
11.	Karnataka	418.29	11.32
12.	Uttaranchal	399.77	-
13.	Jammu & Kashmir	392.69	19.86
14.	Rajasthan	390.36	7.30
15.	Chattisgarh	376.07	-
16.	Tripura	356.75	7.09
17.	Orissa	355.06	13.87
18.	Uttar Pradesh	275.18	9.54
19.	Haryana	255.23	1.45
20.	Assam	211.79	5.21
21.	Jharkhand	87.20	-
22.	Bihar	87.20	5.53
23.	Manipur	81.03	4.90
All States Average		*576.71*	*7.36*

Notes:- denotes not applicable.

Source: Same as source 2 of Table 2.

Diagram 2a

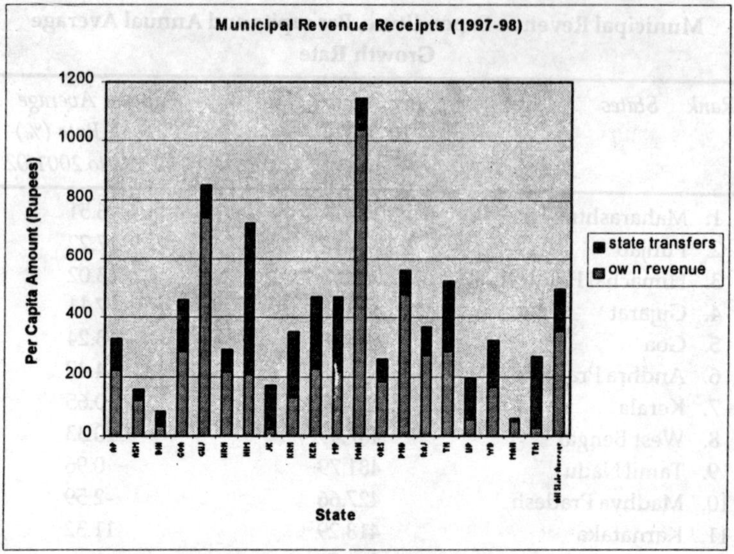

Diagram 2b

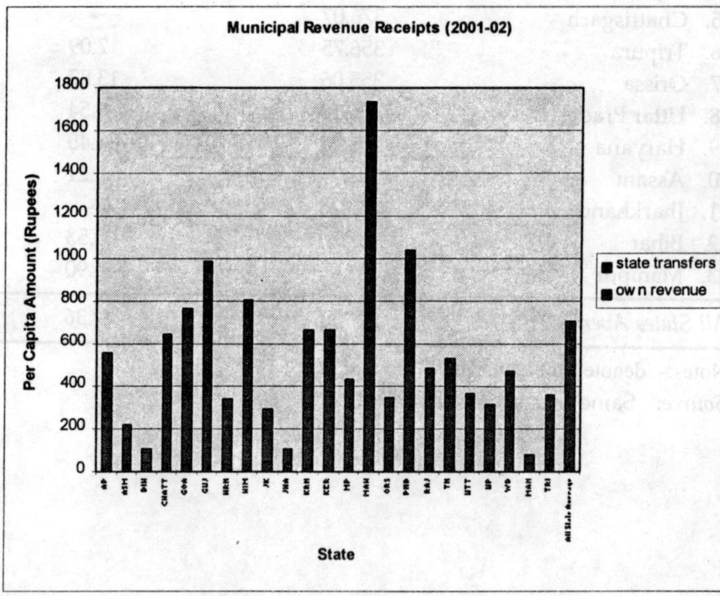

Table 7
Municipal Establishment Expenditure as % of Municipal Revenue Expenditure, 2001/02

Rank	*States*	*Municipal Establishment Expenditure (%)*
1.	Tripura	87.88
2.	Jammu & Kashmir	87.73
3.	Madhya Pradesh	80.41
4.	Manipur	76.64
5.	Chattisgarh	70.00
6.	Haryana	69.71
7.	Assam	65.25
8.	West Bengal	65.17
9.	Uttaranchal	63.76
10.	Rajasthan	63.25
11.	Goa	60.63
12.	Uttar Pradesh	60.00
13.	Tamil Nadu	56.49
14.	Maharashtra	54.38
15.	Orissa	50.59
16.	Kerala	50.27
17.	Himachal Pradesh	49.94
18.	Karnataka	48.51
19.	Gujarat	45.60
20.	Bihar	42.71
21.	Jharkhand	42.71
22.	Punjab	40.82
23.	Andhra Pradesh	33.28
All States Average		54.20

Source: Same as source 2 of Table 2.

Table 8
Expenditure on Municipal Establishment, Per Capita and Annual Average Growth Rate

Rank	States	Per Capita 2001/02	Annual Average Growth Rate (%) 1997/98 to 2001/02
1.	Maharashtra	681.72	4.73
2.	Himachal Pradesh	477.14	11.92
3.	Punjab	411.47	12.65
4.	Gujarat	394.46	8.07
5.	Goa	366.34	8.23
6.	Jammu & Kashmir	344.51	20.13
7.	Madhya Pradesh	343.89	-0.33
8.	West Bengal	317.70	12.80
9.	Tripura	313.52	7.41
10.	Tamil Nadu	272.16	5.87
11.	Chattisgarh	263.25	-
12	Uttaranchal	254.91	-
13.	Kerala	247.90	14.65
14.	Rajasthan	246.92	7.56
15.	Karnataka	202.92	8.99
16.	Orissa	179.64	11.13
17.	Haryana	177.93	-0.51
18.	Andhra Pradesh	169.34	12.08
19.	Uttar Pradesh	165.11	8.35
20.	Assam	138.19	5.71
21.	Manipur	62.10	7.04
22.	Jharkhand	37.24	-
23.	Bihar	37.24	-8.85
All States Average		312.58	6.70

Notes: - denotes not applicable.

Source: Same as source 2 of Table 2.

Table 9
Municipal Expenditure on Operation and Maintenance as % of Municipal Revenue Expenditure, 2001/02

Rank	*States*	*Municipal Expenditure on Operation and Maintenance (%)*
1.	Andhra Pradesh	65.87
2.	Punjab	59.18
3.	Bihar	57.29
4.	Karnataka	51.49
5.	Himachal Pradesh	50.06
6.	Orissa	49.41
7.	Jharkhand	45.19
8.	Kerala	43.70
9.	Tamil Nadu	43.51
10.	Gujarat	43.39
11.	Goa	39.37
12.	Uttaranchal	36.24
13.	West Bengal	34.83
14.	Maharashtra	34.76
15.	Rajasthan	34.66
16.	Assam	33.98
17.	Haryana	30.29
18.	Chattisgarh	30.00
19.	Uttar Pradesh	29.00
20.	Manipur	23.36
21.	Madhya Pradesh	19.59
22.	Jammu & Kashmir	12.27
23.	Tripura	7.26
All States Average		39.93

Source: Same as source 2 of Table 2.

Table 10
Municipal Own Revenue Receipts (-) Expenditure on Municipal Establishment, Per Capita and Annual Average Growth Rate

Rank	States	Per Capita 2001/02	Annual Average Growth Rate (%) 1997/98 to 2001/02
1.	Maharashtra	811.61	13.49
2.	Punjab	520.91	20.02
3.	Gujarat	414.99	-2.27
4.	Andhra Pradesh	217.49	15.77
5.	Goa	144.30	47.47
6.	Kerala	123.21	8.88
7.	Karnataka	119.04	-
8.	Tamil Nadu	83.34	4.12
9.	Chattisgarh	58.30	-
10.	Haryana	29.89	-3.05
11.	Assam	15.05	10.40
12.	Orissa	14.86	-39.24
13.	Jharkhand	2.21	
14.	Bihar	2.21	-
15.	Manipur	-20.55	-
16.	Uttar Pradesh	-85.56	7.08
17.	West Bengal	-101.93	35.43
18.	Uttaranchal	-141.23	-
19.	Himachal Pradesh	-141.59	12.06
20.	Madhya Pradesh	-155.22	4.09
21.	Rajasthan	-166.24	-
22.	Tripura	-254.59	5.32
23.	Jammu & Kashmir	-296.33	-
All States Average		*169.56*	*9.61*

Notes: - denotes not applicable.
Source: Same as source 2 of Table 2.

Table 11
Municipal Revenue Account Deficit (-)/Surplus, Per capita and Annual Average Growth Rate

Rank	*States*	*Per Capita 2001/02*	*Annual Average Growth Rate (%) 1997/98 to 2001/02*
1.	Maharashtra	239.62	30.29
2.	Manipur	-39.48	23.33
3.	Haryana	-47.42	15.48
4.	Bihar	-47.74	7.29
5.	Jharkhand	-47.74	-
6.	***Chattisgarh***	**-54.52**	-
7.	***Gujarat***	**-55.67**	-
8.	***Assam***	**-58.54**	2.95
9.	Punjab	-75.75	28.37
10.	Goa	-93.54	7.02
11.	Karnataka	-96.33	-8.40
12.	Andhra Pradesh	-122.05	15.71
13.	Kerala	-122.06	5.53
14.	Tamil Nadu	-126.29	-8.54
15.	Orissa	-160.56	55.59
16.	Uttar Pradesh	-195.64	9.44
17.	Madhya Pradesh	-238.98	-1.88
18.	West Bengal	-271.73	13.74
19.	Uttaranchal	-286.09	-
20.	Tripura	-297.82	5.25
21.	Rajasthan	-309.68	69.00
22.	Jammu & Kashmir	-344.51	-
23.	Himachal Pradesh	-619.91	13.67
	All States Average	*-94.57*	*5.77*

Note: denotes not applicable.

Source: Same as source 2 of Table 2.

Chart 1: Initiatives Taken by State Governments/Municipal Governments

State/City	KEY INDICATORS						
	Property Tax	*Accounting Reforms*	*E-governance*	*Bond Issue*	*Cost Reduction*	*Participatory Governance Remarks*	*Public Private Partnership Remarks*
(1)	(2)	(3)	(4)	(5)	(6)	(7)	(8)
Andhra Pradesh							
Hyderabad	■	■					■
Vijaywada			■				
Vishakapatnam			■				■ Watersupply
Bihar							
Patna	■						
Gujarat							
Ahmedabad	■	■	■	■			■ Slum networking
Anand		■					
Kodinaar							■ River cleaning
Rajkot					■		■ Privatization
Vadodara					■		■
Karnataka							
Bangalore	■	■		■			■ Municipal effectiveness, street light maintenance
Madhya Pradesh							
Bhopal			MIS system		■ Developing biocompust plant		■ Slum networking
Indore	■		Bill validation software		■ Rain water harvesting, solid waste management		■ Road construction
Jabalpur				■ (improvement of WS)			
Maharashtra							
Greater Mumbai			■			■ Community participatory proving slum dweller, solid waste management	
Nagpur				Arresting unwanted water works, internal road development			
Nashik				■			
Thane					advance billing		

Chart 1: *(Contd.)*

(1)	(2)	(3)	(4)	(5)	(6)	(7)	(8)
Orissa							
Bhubaneshwar							
Puri							■ Development of Bio Compost
Punjab							
Ludhiana						■	
Tamil Nadu (All Cities)							
Coimbature							
Namakkal							■
Tirupur							■ Solid waste management all stakeholders
Tiruvalli			■				■
Rajasthan							
Jaipur					Contracted out photo copying ■		■ Street light privatization
Jodhpur							
Uttar Pradesh							
Mirzapur	■						
Uttaranchal							
Dehradun				■ Registration of birth & death			
West Bengal							
Kolkata					■		

Diagram 3

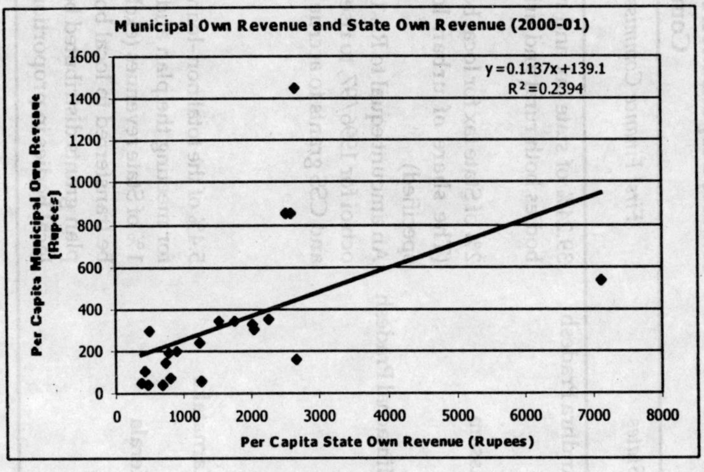

Chart 2. Devolution/Dispensation Package Recommended by the First and Second Finance Commission of States (SFCs)

States	*First Finance Commission of States*	*Second Finance Commission of States*
Andhra Pradesh	39.24% of state tax and non–tax revenue to all local bodies both rural and urban.	40.92% of state tax and non tax revenue to all bodies, both rural & urban bodies. 18.54% is allocated to ULBs alone.
Assam	2% of State tax for local bodies, both rural and urban. (The share of urban local bodies has not been specified).	-
Himachal Pradesh	An amount equal to Rs. 12.2 crore as grants in lieu of octroi for 1996/97, to rise to Rs. 17.9 crore in 2000/01 and CSS grants to accrue to municipalities.	An amount equal to Rs 19.66 crores as development grants for the year 2002-03 with a 10 per cent mark up to neutralize inflation mark up, this would rise to Rs. 28.79 crore by 2006-07, and CSS grants to accrue to municipalities.
Karnataka	5.4% of the total non–loan gross own revenue receipts for meeting the plan and non–plan requirements.	8% of non loan gross own revenue receipts to ULBs.
Kerala	1% of State revenues (excluding from certain sources) be transferred to local bodies as non–statutory non–plan grants distributed between the rural and urban local bodies in proportion to their population.	-

(*Contd.*)

Madhya Pradesh	8.67% of the tax and non-tax revenues of State government.	1.07% of divisible pool of State own tax revenue.
Maharashtra	25% to 100% of entertainment taxes collected from municipalities of different grades, 25% of vehicle tax and 10% of profession tax are recommended shares for local bodies.	
Manipur	Maintenance grant equal to Rs. 88.3 lakh to accrue to municipalities in 1996/97, which varies in subsequent years.	
Orissa	Rs. 179.5 crores is the projected transfer (grant) to urban local bodies between 1998/99 and 2004/05. (The deficit of Rs. 1,378 crores between the estimated income and expenditure and an additional requirement of Rs. 381.48 crore for improvement of core civic services should be met by the Eleventh Finance Commission).	
Punjab	20% of the net proceed for five taxes namely, stamp duty, motor vehicle tax, electricity duty, entertainment tax, and cinematograph shows should be transferred to municipalities, and the projected gap of Rs. 322 crore should be met by the Central Finance Commission.	4 per cent of net tax proceeds of all State taxes to be devolved to all local bodies.

(Contd.)

Rajasthan	2.18% the net proceeds of State taxes should be devolved on the local bodies; the division of these proceeds between rural and urban should be in the ratio of 3.4:1.	Total devolution of Rs. 794.43 crore consisting of 2.25% share in states net own tax revenue (excluding entertainment tax) ; 15% share in entertainment tax for ULBs for the award period 2000-05 and 1% share in royalty receipts from minerals to Gram Panchayats.
Tamil Nadu	8% of the State's net tax revenue should be devolved on to the local bodies in 1997/98; this percentage should gradually increase in successive years to 9%, 10%, 11% and reaching 12% in 2001/02. The division of this amount between rural and urban should be on the basis of population as in the last Census.	8% out of State's Own Tax Revenue after excluding Entertainment Tax to the local bodies for each year from 2002-03 to 2006-07. The shares of PRIs and ULBs in the recommended devolution will be in the ratio 58:42.
Utter Pradesh	7% of the net proceeds of State's total tax revenue should be transferred to urban local bodies.	–
West Bengal	16% of the net proceeds of all taxes collected by the State should be transferred to local bodies. Such funds should be released to the Districts. These proceeds should be divided between urban and rural based on population.	*a*) Nearly 72 per cent tax proceeds from entertainment tax. *b*) 10 per cent allocated from states revenue as untied entitlement fund, the proceeds of which are to be distributed between ULB and Panchayats.

Total 12. Transfers to Municipalities (SFC devolution's grants, Compensatory grants, Assigned and Shared revenues) (Amount in Rs. lakh)

States	*1997-98*	*1998-99*	*1999-2000*	*2000-01*	*2001-02*	*Annual Average Growth Rate (%) 1997/98 to 2001/02*
Andhra Pradesh	*19359.06*	*36600.59*	*26035.45*	*28255.50*	*31784.25*	*12.40*
Assam	*831.70*	*762.64*	*794.23*	*1277.62*	*1624.17*	*16.73*
Bihar	*5670.31*	*5057.60*	*11588.52*	*5593.58*	*5559.28*	*-0.49*
Chattisgarh	*na*	*na*	*na*	*11245.72*	*12624.04*	*-*
Goa	*606.77*	*528.25*	*na*	*628.37*	*941.18*	*10.97*
Gujarat	*17496.18*	*22204.92*	*29049.83*	*34740.94*	*31395.74*	*14.62*
Haryana	*3747.55*	*3059.17*	*6329.39*	*9477.39*	*7891.81*	*18.62*
Himachal Pradesh	*2715.74*	*3418.06*	*2917.90*	*3058.42*	*2787.09*	*0.65*
Jammu & Kashmir	*3224.99*	*3875.11*	*5884.46*	*6127.18*	*6162.01*	*16.19*
Jharkhand	*na*	*na*	*na*	*2453.46*	*2440.30*	*-*
Karnataka	*34079.68*	*40463.38*	*37827.30*	*47949.25*	*60859.27*	*14.50*
Kerala	*15664.76*	*19052.13*	*20506.30*	*16524.09*	*17949.46*	*3.40*
Madhya Pradesh	*40899.91*	*51026.29*	*64010.65*	*59846.32*	*37662.96*	*-2.06*
Maharashtra	*37874.80*	*39272.52*	*70909.64*	*71377.81*	*94176.76*	*22.77*
Manipur	*51.79*	*107.17*	*175.27*	*180.10*	*194.68*	*33.10*
Orissa	*3291.24*	*4103.63*	*7607.45*	*7819.74*	*8046.68*	*22.35*
Punjab	*5753.37*	*9076.79*	*7266.78*	*7845.46*	*8489.52*	*9.73*
Rajasthan	*11041.27*	*31270.86*	*39567.50*	*45612.93*	*51702.74*	*38.60*
Tamil Nadu	*52209.00*	*56953.50*	*54344.00*	*54360.00*	*46770.00*	*-2.75*
Tripura	*880.00*	*750.00*	*1200.00*	*1300.00*	*1100.00*	*5.58*
Uttar Pradesh	*43568.02*	*68064.31*	*70776.81*	*71337.18*	*77488.64*	*14.40*
Uttaranchal	*na*	*na*	*na*	*5104.66*	*5104.66*	*-*
West Bengal	*28535.00*	*32481.00*	*65772.00*	*50217.00*	*50203.00*	*14.12*
All States	*327501.15*	*428127.92*	*522563.48*	*542332.72*	*562958.24*	*13.54*

Notes: denotes not applicable, na denotes not available.

Source: Same as source 2 of Tables 2.

Table 13. Entertainment tax and Profession tax transferred to Municipalities (Amount in Rs. Lakh)

States	*1997-98*	*1998-99*	*1999-2000*	*2000-01*	*2001-02*	*AAGR (%)*
Andhra Pradesh	8,349.27	10,104.08	10,676.90	11,229.44	11,914.77	8.89
Assam	225.85	127.34	200.58	181.22	201.28	-2.88
Bihar	na	na	na	na	na	-
Chattisgarh	na	na	na	na	na	-
Goa	na	na	na	na	na	-
Gujarat	1,920.73	2,311.90	2,408.65	3,350.94	2,894.17	10.25
Haryana	na	na	na	350.00	na	-
Himachal Pradesh	na	na	na	na	na	-
Jammu & Kashmir	na	na	na	na	na	-
Jharkhand	na	na	na	na	na	-
Karnataka	na	na	na	na	na	-
Kerala	na	na	na	na	na	-
Madhya Pradesh	na	na	na	na	na	-
Maharashtra	754.84	1,118.93	676.61	868.70	16.71	-95.26
Orissa	48.22	118.05	na	13.98	na	-
Punjab	na	na	na	na	na	-
Rajasthan	100.17	1,049.84	na	na	na	-
Tamil Nadu	7,179.00	9,202.00	7,283.00	6,261.00	4,495.00	-11.70
Uttaranchal	na	na	na	na	na	-
Uttar Pradesh	na	na	na	na	na	-
West Bengal	6,972.95	10,675.00	37,619.60	3,004.38	4,158.00	-12.93
All States	*18,615.47*	*31,719.85*	*55,126.64*	*20,065.91*	*16,670.79*	-2.76

Notes: denotes not applicable. na denotes not applicable or not available
AAGR (%) is Annual Average Growth Rate.

Source: Same as Source 2 of Table 2.

Table 14: Municipal Transfers as a % of State's Own Revenues

State	*1997-98*	*1998-99*	*1999-00*	*2000-01*
Andhra Pradesh	2.17	3.73	2.27	2.13
Assam	0.66	0.53	0.48	0.66
Bihar	2.03	1.32	2.15	1.50
Chattisgarh	-	-	-	10.83
Goa	1.00	0.76	-	0.67
Gujarat	1.99	2.14	2.62	2.80
Haryana	1.13	0.69	1.40	1.74
Himachal Pradesh	3.95	4.46	1.74	3.38
Jammu & Kashmir	-	-	-	-
Jharkhand	-	-	-	-
Karnataka	4.46	4.84	4.06	4.49
Kerala	3.17	3.74	3.65	2.58
Madhya Pradesh	6.21	7.41	7.75	8.13
Maharashtra	2.19	2.21	3.35	2.82
Manipur	0.01	0.02	0.03	0.03
Orissa	1.68	2.01	3.14	2.73
Punjab	1.07	1.91	1.25	1.27
Rajasthan	2.25	5.91	6.48	6.53
Tamil Nadu	5.34	5.31	4.47	3.92
Tripura	0.18	0.15	0.21	0.18
Uttar Pradesh	5.26	7.25	6.20	5.52
Uttaranchal	-	-	-	14.24
West Bengal	5.76	6.32	11.61	7.07
All States	*3.31*	*3.98*	*4.18*	*3.85*

Notes:- denotes state's own revenues are not available.

Source: Same as source 1 and 2 of Table 2.

Table 15. Revenue Receipts from Entertainment Tax and Taxes on Professions, Trades Callings and Employment Across Major States, 1996/97 to 2000/01 (Rs. Lakh)

States	1996-97		1997-98		1998-99		1999-00		2000-01		Annual Average Growth Rate	
	Entertainment tax	Tax on professions, trades and callings	Entertainment tax	Tax on professions, trades and callings	Entertainment tax	Tax on professions, trades and callings	Entertainment tax	Tax on professions trades and callings	Entertainment tax	Tax on professions, Trades and callings	Enterainment tax	Tax on professions, trades and callings
Andhra Pradesh	6494.0	7226.0	na	7554.0	na	12167.0	8017.0	12437.0	5977.0	13792.0	-2.1	16.2
Assam	1335.0	3503.0	1982.0	3948.0	2330.0	4674.0	2562.0	5862.0	4402.0	6970.0	29.8	17.2
Bihar	2053.0	na	2046.0	na	1983.0	na	3645.0	2.0	1486.0	1.0	-8.1	-
Gujarat	5898.0	4827.0	5951.0	6194.0	6271.0	7533.0	6740.0	8305.0	5300.0	10480.0	-2.7	19.4
Haryana	229.0	na	1305.0	na	1194.0	na	1076.0	na	962.0	93.0	35.9	-
Himachal Pradesh	55.0	na	55.0	na	65.0	na	78.0	na	90.0	na	12.3	-
Jammu & Kashmir	na	na	300.0	na	330.0	na	310.0	na	na	na	nap	-
Karnataka	3420.0	11942.0	5528.0	10296.0	5627.0	11426.0	6011.0	13279.0	5073.0	15156.0	9.9	6.0
Kerala	7.0	na	na	na	2.0		11.0	na	58.0	na	52.9	-
Madhya Pradesh	1710.0	11226.0	1638.0	8151.0	1795.0	10954.0	1559.0	18458.0	2023.0	17191.0	4.2	10.7
Maharashtra	10131.0	38235.0	14881.0	39605.0	16079.0	54627.0	18592.0	80796.0	20092.0	94221.0	17.1	22.5
Orissa	572.0	na	588.0	na	689.0	na	1233.0	na	1460.0	1130.0	23.4	-
Punjab	554.0	na	581.0	na	475.0	na	1029.0	na	875.0	na	11.4	-
Rajasthan	2145.0	na	2391.0	na	2215.0	na	2752.0	na	2426.0	na	3.1	-
Tamil Nadu	11716.0	na	11924.0	an	9198.0	na	9109.0	na	8556.0	na	-7.9	-
Uttar Pradesh	9539.0	614.0	12683.0	632.0	13187.0	643.0	13589.0	585.0	50458.0	444.0	41.6	-8.1
West Bengal	4501.0	11548.0	4343.0	12354.0	4181.0	14000.0	6122.0	19219.0	4969.0	20691.0	2.5	14.6
All States	*60359.0*	*89121.0*	*66196.0*	*88734.0*	*65621.0*	*116024.0*	*82435.0*	*158943.0*	*114207.0*	*180169.0*	*15.9*	*17.6*

Source: State Budget Documents.

Notes: denotes not applicable na not applicable.

Table 16. Municipal Own Revenue and Distribution of Eleventh Finance Commission Grant of Rs. 400 crore* (in Rs. Lakh)

States	*Municipal own revenue 2001-02 (Rs. Lakh)*	*Municipal share of Rs. 400 cr. (Rs. Lakh)*	*Municipal grant as a per cent of municipal own revenue*
Andhra Pradesh	71745.71	3293.20	4.59
Assam	3825.81	430.80	11.26
Bihar	3408.44	1878.00	38.29 #1
Chattisgarh	12555.29	-	-
Goa	1858.72	92.80	4.99
Gujarat	144849.22	2650.40	1.83
Haryana	12106.95	732.80	6.05
Himachal Pradesh	1978.93	78.00	3.94
Jammu & Kashmir	1199.02	313.20	26.12
Jharkhand	1496.17	-	-
Karnataka	56349.68	2496.40	4.43
Kerala	22432.79	1504.80	6.71
Madhya Pradesh	29437.00	3120.40	7.43 #2
Maharashtra	587058.29	6325.20	1.08
Manipur	224.03	88.00	39.28
Orissa	10176.83	799.20	7.85
Punjab	75381.24	1094.40	1.60
Rajasthan	10339.68	1988.40	19.23
Tamil Nadu	92013.00	3867.20	4.39
Tripura	217.67	-	-
Uttaranchal	2320.61	-	-
Uttar Pradesh	26551.00	5032.80	17.43 #3
West Bengal	42201.69	3949.60	9.36
All States	*1209727.77*	*39735.60*	*3.28*
All India (Urban)		*40000.00*	

Note: * Rs. 400 crore amount is EFC's grant amount for ULB's.
denotes not applicable

#1 is combined % of municipal share in Municipal Own Revenue of Bihar and Jharkhand.

#2 is combined % of municipal share in Municipal Own Revenue of Madhya Pradesh and Chattisgarh.

#3 is combined % of municipal share in Municipal Own Revenue of Uttar Pradesh and Uttaranchal.

Table 17. Criteria for interse distribution between ULBs according to second SFC reports

States	*Criteria*										
	Population	*Slum population*	*SC population*	*Density population*	*Illiteracy rate*	*Area excluding slum*	*Efficiency*	*Equity*	*Length of Kutcha drains*	*Asset creation*	*Expenditure*
Andhra Pradesh[1]	Y	Y				Y	Y	Y[2]			
Himachal Pradesh							Y[3]				
Karnataka	Y				Y						
Madhya Pradesh	Y	Y									
Punjab	Y		Y					Y[4]			
Rajasthan	Y							Y[5]			
Tamil Nadu	Y	Y	Y				Y[6]			Y	Y
West Bengal[7]	Y		Y[8]	Y	Y				Y		

Source: Second State Finance Comission Report of the Respective State Government.

Notes:
1. In AP, the criteria are for interse distribution of the amount earmarked for civic amenities.
2. Tax demand is less than the amount required for salaries of the non-teaching staff with the amount distributed in proportion to the gap between the two.
3. The grants will be 75% if the local body imposes house tax on a minimum 7.5%. The balance 25% will be provided if the local body increases the house tax by a percentage point every year.
4. Shortfall of per capita tax income as compared to average per capita tax income of all ULBs.
5. Distributed on the basis of population as additional share to offset their weak resource raising capacity.
6. Per capita own income.
7. In West Bengal, the funds are distributed first between districts on the basis of eight indicators and then amongst the ULBs.
8. ST population as well.

8

Executive Summary of the Seminar

–P. S. N. Rao

The National Seminar on Municipal Finance, conducted by the Indian Institute of Public Administration (IIPA), New Delhi and sponsored by the Twelfth Finance Commission, Government, of India, was held on the 29th and 30th of December, 2003 at the IIPA, New Delhi.

The Seminar began with a Welcome Address by Dr. P. L. Sanjeev Reddy, Director, IIPA, Where he briefly traced the evolution of urban local bodies in India. He made a reference to the various committees set up in the past, such as the Local Finance Enquiry Committee, Rural-Urban Relationship Committee and so on and so forth. He said that the problems are now well known and well documented . He briefly mentioned the Seventy-Fourth Constitutional Amendment, the functions transferred to the urban local bodies and the setting up of the State Finance Commission. Dr. Reddy said that despite all these development, unfortunately, a vast majority of our citizens in the cities and towns are still depried of access to even mere basic services that are essential for day-to-day living. Therefore, he argued, what are needed today are effective practial changes in the system, so that the citizens can ultimately get something out of the local governments. He also referred to the recommendations of the earlier Finance Commissions and the lack of alternative path in case the States choose to go in a different way.

In his Opening remarks, Shir T.R. Prasad, Member of the Twelfth Finance Commission, said that the Finance Commission has a daunting task in front of it from the Centre, the States and the various local bodies. He said that there is a huge unspoken expectation from the milions of people in this country, who are unable to aritculate, that needs to be taken into account and that is where the challenge lies. He also raised the issue of authority versus democracy and stated that only the convergent viewpoint represents the democratic viewpoint. He made a very important point that many of the problems of the urban local bodies are not merely fiscal, the solution is not just stepping up allocations, and the solutions lie somewhere else. Urban problems are not just funding problems. Ther are various issues related to depleting natural resources, lack of human capacity, need for alternative technology and so on and so forth. Therefore, all problems cannot just be circumvented by money. He geve a large number of examples to substantiate this particular point and he called for a more holistic and comprehensive approach to the problem. He concluded that ultimately urban management is more important rather than merely mobilizing money. He also called for addressing the issues of institutional capacity holding and development of governmental process and plans.

The Inaugural Address was delivered by Dr. C. Rangarajan, Chairman of the Twelfth Finance Commission. He started his presentation with a broad overview of the various developments that have occurred over the last 100 years, which have ushered municipal governments in India. He made, reference to the various commissions and committees and stated once again that despite all this there is still a lot of room for improvement and we do not think we have really moved far, as far as the state of urban problems is concerned. He drew particular attention to the Seventy-Fourth Constitutional Amendment and the setting up of various State Finance Commissions and the roles, which they have played. He state that while several states have set up State Finance Commissions, their role in the larger process of fiscal decentralization has not been very satisfactory, particularly in the transfers to be given to ULBs. He stated that slack of uniformity in the approach of the SFCs in terms of the principles laid down for devolution of resources from the states to the ULBs, lack of synchronization of the award period of the SFCs and the absence of rational determination of the gap between normative costs of service delivery and normative capacities to raise resources makes the taks very complx. He outlined the various routes in relation to allocation of financial resources by the Finance Commission to the urban local bodies, such as *ad hoc* grants and so on and so forth and then he hoped that this Seminar would discuss these issues. I think this Seminar did discuss all these issues.

The first Technical Session was on the "Role of National Finance Commission in Fiscal Decentralization". Dr. G.C. Srivastava, Member Secretary of the Twelfth Finance Commission, chaired the session. Prof. Abhijit Datta made the key presentation. He discussed the role of the National Finance Commission and he made very specific reference to vertical and horizontal fiscal equalization, both in short and long term. Ultimately, at the end of his paper, he outlined broadly two options and finally recommeded that the Eleventh Finance Commission strategies of grants to urban local bodies on a per capita basis could continue. However, he did suggest some changes and some modification in the system.

This was followed by presentations from two eminent discussants, Prof. Amaresh Bagchi and Dr. Junaid Ahmed. Prof. Amaresh Bagchi from the National Institute of Public Finance and Policy discussed the paper in very great detail. He said that if some of the recommendations suggested by Prof. Abhijit Datta could be implemented then it would go a long way in improving things. Dr. Junaid Ahmed from the World Bank raised the issue of national public goods, regional public goods and local public goods. He said that in times to come the local public goods are going to become extremely important. He said that without local emphasis, the country would not achieve the desired growth rate at the national level. He felt that more than equalization, it is incentivization that is more of an issue. He felt that giving the right kind of incentives to the urban local bodies is more important, and that can actually help in service delivery, which is what probably the citizens of this country want.

The Technical Session Two was charied by Shri Sompal, another Member of the Twelfth Finance Commission and a Member of the Planning Commission. The theme of the Session was "SFC Recommendations and Performance of States." A presentation was made by Prof. Om Mathur from the National Institute of Public Finance and Policy. He basically explained the study that he conducted for the Commission. He discussed the performance of the various States and the extent to which the SFC recommendations have been implemented. He explained the methodology and approach in which he had carried out his study and the indicators that he had used to carry out the performance assessment of the various states. He also brought out the typology of states emerging from the study of the performance. He highlighted the various factors underlying the kind of differential performances that his study revealed. His paper was very much appreciated. Dr. Y. Anantani of City Managers' Association discussed it. It also attracted a lot of floor participation.

The Third Technical Session was on "Fiscal Capacity of ULBs" vis-a-vis their Responsibilities to Provide Core Services. Shir M.C Gupta, former Director of IIPA, who was also involved in the Tenth Finance Commission earlier, chaired this session. Dr. Nageswara Rao of the Tamil Nadu Institute of Urban Studies made the key presentation. He explained the case of Tamil Nadu and reminded us that this is one of the first states, which implemented municipal reforms on a statewide level. He talked of the silent revolution taking place in Tamil Nadu. He highlighted as many as 8 innovative approaches and 14 major reforms, which were undertaken in Tamil Nadu. He said that the State is now moving from there is no Alternative Situation to There are a Number of Alternatives Situations. There was another excellent presentation by Shri P.K. Srihari, Additional Commissioner, Bangalore Municipal Corporation, who talked about the various innovative reforms in the Bangalore Mahanagar Palika, such as self-assessment scheme, *Saral Katha,* fund based accounting, FDAs and so on. He said that the end of the day the proof of the pudding is in the eating. He made a mention of the report card system, which the Public Affair Centre of Bangalore had brought out, which very clearly indicated the success of the reforms that the Mahanagar Palika in Bangalore have been able to achieve.

On the Second day, the Fourth Techincal Session was held. Prof. D.K. Srivastava charied the session. Prof. P.K. Chaubey, who started off the session, firstly emphasized the role of democracy in local government. He touched on some very fundamental issues like the principle of democracy, autonomy, fraternity, diversity and heterogeneity. He also referred to the state of Indian cities in terms of increasing population and increasing urban problems. He referred to what was mentioned earlier by some of the speakers, namely, multi-body functional domain. He said that in view of the serious data problems that are there, it becomes rather difficult for one to really estimate the adequacy of resources for performing the newly transferred functions in the post-Seventy-Fourth Amendment scenario.

This was followed by a presentation by Dr. Gangadhar Jha. His presentation hinged upon two very key points. He started off with the resurgence of city governance that marked the turn of this century. He referred to globalization and structural adjustment, the whole concept of market eonomy, the emergence of cities competing with each other and so on. In the same vein he also talked about decentralization issues, which have come to the fore at the turn of the century.

He then moved on to talking about three key issues, namely, revenue structure, the trends in own revenues and the dependency syndrome. He brought out some very key points. The cities contribute as much as 60 per cent of the GDP and as much as 90 per cent of the Central revenues. But, then, what they ultimately get in terms of transfer is very very little, althought they have every right to get much more. Therfore, at the end of his elaborate presentation, he discussed a variety of methods by which own resources can be improved, things like private sector participation, accounting reforms, access to capital markets, revenue enhancement throuth a variety of other methods and so on. Finally, he concluded by saying that money is certainly not a problem. What is lacking today is bankable projects or viable projects, where the private investors can fund.

Dr. K.K. Pandey from the Human Settlement Management Institute was the fires Discussant to present his views. He brought out some very important points, which are for the consideration of the National Finance Commission, particularly in the area of devolution of funds. Another Discussant was Shri K.C. Sivaramakrishnan, who referred to the nexus of the city governments with the economy as a whole. He stated that the importance of local governments is going to increase more and more, as compared to the state governments and the national government. This issue of shrinking of sovereign space is a very key point that he had made. He also talked about the creation of an independent tax domain for the consideration of the Twelfth Finance Commission. He further spoke about the spatial character of urbanization, which is not normally discussed in the Finance Commissions. The earlier Finance Commissions have not really talked about the spatial character of the whole scheme of things. Today, we cannot look at cities as cities per se, but as large agglomerations, where the urban spread cuts across the municipal areas into the surrounding panchayats and so on, sometimes crossing the district boundaries or even the state boundaries. So, what we are looking at today is more a kind of corridor development, or an urban sprawl situation, where there will be different geographical boundaries coming in, there will be different levels of jurisdiction coming in. He emphasised that this is again another issue, which needs to be looked into in greater detail.

The final discussant was Dr. Ravi Kant Joshi, make some very interesting points on the great potential that lies within the urban local bodies themselves and said that if we are able to put our own house in order, then we can certainly reduce the overall amount of finances that we need. Therefore, he called for micro reforms first and then macro reforms next.

Index